FINANCIAL
Statements

tutorial

NVQ LEVEL 4
ACCOUNTING

David Cox
Derek Street
Consultant: Roger Petheram

OSBORNE

Published by Osborne Books Limited
Unit 1B Everoak Estate
Bromyard Road
Worcester WR2 5HN
Tel 01905 748071
Email books@osbornebooks.co.uk
Website www.osbornebooks.co.uk

Cover and page design by Hedgehog

Printed by the Bath Press, Bath

British Library Cataloguing in Publication Data
A catalogue record for this book is available from the British Library

ISBN 1 872962 54 8

CONTENTS

ACKNOWLEDGEMENTS

The authors wish to thank the following for their help with the editing and production of the book: Jean Cox, Michael Fardon, Michael Gilbert, Rosemarie Griffiths, Jon Moore and Liz Smith. Particular thanks go to Roger Petheram of Worcester College of Technology for reading the text, commenting upon it, checking answers, and always being prepared to discuss any aspect of the book.

Thanks are also due to the Association of Accounting Technicians for their generous help and advice and to the Lead Body for Accounting for permission to reproduce extracts from the Standards of Competence for Accounting. Thanks also go to The Body Shop International PLC for permission to reproduce extracts from their Report and Accounts, and to the Accounting Standards Board for permission to reproduce extracts from their accounting standards.

AUTHORS

David Cox has had more than twenty years' experience teaching accountancy students over a wide range of levels. Formerly with the Management and Professional Studies Department at Worcester College of Technology, he now lectures on a freelance basis and carries out educational consultancy work in accountancy studies. He is author and joint author of a number of textbooks in the areas of accounting, finance and banking.

Derek Street has had over fifteen years' experience of teaching accountancy students, including the AAT qualification at all three levels. His lecturing experience has been gained at Evesham College of FE, Gloucester College of Arts and Technology (GLOSCAT) and North East Worcestershire College where he is currently Head of Department, Professional Studies.

INTRODUCTION

Osborne tutorials

Financial Statements Tutorial has been written to provide a study resource for students taking courses based on the NVQ Level 4 Accounting Unit 11 'Drafting Financial Statements (Accounting Practice, Industry and Commerce)'. The text also covers Element 1 of the following variant Units:

- Unit 12 Drafting Financial Statements (Central Government)
- Unit 13 Drafting Financial Statements (Local Government)
- Unit 14 Drafting Financial Statements (National Health Service)

Financial Statements Tutorial commences with the purpose of financial statements (including a study of key aspects of 'Statement of principles for financial reporting'). It then develops the preparation and presentation of final accounts of sole traders, partnerships and limited companies – including the use of cash flow statements. The impact of accounting standards on financial statements is considered in detail. The text includes the interpretation of accounts using accounting ratios, and the preparation of consolidated accounts for groups of companies.

Financial Statements Tutorial provides the student with the theoretical background to the subject while at the same time including plenty of opportunity to put theory into practice. The aim has been to introduce the right amount of material at the right level.

The chapters of *Financial Statements Tutorial* contain:

- a clear text with worked examples and case studies
- a chapter summary and key terms to help with revision
- student activities – with answers at the end of the book

The tutorial text – with questions and answers – is therefore useful for classroom use and also for distance learning students. More extended student exercises, without answers in the text, are available in the *Financial Statements Workbook*.

Osborne workbooks

Financial Statements Workbook contains extended student activities and sample Central Assessments. The answers to these tasks are included in a separate Tutor Pack.

If you would like a copy of any of our texts, please telephone Osborne Books Sales Office on 01905 748071 for details of how to order, or visit the Osborne online 24 hour shop on www.osbornebooks.co.uk

WEB DIRECTORY

There are a number of websites which will help to supplement your studies for Unit 11, *Drafting Financial Statements*.

information and accountancy news

www.accountancyage.com	– news and information service – regular newsletter
www.accountingweb.co.uk	– news and information – includes a students' discussion forum
www.asb.org.uk	– website of the Accounting Standards Board – gives details of accounting standards and current projects – links to related sites, including the Financial Reporting Council and the Financial Reporting Review Panel
www.companieshouse.gov.uk	– website of Companies House – gives information about forming and running companies – provides details of how to obtain copies of company accounts and other statutory information

accountancy associations

A selection of accountancy bodies and associations is given below, with their website addresses. As well as details of members' and students' services, they give information on assessment and examination schemes. Some sites also provide a news and information service.

www.aat.co.uk	– The Association of Accounting Technicians
www.acca.org.uk	– The Association of Chartered Certified Accountants
www.cima.org.uk	– The Chartered Institute of Management Accountants

www.cipfa.org.uk	– The Chartered Institute of Public Finance Accountants
www.icaew.co.uk	– The Institute of Chartered Accountants in England and Wales
www.icas.org.uk	– The Institute of Chartered Accountants of Scotland

firms of accountants

A selection of accountancy firms is given below. As well as advertising the firms and their services, a number of sites include technical information and notes on recent developments in accounting.

www.andersen.com	– Andersen
www.deloitte.co.uk	– Deloitte & Touche
www.ey.com	– Ernst & Young
www.grant-thornton.co.uk	– Grant Thornton
www.kpmg.co.uk	– KPMG
www.pwcglobal.com	– PricewaterhouseCoopers

updating of *Financial Statements*

The Osborne Books website www.osbornebooks.co.uk will be used to give information about changes and updating of the topics covered in this book.

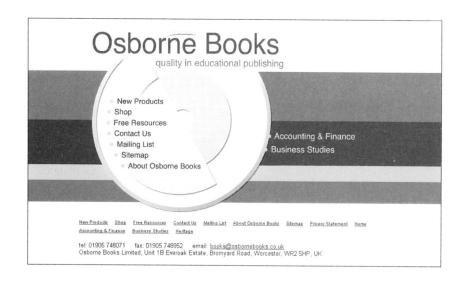

1 PURPOSE OF FINANCIAL STATEMENTS

this chapter covers . . .

Technician Level Unit 11 'Drafting Financial Statements (Accounting Practice, Industry and Commerce)' builds on earlier studies of financial accounting at Intermediate Level. Unit 11 comprises two elements:

- interpret financial statements
- draft limited company, sole trader and partnership year end financial statements

In this chapter we begin our studies by considering the

- general purpose of financial statements
- elements of financial statements
- accounting equation
- development of the regulatory framework of accounting
- Statement of Principles for Financial Reporting
- accounting concepts

NVQ PERFORMANCE CRITERIA COVERED

unit 11: DRAFTING FINANCIAL STATEMENTS

element 1

interpret financial statements

- the general purpose of financial statements used in various organisations is identified
- elements of financial statements used in various organisations are identified

TYPES OF ORGANISATION

A walk or a drive around any medium-sized town will reveal evidence of a wide variety of organisations that operate buses and trains, telephones, shops, the Post Office, banks, restaurants, pubs and clubs, hospitals, the town hall, government offices, schools and colleges, churches, societies, etc. All of these organisations use economic resources – land, labour, capital, enterprise – in varying amounts to achieve their objectives. In so doing they contribute to the local and national economies through, for example:

- the payment of wages to employees
- the payment of rates to the local authority
- the purchase of goods and services, both locally and nationally
- the collection of Value Added Tax on sales
- the payment of tax on profits

We can classify the different types of organisations by distinguishing between private sector, public sector and not-for-profit organisations, as illustrated in the following diagram and explained below:

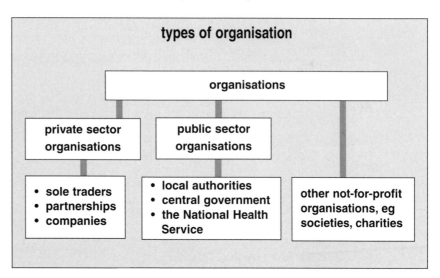

- **private sector organisations** are 'profit-making' and owned by private 'individuals', ie companies, partnerships and sole trader businesses; examples include well-known names such as Virgin, Sainsbury's and BT
- **public sector organisations** are mostly 'not-for-profit' and are owned directly or indirectly by central or local government; examples include the National Health Service and local authorities
- **other 'not-for-profit' organisations**, such as societies and charities, provide mutual services for their members and the community

objectives of organisations

For the **private sector** the profit motive is commonly the most important objective. Profit is measured as the excess of income over expenditure; sufficient profit needs to be generated each year to enable the owners to be able to draw a reasonable amount from the business, or for shareholders to be paid dividends. Often there is a conflict within business between short-term profit and long-term profit: for example, a major investment in training will reduce this year's profit, but may well help to increase profit in future years. Once the profit motive has been satisfied, and particularly as a business increases in size, a range of other objectives is developed: examples include environmental issues – taking initiatives to improve the environment through becoming more energy efficient and reducing waste – and being a good employer – adding value to the output by providing better facilities and better training for the workforce.

In the **public sector** the most important objective is to provide 'best value' – ie to ensure that the best product or service is provided from the resources available to the satisfaction of all parties, including users and those who provide the finance. Best value, as an objective, incorporates application of the three 'E's:

- **effectiveness** – that the actual output achieved, in terms of products or services, is the same as the planned output for the period
- **efficiency** – that output is achieved with the lowest level of resources, ie there is no waste or slack capacity
- **economy** – that goods and services used by the organisation are bought at the lowest possible price consistent with quality and quantity

The level of success in achieving these objectives can often be measured by the financial statements of the organisations.

FINANCIAL STATEMENTS AND THEIR PURPOSES

financial statements

The two main financial statements used by all types of organisations are:

- an **income statement** (for example: profit and loss account, income and expenditure account), which measures the financial performance of the organisation for a particular time period (the accounting period)
- a **balance sheet**, which provides a statement of the financial position of the organisation at a particular date

Income statements usually cover a twelve-month time period (but do not necessarily run to 31 December – the end of the calendar year); the accompanying balance sheet shows the financial position of the organisation at the end of the accounting period.

objective of financial statements

What is the principal objective of financial statements?

'The objective of financial statements is to provide information about the reporting entity's financial performance and financial position that is useful to a wide range of users for assessing the stewardship of the entity's management and for making economic decisions'

This quotation is taken from *Statement of principles for financial reporting* issued by the Accounting Standards Board (see page 22).

Note the following from this definition:

- **entity** – an organisation, eg a business, whose activities and resources are kept separate from those of the owner(s)
- **financial performance** – is reported through an income statement
- **financial position** – is reported through a balance sheet
- **wide range of users** – financial statements are used by a number of interested parties (see below), from existing and potential shareholders through to lenders, employees and government agencies
- **stewardship** – the entity's management is accountable for the safe-keeping of the organisation's resources and for their proper, efficient and profitable use; the financial statements enable users to assess the effectiveness of management in this role
- **economic decisions** – information from the financial statements is used to help in making decisions about investment or potential investment in the entity, eg to buy or sell a company's shares, to make a loan to the entity, or to help in deciding whether to supply goods or services

users of financial statements

There is a wide variety of users – both internal and external – of financial statements, as shown by the diagrams on the next two pages.

Internal users include existing shareholders, members of societies, managers of a company, employees.

External users include potential shareholders and members, lenders, government agencies, etc.

Each user, depending on the type of organisation, is interested in a number of different aspects, as the following diagrams show.

FINANCIAL STATEMENTS: PRIVATE SECTOR

Who is interested?	What are they interested in?	Why are they interested?
Existing and potential investors in a business	• Is the business making a profit? • Can the business pay its way? • What was the sales (turnover) figure?	• To assess the performance of management • To see how much money can be paid in dividends • To see if the business will continue in the foreseeable future • To see if the business is expanding or declining
Lenders	• Has the business made a profit? • What amount is currently loaned? • What is the value of the assets?	• To check if the business will be able to pay interest and make loan repayments • To assess how far the lender is financing the business • To assess the value of security available to the lender
Suppliers and creditors	• Can the business pay its way? • What is the value of the assets?	• To decide whether to supply goods and services to the business • To assess if the business is able to pay its debts
Employees and trade unions	• Has the business made a profit? • Can the business pay its way?	• To assess whether the business is able to pay wages and salaries • To consider the stability of the business in offering employment opportunities in the future
Customers	• Is the business profitable? • What is the value of the assets? • Can the business pay its way?	• To see if the business will continue to supply its products or services • To assess the ability of the business to meet warranty liabilities, and provision of spare parts
Governments and government agencies	• Has the business made a profit? • What was the sales (turnover) figure?	• To calculate the tax due • To ensure that the business is registered for VAT and completes VAT returns on time • To provide a basis for government regulation and statistics • To see how grants provided have been spent
The public	• Is the business profitable? • Can the business pay its way?	• To assess employment prospects • To assess the contribution to the local economy
Managers	• Is the business making a profit? • Can the business pay its way? • How efficiently is the business using its resources?	• To see if the business is expanding or declining • To see if the business will continue in the foreseeable future • To examine the efficiency of the business and to make comparisons with other, similar, businesses

FINANCIAL STATEMENTS: PUBLIC SECTOR

Who is interested?	What are they interested in?	Why are they interested?
Providers of funds (eg central government, taxpayers, banks)	• What is the income of the organisation? • What is the expenditure of the organisation?	• To see if the income is sufficient to provide the services required of the organisation • To examine the expenditure headings of the organisation and to make comparisons with other, similar, organisations • To see if the organisation's spending is within its authority
The public	• What is the expenditure of the organisation? • How has this changed when compared with previous accounting periods	• To assess the level of spending in relation to the services provided • To see if 'best value' has been achieved • To determine the application of the three 'E's: effectiveness, efficiency and economy
Government and government agencies	• What is the income and expenditure of the organisation? • What resources are used by the organisation?	• To make comparisons of service levels, and income and expenditure with other, similar organisations • To see how grants provided have been spent
Banks/creditors	• Does the organisation have a surplus of income over expenditure? • What is the value of the assets?	• To assess whether to grant a loan or to supply goods or services • To assess the speed and affordability of repayment

FINANCIAL STATEMENTS: NOT-FOR-PROFIT ORGANISATIONS

Members (eg of societies)	• What is the income and expenditure of the organisation? • What resources are used by the organisation?	• To assess the stewardship of elected officers of the organisation in the use of its resources • To establish if the organisation's objectives are being achieved
Donors (eg to charities)	• What is the expenditure of the organisation?	• To decide whether donations have been used effectively
Banks/creditors	• Does the organisation have a surplus of income over expenditure? • What is the value of the assets?	• To assess whether to grant a loan or to supply goods or services • To assess the speed and affordability of repayment

contents of the financial statements

As financial statements are the principal means of communicating accounting information to users they must provide details of:

financial performance

- they assess the stewardship of management
- they make possible an assessment of the effectiveness of the use of the organisation's resources in achieving its objectives, eg in profitability
- they allow comparison to be made with the financial performance from previous accounting periods

financial position

- they provide information about the economic resources used by the organisation
- they provide information about the liquidity, efficient use of resources, and financial position of the organisation

ELEMENTS OF FINANCIAL STATEMENTS

Elements of financial statements are the building blocks from which financial statements are constructed – that is, they are the classes of items which comprise financial statements.

The elements of financial statements are as follows:

- assets
- liabilities
- ownership interest
- income
- expenditure
- contributions from owners
- distributions to owners
- gains
- losses

The way in which the elements link together in the financial statements of income statement and balance sheet, together with definitions, are shown on the next page.

Study the diagrams and then read the text on page 18.

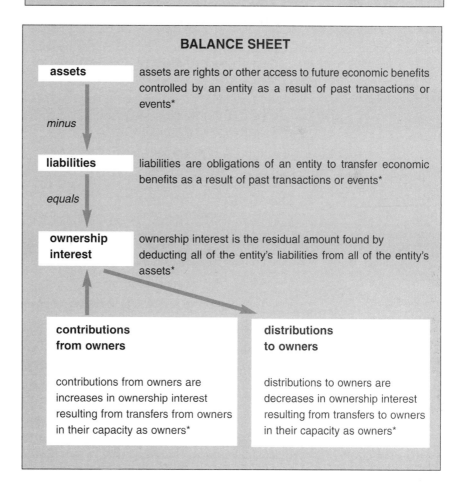

INCOME STATEMENT

| income | income incorporates all forms of income and revenues |

minus

| expenditure | expenditure incorporates all forms of expenses, sometimes referred to as revenue expenditure |

equals

| gains or losses | gains are increases in ownership interest not resulting from contributions from owners* |

losses are decreases in ownership interest not resulting from contributions from owners*

Note: gains and losses also incorporate gains and losses arising from non-revenue items, such as the disposal of fixed assets and the revaluation of assets and liabilities

BALANCE SHEET

| assets | assets are rights or other access to future economic benefits controlled by an entity as a result of past transactions or events* |

minus

| liabilities | liabilities are obligations of an entity to transfer economic benefits as a result of past transactions or events* |

equals

| ownership interest | ownership interest is the residual amount found by deducting all of the entity's liabilities from all of the entity's assets* |

contributions from owners

contributions from owners are increases in ownership interest resulting from transfers from owners in their capacity as owners*

distributions to owners

distributions to owners are decreases in ownership interest resulting from transfers to owners in their capacity as owners*

* definitions taken from *Statement of principles for financial reporting* – see page 22.

importance of elements of financial statements

The importance of the elements of financial statements is that they define the items which can be included in financial statements – if an item does not meet the definitions it cannot be included. The elements are appropriate for the financial statements of all types of organisations:

- private sector organisations produce a profit and loss account to show net profit or loss, together with a balance sheet

- public sector and other not-for-profit organisations produce an income and expenditure account to show a surplus or deficit, together with a balance sheet

THE ACCOUNTING EQUATION

The accounting equation underlies the balance sheet of an organisation and relates to the following elements:

assets *minus* liabilities *equals* ownership interest

In the balance sheet, ownership interest is represented in different forms depending on the type of organisation:

- private sector – capital (for a limited company share capital and reserves)
- public sector – fund accounts
- not-for-profit organisation – accumulated fund

Ownership interest increases with

- gains from the income statement
- gains from non-revenue items, eg upwards revaluation of assets
- contributions from the owners

Ownership interest decreases with

- losses from the income statement
- loss from non-revenue items, eg downwards revaluation of assets
- distributions to owners

For a **company**, the ownership interest is represented by the capital of the company. The profit and loss account links directly to the balance sheet where profits are added to, or losses are deducted from, the capital – thus the profit and loss account explains how the change in capital came about, together with any changes in capital made by the owners – capital introduced or repaid. Some non-revenue gains or losses are reported separately from profit and loss account – for a company, a statement of total recognised gains and losses (see page 139) is used.

For a **public sector organisation** and **not-for-profit organisation**, the ownership interest in the balance sheet is based on fund accounts. A fund represents amounts allocated, earned, or donated for the purposes of the organisation. Examples: a 'task force' is set up by central government to undertake certain activities and is allocated a fund of money for the purpose; a club or society is set up with donations made by the members. Gains or losses are added to, or deducted from, the fund – as with a company, the income and expenditure account of the organisation explains how the change in the fund came about, together with any changes from donations or allocations. Thus, in the balance sheet of a public sector organisation and not-for-profit organisation, the amount of the fund is the equivalent of the capital of a private sector organisation. The accounting equation is therefore:

assets *minus* liabilities *equals* ownership interest

OWNERSHIP INTEREST	
private sector	**public sector/not for profit**
capital from owners	funds allocated or donated
profit or loss from profit and loss account	surplus or deficit from income and expenditure account
other gains or losses	other gains or losses

THE REGULATORY FRAMEWORK OF ACCOUNTING

The regulatory framework forms the 'rules' of accounting. When drafting financial statements, accountants seek to follow the same set of rules – thus enabling broad comparisons to be made between the financial results of different organisations.

The regulatory framework comprises

* accounting standards (in the form of Statements of Standard Accounting Practice, and Financial Reporting Standards)
* company law
* Statement of principles for financial reporting

Collectively, this regulatory framework is often referred to as 'UK GAAP', ie the United Kingdom's Generally Accepted Accounting Practice. For companies quoted on the Stock Exchange, UK GAAP will also include the Stock Exchange's *Listing Regulations*.

The diagram on the next page shows how the regulatory framework developed during the last three decades of the twentieth century.

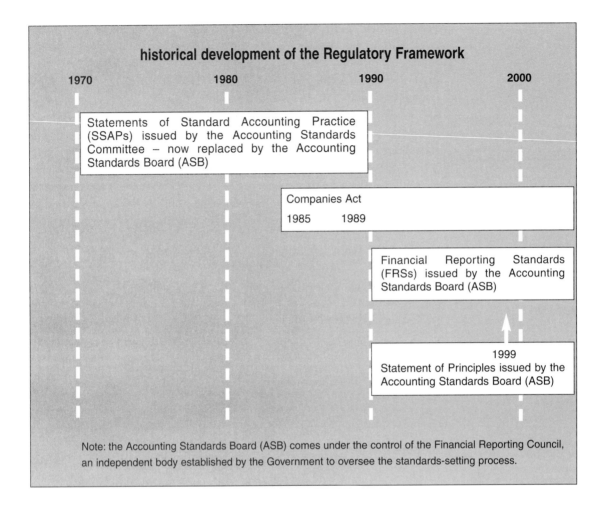

historical development of the Regulatory Framework

1970	1980	1990	2000

Statements of Standard Accounting Practice (SSAPs) issued by the Accounting Standards Committee – now replaced by the Accounting Standards Board (ASB)

Companies Act

1985   1989

Financial Reporting Standards (FRSs) issued by the Accounting Standards Board (ASB)

1999
Statement of Principles issued by the Accounting Standards Board (ASB)

Note: the Accounting Standards Board (ASB) comes under the control of the Financial Reporting Council, an independent body established by the Government to oversee the standards-setting process.

accounting standards

Since 1971 a number of accounting standards have been produced to provide a framework for accounting and to reduce the variety of accounting treatments which companies may use in their financial statements.

Statements of Standard Accounting Practice (SSAPs) were issued by the Accounting Standards Committee (replaced by the Accounting Standards Board in 1990) between 1971 and 1990. Twenty-five standards were issued – over half of these have now been withdrawn and replaced by Financial Reporting Standards.

Financial Reporting Standards (FRSs) have been issued by the Accounting Standards Board (ASB) since 1991. A list of current FRSs, at the time of writing, is shown on pages 175-176. The ASB's aim has been to develop standards that are consistent with one another and to reduce the number of options allowed in the preparation of financial statements.

Company Law

The Companies Act 1985 (as amended by the Companies Act 1989) states the detailed accounting requirements that must be shown when preparing the financial statements of limited companies (see Chapter 6).

In particular, the 1989 Act introduced a requirement that company accounts must state that they have been prepared in accordance with applicable accounting standards and, if there have been any material departures, must give details and the reasons for such departures.

Statement of Principles for Financial Reporting

Although not an accounting standard, Statement of Principles has been developed by the Accounting Standards Board to set out the principles that should underlie the preparation and presentation of financial statements. It is designed to:

- provide a coherent frame of reference to be used in the development and review of accounting standards
- reduce the need to debate fundamental issues when accounting standards are developed or revised
- help preparers and auditors of accounts to analyse issues not covered by accounting standards

Financial Reporting Standard for Smaller Entities (FRSSE)

FRSSE has been developed for small companies and, generally, it provides a simplified version of the requirements from other accounting standards. It also allows for some disclosure requirements required by accounting standards to be excluded.

A small company satisfies two or more of the following criteria:

- turnover (sales) does not exceed £2.8m per year
- assets do not exceed £1.4m
- average number of employees does not exceed 50

THE STANDARDS-SETTING PROCESS

In later chapters we will focus on the use of accounting standards – both Statements of Standard Accounting Practice (SSAPs) and Financial Reporting Standards (FRSs). Here we will look in more detail at the standards-setting process.

Accounting Standards Board – role and structure

The Accounting Standards Board (ASB) was set up in 1990 to develop, issue and withdraw accounting standards. It comes under the control of the Financial Reporting Council, which is an independent body established by the Government to oversee the standards-setting process.

ASB has a full-time Chairman and Technical Director. There is a maximum of nine board members, supported by technical and administrative staff.

accounting standards – the development process

The SSAPs which were current in 1990 at the time of the formation of the ASB were adopted by the Board. (The SSAPs had been developed between 1971 and 1990 by the ASB's predecessor, the Accounting Standards Committee.) Since 1990 a number of SSAPs have been replaced by FRSs.

The procedure for developing new standards is that appropriate topics are identified by the Board from either its own research or submissions made by interested parties. A discussion paper and consultation process then follows which may lead to the publication of a Financial Reporting Exposure Draft (FRED). A wider consultation process now takes place, with views being taken into account, before the FRED is issued as an FRS by the board (a two-thirds majority of the board is required).

authority of accounting standards

Although not laws in themselves, accounting standards are defined in the Companies Act 1989. The Act requires directors of companies – other than small or medium-sized companies – to disclose whether the accounts have been prepared in accordance with applicable accounting standards, particulars of any material departure from those standards, and the reasons for any such departure.

STATEMENT OF PRINCIPLES FOR FINANCIAL REPORTING

As we have seen earlier, Statement of Principles sets out the principles that should underlie the preparation and presentation of financial statements. It comprises eight chapters, each dealing with key issues:

1   The objective of financial statements

2   The reporting entity

3   The qualitative characteristics of financial information

4   The elements of financial statements

5   Recognition in financial statements

6   Measurement in financial statements

7   Presentation of financial information

8   Accounting for interests in other entities

For a study of this Unit the relevant chapters are 1 to 5, and 7.

Chapter 1   The objective of financial statements

As we saw earlier (page 13), the objective of financial statements is *'to provide information about the reporting entity's financial performance and financial position that is useful to a wide range of users for assessing the stewardship of the entity's management and for making economic decisions'*.

Users of financial statements are:

- present and potential investors
- lenders
- suppliers and other trade creditors
- employees
- customers
- governments and their agencies
- the public

Of these users, Statement of Principles sees investors as being the primary group for whom the financial statements are prepared.

Information for users is to be provided in four areas:

1   **financial performance** – the return (from profit and loss account) an entity obtains from the resources it controls

2   **financial position** – as shown by the balance sheet, including

- the economic resources (ie assets and liabilities) controlled by an entity
- the financial structure (ie capital gearing)
- liquidity and solvency
- capacity to adapt to changes

3   **generation and use of cash** – information from the cash flow statement to show the cash from operations, investment activities and financial activities

4   **financial adaptability** – the ability of an entity to take effective action to alter the amount and timing of its cash flows, including the ability to

- raise new capital
- repay capital or debt
- sell assets (without disrupting continuing operations)
- rapidly improve cash inflows from operations

Chapter 2   The reporting entity

- an entity should prepare and publish financial statements
  - when there is a legitimate demand for the information
  - when it is a cohesive economic unit
- what activities to include
  - those activities that are under the direct or indirect control of the entity

Chapter 3   Qualitative characteristics of financial information

Four characteristics are identified by Statement of Principles:

1 relevance
2 reliability   ⟩ these relate to the content of information

3 comparability
4 understandability ⟩ these relate to the presentation of information

The diagram below shows these characteristics:

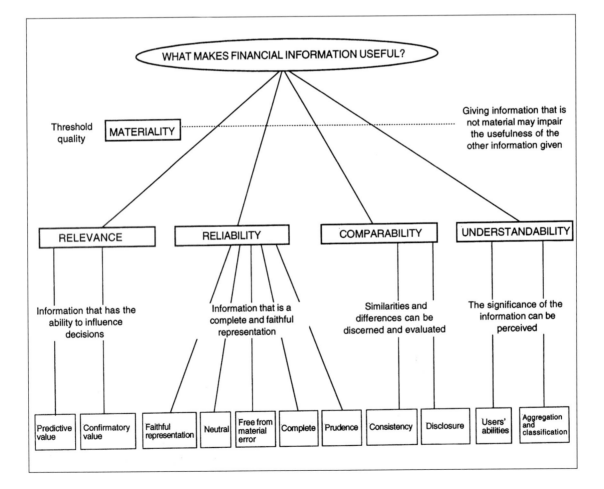

relevant information

The diagram shows that, for information to be *relevant* it must have:

- the ability to influence the economic decisions of users
- predictive value, which helps users to evaluate or assess past, present or future events
- confirmatory value, which helps users to confirm their past evaluations

reliable information

For information to be *reliable* it must be

- a faithful representation, ie it corresponds to the effect of transactions or events
- neutral, ie it is free from deliberate or systematic bias
- free from material error, ie it is accurately recorded and reported
- complete, within the bounds of materiality
- prudent, ie a degree of caution has been applied when making judgements and estimates

comparability

Comparability enables other financial statements for the entity from other time periods to be compared so as to identify trends. It incorporates

- consistency, ie the same accounting techniques have been used throughout the entity both within the same accounting period and also from one period to the next
- disclosure of accounting policies used in the preparation of the financial statements

understandability

Understandability means that the users of financial statements should be able to perceive the significance of the information.

materiality

This chapter of Statement of Principles also incorporates the test of *materiality*. Although materiality is rarely defined in law or accounting standards, the preparer of financial statements must make judgements as to whether or not an item is material. As Statement of Principles says: 'An item of information is material to the financial statements if its misstatement or omission might reasonably be expected to influence the economic decisions of users of those financial statements, including their assessments of management's stewardship'. It goes on to say: 'Whether information is material will depend on the size and nature of the item in question judged in the particular circumstances of the case'. Thus materiality depends very much on the size of the business: a large company may consider that items of less than £1,000 are not material; a small company will use a much lower figure. What is material, and what is not, becomes a matter of judgement, based on the overall usefulness of the financial information.

Chapter 4 The elements of financial statements

Elements of financial statements are the classes of items that financial statements comprise. The elements are listed as being:

- assets
- liabilities
- ownership interest
- gains
- losses
- contributions from owners
- distributions to owners

Statement of Principles gives a definition of each element and these have already been given earlier in this Chapter (page 13).

Chapter 5 Recognition in financial statements

The term 'recognition' means the recording in financial statements of transactions or events, eg bought vehicles for £20,000, paying by cheque; bought a stock of goods for resale £2,000 on credit; sold goods for cash £250.

There are three stages in the recognition process:

- **initial recognition**, which is where an item is recorded in the financial statements for the first time, eg bought vehicles for £20,000

- **subsequent remeasurement**, which involves changing the amount at which an already recognised asset or liability is stated in the financial statements, eg depreciation on vehicles for the year £5,000

- **derecognition**, which is where an item that has previously been recognised ceases to be recognised, eg sold vehicles for £15,000

Statement of Principles acknowledges that there are often areas of uncertainty in the recognition process – for example, in a manufacturing business, there may be uncertainty as to the point at which raw materials stock becomes work-in-progress, and again as to the point at which work-in-progress becomes finished goods. The Statement indicates that the effect of a transaction to create a new asset or liability, or add to an existing asset or liability, will be recognised if:

- sufficient evidence exists that the new asset or liability has been created or that there has been an addition to an existing asset or liability; and

- the new asset or liability or the addition to the existing asset or liability can be measured at a monetary amount with sufficient reliability

Statement of Principles acknowledges that entities operate in an uncertain business environment which can lead to uncertainty in the recognition process:

- **element uncertainty**
  - does the item exist?
  - does it meet the definitions of the elements of financial statements?
- **measurement uncertainty**
  - at what money amount should the item be recognised?

Uncertainty in the recognition process also requires the exercise of **prudence**. In particular, there needs to be stronger evidence of existence, and a greater reliability of measurement, for assets and gains when compared with liabilities and losses. However, the exercise of prudence must not lead to the omission or understatement of assets and gains, nor the deliberate overstatement of liabilities and losses.

Chapter 7   Presentation of financial information

This chapter of Statement of Principles is concerned with the good presentation of financial information so that the essential messages of the financial statements are communicated clearly and effectively and in as simple and straightforward a manner as possible.

The term 'financial statements' comprises the primary financial statements – financial performance (profit and loss account or income statement), balance sheet, and cash flow statement – together with supporting notes that amplify and explain the statements.

Statement of financial performance

Good presentation of profit and loss account (or income statement) involves:

- recognising only gains or losses
- classifying the components of the statement by function (eg production, selling, administrative) and by nature (eg employment costs, interest payable)
- identifying separately amounts that are affected by changes in economic conditions or business activity (eg from continuing and discontinued activities of the business; from geographical areas)
- identifying separately
  - items of an unusual amount
  - special items such as interest payable and taxation
  - items that relate mainly to future profits, eg research and development expenditure

Balance sheet

Good presentation of balance sheet involves:

- recognising only assets, liabilities and ownership interest
- classifying assets to help users to assess the nature, amounts and liquidity of available resources
- classifying liabilities to help users to assess the nature, amounts and timing of obligations
- classifying assets by function, eg fixed assets; current assets

Cash flow statement

Good presentation involves showing the extent to which the entity's activities generate and use cash. In particular, a distinction needs to be made between cash flows from the operations of the entity (eg from selling products), and from other activities (eg purchase or sale of fixed assets).

Accompanying information

This is information which accompanies and complements the financial statements, but which does not form part of the financial statements. Examples of accompanying information include directors' reports, chairman's statement, operating and financial reviews.

Good presentation involves a discussion of:

- the main factors underlying the financial performance, including the principal risks, uncertainties and trends of the main business areas and how the entity is responding to them
- the strategies being adopted on capital structure
- the activities and expenditure that are being invested for the future

ACCOUNTING CONCEPTS

There are a number of accounting concepts which form the 'bedrock' of the preparation of financial statements. Some are included in Statement of Principles (see previous section), while others are discussed further in FRS 18, entitled *Accounting policies*.

Accounting concepts are illustrated in the diagram opposite and include:

business entity

This refers to the fact that financial statements record and report on the activities of one particular entity. They do not include the personal assets and liabilities of those who play a part in owning or running the entity.

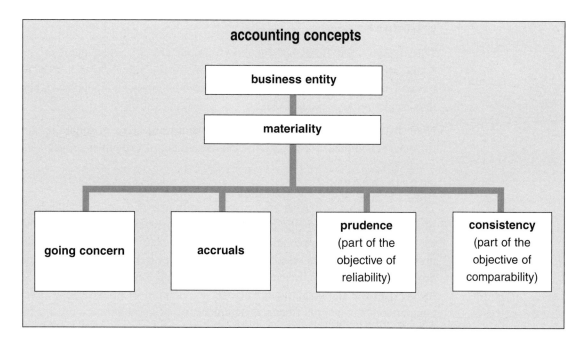

materiality

Some items are of such low value that it is not worth recording them separately in the accounting records, ie they are not 'material'. Examples include

- small expense items grouped together as sundry expenses
- small end-of-year stocks of office stationery not valued for the purpose of financial statements
- low-cost fixed assets being charged as an expense in profit and loss account

going concern

This presumes that the entity to which the financial statements relate will continue in the foreseeable future, ie there is no intention to reduce significantly the size of the entity or to liquidate it. Values based on break-up amounts – a 'gone concern' – tend not to be relevant to users seeking to assess the entity's ability to generate cash or to adapt to changing circumstances.

accruals

This means that expenses and revenues are matched so that they concern the same goods or services and the same time period. Profit and loss account shows the amount of the expense that should have been incurred and the amount of income that should have been received.

prudence

This requires that financial statements should always, when there is any doubt, report a conservative figure for profit or the valuation of assets. To this end, profits are not to be anticipated and should only be recognised when they can be reliably measured.

Note that prudence is one aspect of the overall objective of reliability for financial statements – see diagram from Statement of Principles on page 24.

consistency

This requires that, when an entity adopts particular accounting methods, it should normally continue to use such methods consistently. For example, the use of straight-line depreciation for a particular class of fixed asset would normally continue to be used in the future; however, changes can be made provided there are good reasons for so doing, and a note of explanation is included in the financial statements. By application of consistency, direct comparison between the financial statements of different years can be made.

Note that consistency is one aspect of the overall objective of comparability for financial statements – see diagram from Statement of Principles on page 24.

other concepts

There are other concepts – such as money measurement, historical cost, duality – which are followed when preparing financial statements. These will have been covered in earlier studies at NVQ Level in Accounting.

CHAPTER SUMMARY

- The different types of organisations are classified between those in the private sector, the public sector and other not-for-profit organisations

- The objectives of organisations are
  - profit in the private sector
  - best value in the public sector
  - provision of mutual services by other not-for-profit organisations

- The two main financial statements used by all types of organisations comprise an income statement (eg profit and loss account) and a balance sheet.

- There is a wide variety of users of financial statements – investors, lenders, employees, the public, etc.

- The elements of financial statements are: assets, liabilities, ownership interest, income, expenditure, contributions from owners, distributions to owners, gains, losses.

- The regulatory framework of accounting, often referred to as UK GAAP, comprises
  - Companies Act 1985, 1989
  - Statements of Standard Accounting Practice
  - Financial Reporting Standards
  - Statement of Principles

- Statement of Principles for Financial Reporting sets out the principles that should underlie the preparation and presentation of financial statements. It comprises eight chapters, each dealing with key issues.

- Accounting concepts form the 'bedrock' of the preparation of financial statements; they include: business entity, materiality, going concern, accruals, prudence and consistency

private sector organisations	owned by private individuals, in the form of companies, partnerships and sole trader businesses
public sector organisations	owned directly or indirectly by central or local government
other not-for-profit organisations	provide mutual services to their members and the community
stewardship	the accountability of the entity's management for the safe-keeping of the organisation's resources and for their proper, efficient and profitable use
economic decisions	making use of information from financial statements to help in making decisions about investment or potential investment in the entity
elements of financial statements	the building blocks from which financial statements are constructed
income statement	income *minus* expenditure *equals* gains or losses
balance sheet	assets *minus* liabilities *equals* ownership interest
SSAP	Statement of Standard Accounting Practice
FRS	Financial Reporting Standard
FRSSE	Financial Reporting Standard for Smaller Entities

STUDENT ACTIVITIES

Osborne Books is grateful to the AAT for their kind permission to use Central Assessment task material for the following activities: 1.8, 1.9, 1.10, 1.11.

1.1 Which of the following cannot be described as a public sector or not-for-profit organisation?

(a) The National Health Service

(b) A registered charity

(c) A Local Authority

(d) A private limited company

1.2 Which of the following statements is correct?

(a) Assets – Liabilities = Ownership interest

(b) Assets + Liabilities = Ownership interest

(c) Current Assets – Current Liabilities = Ownership interest

(d) Current Assets + Current Liabilities = Ownership interest

1.3 An income and expenditure account is similar to a:

(a) Bank reconciliation statement

(b) Trial Balance

(c) Profit and Loss Account

(d) Balance Sheet

1.4 Name three user groups of private sector financial statements indicating the type of financial information each group might be interested in.

1.5 Distinguish between 'stewardship' and 'economic decisions' in relation to Financial Statements.

1.6 Explain the following terms used in financial accounting.

(a) Going concern

(b) Prudence

(c) Business entity

(d) Matching/accruals

1.7   In preparing the accounts of Harold for the year to 31st March 20-2 a number of problems were encountered. These were as follows:

(a)   The business bank account had paid Harold's daughters' school fees for the year.

(b)   At 31st March 20-2 there was a box of pencils left in the stationery cupboard, and Harold was not sure if this should be included as closing stock.

(c)   The short-term viability of Harold's business seems extremely uncertain.

(d)   During the year Harold paid £6,000 rent but he is puzzled because only £5,000 appears in the profit and loss account and £1,000 appears in the balance sheet as a prepayment.

(e)   It was rumoured that one of Harold's customers had gone into liquidation, owing the business £500.

(f)   In previous years Harold had valued his closing stock on a FIFO (first in first out) basis, but this year he believed he would pay less income tax if he valued the same stock on a LIFO (last in first out) basis.

REQUIRED

State which accounting concept(s) relates to each of the above problems (a) - (f) and show how each concept should be applied in the case of Harold's business.

1.8   You have been asked to advise Jonathan Brown, a sole trader, on the accounting treatment of certain transactions which he considers might affect his financial statements for the year ended 31 December 20-5. The matters on which he would like your advice are set out below.

(a)   The business paid for an advertising campaign during the year at a cost of £2,800. It is estimated by Jonathan Brown that this will lead to an overall increase in sales of 15%. Half of this increase was achieved in 20-5 and the other half is expected to be achieved in 20-6.

(b)   Jonathan Brown took stock costing £500 from the business at the end of the year for his own use. He removed the stock on 31 December 20-5 after the year-end stock count had taken place. No adjustment was made to the stock balance to take account of this action.

(c)   Jonathan Brown has put his own house up as security for a loan made by the bank to his business. The loan was made specifically for the business and not for the personal use of Jonathan Brown.

REQUIRED

Advise Jonathan Brown on the accounting treatment of these transactions in his financial statements for the year ended 31 December 20-5. Explain your treatment, where relevant, by reference to accounting concepts and accounting principles.

1.9 **Task 1**

(a) What is the objective of financial statements?

(b) Illustrate how this objective is fulfilled by considering the financial statements of one type of profit-making body and one type of public sector or not-for-profit organisation.

Task 2

(a) Identify the elements of financial statements.

(b) Explain how the elements are related in the balance sheet and in the profit and loss account of a profit-making organisation and the relationship between the two financial statements.

(c) What major difference would you expect to find in the balance sheet of a public sector or not-for-profit organisation when compared with that of a profit-making organisation?

1.10 **Task 1**

State one type of profit-making and one type of public sector or not-for-profit organisation. For each type of organisation:

(a) give one example of an external user of the financial statements, and

(b) describe one type of decision which would be made by the users with the assistance of the financial statements of the organisation.

Task 2

The accounting equation is often expressed as:

ASSETS – LIABILITIES = OWNERSHIP INTEREST

(a) Explain what each of the terms 'assets', 'liabilities' and 'ownership interest' means.

(b) Identify, in general terms only, the balances that would appear in the 'ownership interest' section of the balance sheet of one profit-making and one public sector or not-for-profit organisation.

1.11 The directors of Machier Ltd have asked you a number of questions about financial statements. Prepare notes for the directors answering the following questions:

(a) What are the elements in a balance sheet of a company? State which of the balances in the balance sheet of Machier Ltd (shown on the opposite page) fall under each element.

(b) How are the elements related in the Accounting Equation? Show numerically that the accounting equation is maintained in the balance sheet of Machier Ltd.

(c) What is the difference between an income and expenditure account of a not-for-profit organisation and a profit and loss account for a commercial company?

(d) What is the equivalent of the capital balances in a not-for-profit organisation?

Machier Ltd

Balance Sheet as at 31 March 20-9

	£000
Fixed assets	4,282
Current assets	
Stocks	448
Debtors	527
Cash	–
	975
Current liabilities	
Trade creditors	381
Dividends payable	20
Taxation	165
Bank overdraft	183
	749
Net current assets	226
Long-term loan	2,800
	1,708
Captial and reserves	
Called up share capital	200
Share premium	100
Profit and loss account	1,408
	1,708

2 SOLE TRADER FINAL ACCOUNTS

this chapter covers . . .

This chapter examines the financial statements (or final accounts) of a sole trader business which are produced at the end of each accounting period. The final accounts comprise profit and loss account and balance sheet. The chapter covers:

- extended trial balance

- conventional format final accounts used by accountants

- adjustments to final accounts for

  - closing stock

  - accruals and prepayments

  - depreciation of fixed assets

  - bad debts written off and provision for bad debts

- accounts of service sector businesses

NVQ PERFORMANCE CRITERIA COVERED

unit 11: DRAFTING FINANCIAL STATEMENTS

element 2

draft limited company, sole trader and partnership year end financial statements

- financial statements are accurately drafted from the appropriate information

- subsequent adjustments are correctly implemented

- year end financial statements are presented for approval to the appropriate person in clear form

- confidentiality procedures are followed at all times

- the organisation's policies, regulations, procedures and timescales relating to financial statements are observed at all times

- discrepancies, unusual features or queries are identified and either resolved or referred to the appropriate person

SOLE TRADERS

Sole traders are people who are in business on their own: they run shops, factories, farms, garages, local franchises, etc. The businesses are generally small because the owner usually has a limited amount of capital. Profits are often small and, after the owner has taken out drawings, are usually ploughed back into the business.

People set up as sole traders for various reasons:

• the owner has independence and can run the business, by and large, without the need to consult others

• in a small business with few, if any, employees, personal service and supervision by the owner are available at all times

• the business is easy to establish legally – either using the owner's name, or a trading name such as 'Wyvern Plumbers'

The disadvantages of a sole-trader business are:

• the owner has unlimited liability for the debts of the business – this means that if the sole trader should become insolvent, the owner's personal assets may be used to pay creditors

• expansion is limited because it can only be achieved by the owner ploughing back profits, or by borrowing from a lender such as a bank

• the owner usually has to work long hours and it may be difficult to find time to take holidays; if the owner should become ill the work of the business will either slow down or stop altogether

CONFIDENTIALITY PROCEDURES

Sole traders often seek professional help with the financial affairs of the business – especially for the preparation of final accounts. All financial information should be treated with confidentiality by outsiders and

– should not be revealed to anyone outside the business (unless authorisation is given by the owner, for example to give information to the bank or Inland Revenue)

– should be revealed only within the business to the sole trader, or to those within the business whom the sole trader has authorised to receive it

The financial statements of sole traders have to be disclosed to very few people – the Inland Revenue (for income tax), and lenders (if any) such as banks. Apart from these, sole traders can keep their financial statements private.

FINANCIAL STATEMENTS AND THE TRIAL BALANCE

financial statements

The financial statements (or final accounts) of a sole trader comprise:

- an **income statement**, which normally takes the form of a profit and loss account (and incorporates a trading account for businesses that buy and sell goods) and shows the profit or loss of the business

- a **balance sheet**, which shows the assets and liabilities of the business together with the owner's capital

These financial statements can be produced more often than once a year in order to give information to the owner on how the business is progressing. However, it is customary to produce annual accounts for the benefit of the Inland Revenue, bank manager and other interested parties. In this way the profit and loss account covers an accounting period of a financial year (which can end at any date – it doesn't have to be the calendar year), and the balance sheet shows the state of the business at the end of the accounting period.

trial balance

The starting point for preparing final accounts is the **trial balance** prepared by the book-keeper: all the figures recorded on the trial balance are used in the final accounts. The book-keeper's two-column trial balance is often extended into a spreadsheet with a number of columns – this format is called the **extended trial balance** (ETB).

The extended trial balance gives an understanding of the principles of final accounts by showing:

- the profit or loss made by the business during the accounting period

- the assets, liabilities and capital of the business at the end of the accounting period

The extended trial balance format is often used by accountancy firms as a first step towards preparing year-end accounts for their clients. The use of ETBs is covered fully at NVQ level 3 in Accounting. Here we will use them as the starting point in the preparation of final accounts in the conventional format used by accountants.

The following Case Study starts with the book-keeper's two-column trial balance and then shows how the extended trial balance format uses columns and rows to prepare the final accounts. A reminder of the steps to complete the extended trial balance is given on page 41. Later on we will see how the ETB is used in the preparation of accounts in the conventional format.

CASE STUDY

TARA SMITH:
THE EXTENDED TRIAL BALANCE

situation

Tara Smith runs a designer fashion shop in town. Her book-keeper has just extracted the year-end trial balance shown below. Note that the trial balance includes the stock value at the *start* of the year, while the end-of-year stock valuation is given *after* the trial balance. For the purposes of financial accounting, the stock of goods for resale is valued by the business (and may be verified by the auditor) at the end of each financial year, and the valuation is subsequently entered into the book-keeping system.

TARA SMITH, TRADING AS 'THE FASHION SHOP'
Trial balance as at 31 December 2002

	Dr £	Cr £
Stock at 1 January 2002	12,500	
Purchases	105,000	
Sales		155,000
Administration expenses	6,200	
Wages	23,500	
Rent paid	750	
Telephone	500	
Interest paid	4,500	
Travel expenses	550	
Premises	100,000	
Shop fittings	20,000	
Debtors	10,500	
Bank	5,450	
Cash	50	
Capital		75,000
Drawings	7,000	
Loan from bank		50,000
Creditors		14,500
Value Added Tax		2,000
	296,500	296,500

Note: stock at 31 December 2002 was valued at £10,500

solution

The layout on the next page shows how an extended trial balance uses columns and rows to prepare the final accounts of Tara Smith. Note that the profit and loss account column incorporates the trading account. The steps to complete the extended trial balance are set out on page 41 and the layout of Tara's financial statements is shown on pages 43 to 45.

EXTENDED TRIAL BALANCE   TARA SMITH TRADING AS 'THE FASHION SHOP'   31 DECEMBER 2002

Description	Ledger balances		Adjustments		Profit and loss		Balance sheet	
	Dr £	Cr £	Dr £	Cr £	Dr £	Cr £	Dr £	Cr £
Stock at 1 Jan 2002	12,500				12,500			
Purchases	105,000				105,000			
Sales		155,000				155,000		
Administration expenses	6,200				6,200			
Wages	23,500				23,500			
Rent paid	750				750			
Telephone	500				500			
Interest paid	4,500				4,500			
Travel expenses	550				550			
Premises	100,000						100,000	
Shop fittings	20,000						20,000	
Debtors	10,500						10,500	
Bank	5,450						5,450	
Cash	50						50	
Capital		75,000						75,000
Drawings	7,000						7,000	
Loan from bank		50,000						50,000
Creditors		14,500						14,500
Value Added Tax		2,000						2,000
Closing stock: Profit and loss				10,500		10,500		
Closing stock: Balance sheet			10,500				10,500	
Accruals								
Prepayments								
Depreciation								
Bad debts								
Provision for bad debts: adjustment								
Net profit/loss					12,000			12,000
	296,500	296,500	10,500	10,500	165,500	165,500	153,500	153,500

completing the extended trial balance . . .

1 Enter the trial balance details into the description and ledger balances columns. Total the debit and credit columns of ledger balances to show that the trial balance proves the arithmetical accuracy of the book-keeping. Note that the blank lines after premises and shop fittings will be used for depreciation amounts – see the Case Study on page 48

2 Deal with adjustments – in this example, the only adjustment is for the valuation of closing stock at 31 December 2002. In the adjustments columns the amount of closing stock is credited to the profit and loss account and debited to the balance sheet. Now total the debit and credit adjustment columns; note that totals are the same, ie they balance. We shall be using the other adjustment items in the Case Study on page 48.

3 Transfer to the profit and loss columns (which incorporate the trading account) the rows for

- opening stock
- closing stock (from the adjustments column)
- purchases made by the business
- sales made by the business (together with any small amounts of income)
- revenue expenditure of the business

From the trial balance and adjustment columns, ensure that debit balances are entered in the debit column of profit and loss account and credit balances are entered in the credit column.

4 Transfer to the balance sheet columns the remaining rows from the trial balance and adjustments columns. These represent:

- assets
- liabilities
- capital
- drawings

5 In the profit and loss columns, total the money amounts and then, just like balancing an account, enter the amount required to make both debit and credit sides equal: here it is £12,000. If the amount is entered on the debit side, it represents the net profit of the business for the accounting period; if on the credit side, it is a loss. For Tara Smith, it is a profit of £12,000 for the financial year.

6 Enter the net profit or loss in the balance sheet column, but on the opposite side to that in profit and loss. For example, with Tara Smith's business, the amount of the net profit row is £12,000, which is:

- entered in the debit column of profit and loss
- entered in the credit column of the balance sheet

Now total the debit and credit balance sheet columns. They balance with the same total – here £153,500 – which proves that the balance sheet balances.

Trading account shows gross profit for the accounting period. **Profit and loss account** shows net profit for the accounting period. Note that 'profit and loss account' is often used as a general heading which includes both of these financial statements.

The amounts for **sales** and **purchases** include only items in which the business trades – eg a clothes shop buying clothes from the manufacturer and selling to the public. Note that items bought for use in the business, such as a new till for the shop, are not included with purchases but are shown as assets on the balance sheet.

Cost of sales represents the cost to the business of the goods which have been sold in this financial year. Cost of sales is:

	opening stock	(stock bought previously)
plus	purchases	(purchased during the year)
minus	closing stock	(stock left unsold at the end of the year)
equals	cost of sales	(cost of what has actually been sold)

Gross profit is calculated as:

sales – cost of sales = gross profit

If cost of sales is greater than sales, the business has made a gross loss.

Overheads are the running costs of the business – known as *revenue expenditure*. The categories of overheads used vary according to the needs of each business.

Net profit is calculated as:

gross profit – overheads = net profit

If overheads are more than gross profit, the business has made a net loss.

The net profit is the amount the business earned for the owner during the year, and is subject to taxation. The owner can draw some or all of the net profit for personal use in the form of drawings. Part of the profit might well be left in the business in order to help build up the business for the future.

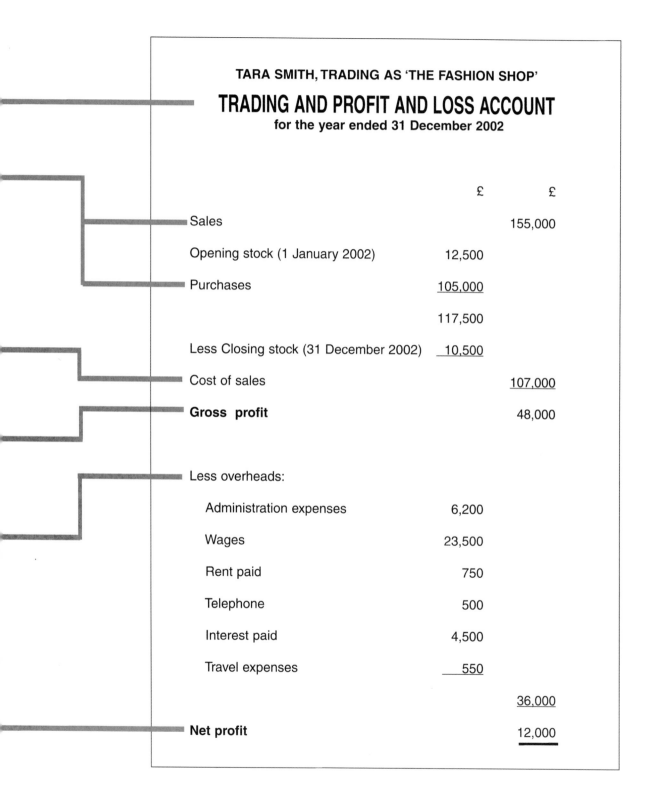

TARA SMITH, TRADING AS 'THE FASHION SHOP'

TRADING AND PROFIT AND LOSS ACCOUNT
for the year ended 31 December 2002

	£	£
Sales		155,000
Opening stock (1 January 2002)	12,500	
Purchases	105,000	
	117,500	
Less Closing stock (31 December 2002)	10,500	
Cost of sales		107,000
Gross profit		48,000
Less overheads:		
Administration expenses	6,200	
Wages	23,500	
Rent paid	750	
Telephone	500	
Interest paid	4,500	
Travel expenses	550	
		36,000
Net profit		12,000

Fixed assets comprise the long-term items owned by a business which are not bought with the intention of selling them off in the near future, eg premises, machinery, motor vehicles, office equipment, shop fittings, etc.

Current assets comprise short-term assets which change regularly, eg stock of goods for resale, debtors, bank balances and cash. These items will alter as the business trades, eg stock will be sold, or more will be bought; debtors will make payment to the business, or sales on credit will be made; the cash and bank balances will alter with the flow of money paid into the bank account, or as withdrawals are made.

Current liabilities are due for repayment within twelve months of the date of the balance sheet, eg creditors, and bank overdraft (which is usually repayable on demand, unlike a bank loan which is negotiated for a particular time period).

Working capital is the excess of current assets over current liabilities, ie current assets minus current liabilities = working capital. Without adequate working capital, a business will find it difficult to continue to operate. Working capital is also often referred to as net current assets.

Long-term liabilities are where repayment is due in more than one year from the date of the balance sheet; they are often described by terms such as 'bank loan,' 'long-term loan,' or 'mortgage.'

Net assets is the total of fixed and current assets, less current and long-term liabilities. The net assets are financed by the owner of the business, in the form of capital. Net assets therefore equals the total of the 'financed by' section – the balance sheet 'balances'.

Capital is the owner's investment, and is a liability of a business, ie it is what the business owes the owner.

TARA SMITH, TRADING AS 'THE FASHION SHOP'

BALANCE SHEET

as at 31 December 2002

	£	£
Fixed Assets		
Premises		100,000
Shop fittings		20,000
		120,000
Current Assets		
Stock	10,500	
Debtors	10,500	
Bank	5,450	
Cash	50	
	26,500	
Less Current Liabilities		
Creditors	16,500	
Working Capital		10,000
		130,000
Less Long-term Liabilities		
Loan from bank		50,000
NET ASSETS		80,000
FINANCED BY		
Capital		
Opening capital		75,000
Add net profit		12,000
		87,000
Less drawings		7,000
Closing capital		80,000

THE ETB AND CONVENTIONAL ACCOUNTS

The extended trial balance does not present final accounts in the conventional format used by accountants. The figures are taken from the profit and loss and balance sheet columns of the ETB and presented in the vertical format – running down the page – shown on page 43 (trading and profit and loss account) and on page 45 (balance sheet) for Tara Smith; notes to explain various aspects of these conventional accounts are given on pages 42 and 44.

FINAL ACCOUNTS – THE SIX ADJUSTMENTS

Whilst the starting point for the preparation of final accounts is the book-keeper's two-column trial balance, if we used only the trial balance figures (which record the financial transactions that have taken place) the resultant final accounts would show an inaccurate picture of the state of the business. Adjustments are made with the aim of improving the accuracy of the financial statements in showing the profit, and the assets and liabilities of the business.

The six main adjustments to final accounts are for:

1 closing stock

2 accruals

3 prepayments

4 depreciation of fixed assets

5 bad debts written off

6 provision for bad debts

These adjustments are covered fully at NVQ level 3 in Accounting. The effect of each on the final accounts is summarised as follows:

1 closing stock

- deduct from purchases in trading account
- current asset in balance sheet

Note that this adjustment was incorporated into the Case Study on page 39.

2 accrual of expenses

- increase expense in profit and loss account
- current liability in balance sheet

Note: there may also be accruals and prepayments at the start of the year which need to be allowed for when calculating the expense amount for profit and loss account. Income items, eg rent received, can also be accrued – increase income, current asset in balance sheet.

3 **prepayment of expenses**

– decrease expense in profit and loss account

– current asset in balance sheet

Note: there may also be accruals and prepayments at the start of the year which need to be allowed for when calculating the expense amount for profit and loss account. Income items can also be prepaid – decrease income, current liability in balance sheet.

4 **provision for depreciation of fixed assets**

– expense in profit and loss account

– fixed asset value reduced in balance sheet

5 **bad debts written off**

– expense in profit and loss account

– debtors' figure reduced in balance sheet

6 **provision for bad debts**

increase in provision for bad debts

– expense in profit and loss account

– debtors' figure reduced in balance sheet by amount of total provision

decrease in provision for bad debts

– income in profit and loss account

– debtors' figure reduced in balance sheet by amount of remaining provision

Using the extended trial balance format, we start with the trial balance from the book-keeping records and then use the adjustments column to record closing stock, accruals and prepayments, depreciation, bad debts, and provision for bad debts. The adjusted figures are then recorded under the appropriate headings of profit and loss account and balance sheet.

The following Case Study develops the trial balance of Tara Smith (from the Case Study seen earlier on page 39) and incorporates the six adjustments into the extended trial balance.

In a further Case Study (page 51), the 'profit and loss' and 'balance sheet' columns of the ETB are used to present the final accounts in the conventional format used by accountants.

TARA SMITH: ADJUSTMENTS TO FINAL ACCOUNTS

situation

Using the trial balance of Tara Smith at 31 December 2002, shown on page 39, we will make the following adjustments at that date:

- stock was valued at £10,500
- telephone expenses accrued £100
- rent prepaid £75
- depreciate the premises (which were bought during the year) at 2 per cent per annum, using the straight-line method
- depreciate the shop fittings (which were bought during the year) at 25 per cent per annum, using the reducing balance method
- write off bad debts of £100
- create a provision for bad debts of £250

solution

The layout on the next page shows how these adjustments are incorporated into the extended trial balance. The adjustment for closing stock was explained in the Case Study on page 39.

accrual of expenses

- in the adjustments columns:
  - record £100 on the debit side of the telephone row
  - record £100 on the credit side of the accruals row
- on the debit side of the profit and loss account columns the total cost of the telephone row is now £600 (ie £500 from the trial balance, plus £100 accrual)
- on the credit side of the balance sheet columns £100 from the accruals row is shown as a liability of the business

prepayment of expenses

- in the adjustments columns:
  - record £75 on the credit side of the rent paid row
  - record £75 on the debit side of the prepayments row
- on the credit side of the profit and loss columns the total cost of rent paid is now £675 (ie £750 from the trial balance, less £75 prepaid)
- on the debit side of the balance sheet columns £75 from the prepayments row is shown as an asset of the business

depreciation of fixed assets

The depreciation amounts are:

- premises: 2 per cent per annum straight-line, ie £2,000
- shop fittings: 25 per cent per annum reducing balance, ie £5,000

EXTENDED TRIAL BALANCE   TARA SMITH TRADING AS 'THE FASHION SHOP'   31 DECEMBER 20-2

Description	Ledger balances Dr £	Cr £	Adjustments Dr £	Cr £	Profit and loss Dr £	Cr £	Balance sheet Dr £	Cr £
Stock at 1 Jan 20-2	12,500				12,500			
Purchases	105,000				105,000			
Sales		155,000				155,000		
Administration expenses	6,200				6,200			
Wages	23,500				23,500			
Rent paid	750			75	675			
Telephone	500		100		600			
Interest paid	4,500				4,500			
Travel expenses	550				550			
Premises	100,000						100,000	
Provision for depreciation: premises				2,000				2,000
Shop fittings	20,000						20,000	
Provision for depreciation: shop fittings				5,000				5,000
Debtors	10,500			100			10,400	
Bank	5,450						5,450	
Cash	50						50	
Capital		75,000						75,000
Drawings	7,000						7,000	
Loan from bank		50,000						50,000
Creditors		14,500						14,500
Value Added Tax		2,000						2,000
Provision for bad debts				250				250
Closing stock: Profit & loss				10,500		10,500		
Closing stock: Balance sheet			10,500				10,500	
Accruals				100				100
Prepayments			75				75	
Depreciation			7,000		7,000			
Bad debts			100		100			
Provision for bad debts: adjustment			250		250			
Net profit/loss					4,625			4,625
	296,500	296,500	18,025	18,025	165,500	165,500	153,475	153,475

The depreciation is shown in the extended trial balance as follows:

- in the description columns:
  - on the blank line below premises write in 'provision for depreciation: premises'
  - on the blank line below shop fittings write in 'provision for depreciation: shop fittings'
- in the adjustment columns:
  - record £7,000 (ie £2,000 + £5,000) on the debit side of the 'depreciation for year' row
  - record £2,000 on the credit side of the 'provision for depreciation: premises' row
  - record £5,000 on the credit side of the 'provision for depreciation: shop fittings' row
- on the debit side of the profit and loss columns record the depreciation for year of £7,000
- on the credit side of the balance sheet columns record the £2,000 and £5,000 provision for depreciation made on the two classes of assets

As this is the first year that Tara Smith has recorded depreciation, both depreciation for year and provision for depreciation amounts are the same.

bad debts written off

The adjustment to write off bad debts is shown in the extended trial balance as follows:

- in the adjustments columns:
  - record £100 on the debit side of the bad debts row
  - record £100 on the credit side of the debtors row
- on the debit side of the profit and loss account columns record the bad debts written off amount of £100
- on the debit side of the balance sheet columns show debtors as a net figure of £10,400 (ie £10,500 less £100 written off)

provision for bad debts

Here Tara Smith is creating a new provision for bad debts of £250; it is shown in the extended trial balance as follows:

- in the adjustments columns:
  - record £250 on the debit side of the 'provision for bad debts: adjustment' row
  - record £250 on the credit side of the provision for bad debts row
- in the profit and loss account columns record the £250 amount of the 'provision for bad debts: adjustment' as an expense in the debit column
- in the balance sheet columns show provision for bad debts £250 on the credit side

Note that, where an existing provision for bad debts is to be increased, the above principles are followed, with the balance sheet columns showing the total amount, ie existing provision plus increase. To reduce an existing provision, then the reverse entries will be made.

In the extended trial balance:

- 'provision for bad debts: adjustment' is shown in the profit and loss account and records the amount to create, increase or decrease the provision each year
- 'provision for bad debts' is shown in the credit column of the balance sheet and is the accumulated total of the provision

extended trial balance

The extended trial balance of Tara Smith, incorporating the above adjustments is shown on page 49. The altered figures have been shaded for illustrative purposes. Note that net profit will be different from that shown in the first Case Study because of the effect of the adjustments.

TARA SMITH:
PREPARING CONVENTIONAL ACCOUNTS

situation

The extended trial balance does not present final accounts in the conventional format used by accountants, but it does ensure that the dual aspect of each adjustment is dealt with correctly, and that no item from the trial balance is overlooked. ETBs are often used by accountancy firms in the preparation of year-end final accounts.

Using the extended trial balance of Tara Smith shown on page 49, present the final accounts in the conventional format used by accountants.

solution

Using the conventional format, the final accounts of Tara Smith will be presented as shown below and on the next page.

TARA SMITH, TRADING AS 'THE FASHION SHOP'

TRADING AND PROFIT AND LOSS ACCOUNT
for the year ended 31 December 2002

	£	£
Sales		155,000
Opening stock (1 January 2002)	12,500	
Purchases	105,000	
	117,500	
Less Closing stock (31 December 2002)	10,500	
Cost of sales		107,000
Gross profit		48,000
Less overheads:		
Administration expenses	6,200	
Wages	23,500	
Rent paid	675	
Telephone	600	
Interest paid	4,500	
Travel expenses	550	
Provision for depreciation: premises	2,000	
shop fittings	5,000	
Bad debts written off	100	
Provision for bad debts	250	
		43,375
Net profit		4,625

TARA SMITH, TRADING AS 'THE FASHION SHOP'

BALANCE SHEET OF TARA SMITH
as at 31 December 2002

	£	£	£
Fixed Assets	Cost	Dep'n to date	Net
Premises	100,000	2,000	98,000
Shop fittings	20,000	5,000	15,000
	120,000	7,000	113,000
Current Assets			
Stock		10,500	
Debtors	10,400		
Less provision for bad debts	250		
		10,150	
Prepayment		75	
Bank		5,450	
Cash		50	
		26,225	
Less Current Liabilities			
Creditors	14,500		
Accrual	100		
Value Added Tax	2,000		
		16,600	
Working Capital			9,625
			122,625
Less Long-term Liabilities			
Loan from bank			50,000
NET ASSETS			72,625
FINANCED BY			
Capital			
Opening capital			75,000
Add net profit			4,625
			79,625
Less drawings			7,000
Closing capital			72,625

SOLE TRADER FINAL ACCOUNTS: EXAMPLE LAYOUT

An example layout for the final accounts of a sole trader can be downloaded from the website: www.osbornebooks.co.uk. This format shows:

– an example layout for a trading and profit and loss account

– an example layout for a balance sheet

Note that when used for partnerships (see Chapter 3), the layout will need to be adjusted to take note of the appropriation of profits and of the partners' capital and current accounts.

PRIVATE EXPENSES AND GOODS FOR OWN USE

Adjustments also have to be made in the final accounts for the amount of any business facilities that are used by the owner for private purposes. These adjustments are for private expenses and goods for own use.

private expenses

Sometimes the owner of a business uses business facilities for private purposes, eg telephone or car. The owner will agree that part of the expense shall be charged to him or her as drawings, while the other part represents a business expense.

For example, the balance of the telephone account is £600 at the year-end, and the owner agrees that this should be split as one-quarter private use, and three-quarters to the business. The book-keeping entries to record such adjustments are:

– debit drawings account with the amount of private use, ie £150

– credit telephone account with the amount of private use, ie £150

– debit profit and loss account with the amount of business use, ie £450

– credit telephone account with the amount of business use, ie £450

goods for own use

When the owner of a business takes some of the goods in which the business trades for his or her own use, the double-entry book-keeping is:

– debit drawings account

– credit purchases account

Note that where a business is VAT-registered, VAT must be accounted for on goods taken by the owner.

ADDITIONAL ITEMS IN FINAL ACCOUNTS

As well as the adjustments to final accounts, there are a number of additional items that are shown in the trading and profit and loss account. These include:

- carriage in
- carriage out
- sales returns
- purchases returns
- discount received
- discount allowed

carriage in

This is the expense to a buyer of the carriage (transport) costs. For example, if an item is purchased by mail order, the buyer usually has to pay the additional cost of delivery.

In the trading account, the cost of carriage in is added to the cost of purchases. The reason for doing this is so that all purchases are at a 'delivered to your door' price.

carriage out

This is where the seller pays the expense of the carriage charge. For example, an item is sold to the customer and described as 'post free'.

In the profit and loss account, the cost of carriage out incurred on sales is shown as an expense of the business.

sales returns

Sales returns (or *returns in*) is where a debtor returns goods to the business. In final accounts, the amount of sales returns is deducted from the figure for sales in trading account.

purchases returns

Purchases returns (or *returns out*) is where a business returns goods to a creditor.

In final accounts, the amount of purchases returns is deducted from the figure for purchases in trading account.

discount received

Discount received is an allowance offered by creditors on purchases invoice amounts for quick settlement, eg 2% cash discount for settlement within seven days.

In final accounts, the amount of discount received is shown in profit and loss account as income received.

discount allowed

This is an allowance offered to debtors on sales invoice amounts for quick settlement.

In final accounts, the amount of discount allowed is shown in profit and loss account as an expense.

CASE STUDY

NATASHA MORGAN: TRADING AND PROFIT AND LOSS ACCOUNT – ADDITIONAL ITEMS

situation

An extract from the trial balance of Natasha Morgan, sole trader, is as follows:

Trial balance (extract) as at 30 June 2003

	Dr £	Cr £
Stock at 1 July 2002	12,350	
Sales		250,000
Purchases	156,000	
Sales returns	5,400	
Purchases returns		7,200
Carriage in	1,450	
Carriage out	3,250	
Discount received		2,500
Discount allowed	3,700	
Other expenses	78,550	

Note: stock at 30 June 2003 was valued at £16,300

Natasha asks for your help in the preparation of the trading and profit and loss account in the conventional format.

solution

There are a number of additional items to be incorporated into the layout of the trading and profit and loss account. In particular, the calculation of cost of sales is made in the following way:

      opening stock

  +   purchases

  +   carriage in

  −   purchases returns

  −   closing stock

  =   cost of sales

For Natasha Morgan's business, the trading and profit and loss account is as follows (note the use of three money columns):

NATASHA MORGAN, SOLE TRADER
TRADING AND PROFIT AND LOSS ACCOUNT
for the year ended 30 June 2003

	£	£	£
Sales			250,000
Less Sales returns			5,400
Net sales			244,600
Opening stock (1 July 2002)		12,500	
Purchases	156,000		
Add Carriage in	1,450		
	157,450		
Less Purchases returns	7,200		
Net purchases		150,250	
		162,600	
Less Closing stock (30 June 2003)		16,300	
Cost of sales			146,300
Gross profit			98,300
Add Discount received			2,500
			100,800
Less overheads:			
Discount allowed		3,700	
Other expenses		78,550	
			82,250
Net profit			18,550

SERVICE SECTOR BUSINESSES

The final accounts of a service sector business – such as a secretarial agency, solicitor, estate agent, doctor – do not normally include a trading account. This is because the business, instead of trading in goods, supplies services. Thus the final accounts consist of:

- profit and loss account
- balance sheet

The profit and loss account, instead of starting with gross profit from the trading account section, commences with the income from the business activity – such as 'fees', 'income from clients', 'charges', 'work done'. Other items of income – such as discount received – are added, and the overheads are then listed and deducted to give the net profit, or net loss, for the accounting period. An example of a service sector profit and loss account is shown below:

JEMMA SMITH, TRADING AS 'WYVERN SECRETARIAL AGENCY'
PROFIT AND LOSS ACCOUNT
for the year ended 31 December 2002

	£	£
Income from clients		110,000
Less overheads:		
Salaries	64,000	
Heating and Lighting	2.000	
Telephone	2.000	
Rent and Rates	6,000	
Sundry Expenses	3,000	
		77,000
Net profit		33,000

The balance sheet layout of a service sector business is identical to that seen earlier (page 52); the only difference is that there is unlikely to be much, if any, stock in the current assets section.

CHAPTER SUMMARY

- The financial statements (or final accounts) of a sole trader comprise an income statement (usually in the form of a profit and loss account) and a balance sheet.

- The starting point for preparing final accounts is the book-keeper's two-column trial balance.

- Adjustments to the trial balance are made for:
  - closing stock
  - accruals
  - prepayments
  - depreciation of fixed assets
  - bad debts written off
  - provision for bad debts

- The adjustments are often incorporated into the final accounts through an extended trial balance into the conventional format used by accountants.

KEY TERMS

financial statements	also known as final accounts, comprise income statement and balance sheet
income statement	normally a profit and loss account, which shows the profit or loss for the accounting period
balance sheet	the assets, liabilities and capital at the end of the accounting period
accounting period	time period covered by the final accounts – usually produced annually
extended trial balance	spreadsheet format used in the preparation of final accounts
conventional accounts	vertical format presentation of final accounts used by accountants
service sector business	business that supplies services instead of trading in goods

STUDENT ACTIVITIES

Osborne Books is grateful to the AAT for their kind permission to use Central Assessment task material for the following activity: 2.8

2.1 A trading account for a business shows:

(a) Net Profit

(b) Gross profit

(c) Net assets

(d) Gross assets

2.2 Net profit is calculated as:

(a) Sales minus cost of sales

(b) Sales plus overheads

(c) Gross profit minus overheads

(d) Gross profit minus cost of sales

2.3 On a balance sheet current assets minus current liabilities equals:

(a) Owners capital

(b) Working capital

(c) Net assets

(d) Fixed assets

2.4 What are the main differences between Fixed and Current Assets on a balance sheet?

2.5 The following is the latest trial balance for William Blakeney, who runs an art and antiques business. You have been asked to assist in the preparation of his financial statements for the year ended 31 July 20-2

	Dr £	Cr £
Premises at cost	86,000	
Delivery van at cost	24,000	
Fixtures and Fittings at cost	29,500	
Accumulated Depreciation as at 01.08.20-1		
– Premises		8,600
– Delivery van		8,640
– Fixtures and Fittings		14,750

Drawings	10,000	
Stock at 01.08.20-1	43,750	
Debtors	5,350	
Cash in hand	250	
Cash at bank		12,160
Creditors		29,450
Provision for doubtful debts		125
Capital		12,865
Bank Loan Account		35,000
Sales		198,630
Purchases	84,550	
Delivery van expenses	6,290	
Shop expenses	3,370	
Heat and Light	2,840	
Postage, Stationery and Telephone	4,910	
Wages and salaries	15,220	
Advertising	2,660	
Bad debts	450	
General expenses	1,080	
	320,220	320,220

Additional information

- Closing stock has been counted and valued at £52,170

- Depreciation charges for the year are based upon the following annual policy rates:

    Premises 2% on cost (straight line method)

    Delivery Van 20% on the reducing balance method

    Fixtures and Fittings 10% on cost (straight line method)

- A further £380 is owed for heat and light and should now be accrued.

- The provision for doubtful debts should now be adjusted to 4% of the closing debtor balances.

- Advertising prepaid amounted to £560 as at 31 July 20-2

REQUIRED

Task 1

Draft a profit and loss account for William Blakeney for the year to 31 July 20-2, incorporating the adjustments shown above.

Task 2

Prepare the business balance sheet as at 31 July 20-2

2.6 The following trial balance has been taken from the accounts of Malcolm Walker as at 30 September 20-2 after the drafting of his profit and loss account:

	Dr £	Cr £
Stocks as at 30.09.20-2	98,500	
Debtors	86,500	
Provision for bad and doubtful debts		4,000
Capital		425,000
Bank loan account		65,000
Creditors		72,500
HMCE (VAT account)		21,400
Bank account		12,500
Accruals		3,600
Prepayments	2,400	
Net profit for the year		106,250
Drawings	48,750	
Land at cost	133,725	
Premises at cost	300,000	
Machinery and equipment at cost	125,800	
Fixtures and Fittings at cost	55,250	
Motor vehicles at cost	88,000	
Accumulated depreciation		
- Premises		96,000
- Machinery and equipment		62,900
- Fixtures and Fittings		16,575
- Motor vehicles		53,200
	938,925	938,925

Additional information:

- There is an additional accrual for accountancy charges totalling £16,000 which now needs to be incorporated into this year's accounts.

- The provision for bad and doubtful debts needs to be adjusted to 3% of the closing debtors balances.

REQUIRED

Task 1

Adjust the draft profit figure contained in the above trial balance to take into account the 'Additional information' provided above.

Task 2

Prepare a balance sheet for Malcolm Walker as at 30 September 20-2 based on the revised profit figure calculated in Task 1 above.

2.7 The extended trial balance of Murtagh and Company is set out on the next page. You have been asked to prepare the financial statements for the company for the year ended 31 August 20-2.

First, however, you need to make the following adjustments:

1   The provision for bad debts needs to be adjusted to 5% of the closing debtors balances.

2   No account has been taken for this years' depreciation charges. It is company policy to use the straight line method based on the following annual rates:

	%
Buildings	2
Furniture and Fittings	10
Plant and Equipment	25
Motor Vehicles	20

REQUIRED

Task 1

Draft a trading profit and loss account for the year ended 31 August 20-2 after adjusting for points 1 and 2 above.

Task 2

Prepare a balance sheet as at the same date.

EXTENDED TRIAL BALANCE

name: Murtagh & Co.   date: 31 August 20-2

Description	Ledger balances		Adjustments		Profit and loss		Balance sheet	
	Dr £	Cr £	Dr £	Cr £	Dr £	Cr £	Dr £	Cr £
Land at Cost	400,000						400,000	
Buildings at Cost	250,000						250,000	
Furniture and Fittings at Cost	100,000						100,000	
Plant and Equipment at Cost	175,000						175,000	
Motor Vehicles at Cost	125,000						125,000	
Accumulated Depreciation as at 01.09.2001								
Buildings		30,000						30,000
Furniture and Fittings		40,000						40,000
Plant and Equipment		43,750						43,750
Motor vehicles		50,000						50,000
Sales and work completed		480,000				480,000		
Wages and NIC	100,000		6,190		106,190			
Postage and Stationery	5,750				5,750			
Purchases	260,250				260,250			
Rent, Rates and Insurance	40,250			4,925	35,325			
Bank Interest Received		6,720				6,720		
Commissions Received		5,250				5,250		
Telephone	26,100		2,820		28,920			
Light and Heat	19,250		1,410		20,660			
Motor Expenses	24,950			2,470	22,480			
Discounts Allowed	4,800				4,800			
Bad debts	6,500		1,250		7,750			
Provision for Doubtful Debts		1,830						1,830
Repairs to buildings	4,375				4,375			
Advertising	22,400				22,400			
Stock	78,750		86,150	86,150	78,750	86,150	86,150	
Debtors	48,250			1,250			47,000	
Bank Account		8,350						8,350
Cash In Hand	500						500	
Trade Creditors		29,150						29,150
HMCE Vat Account		8,390						8,390
Inland Revenue – PAYE NIC		6,250						6,250
Loan Mid West Bank		32,350						32,350
Bank Deposit Account	10,240						10,240	
Capital 01.09.01		986,325						986,325
Drawings	26,000						26,000	
Prepayments			7,395				7,395	
Accruals				10,420				10,420
Net profit/loss					19,530			19,530
	1728365	1728365	105,215	105,215	597,650	597,650	1246815	1,246,815

2.8 You have been approached by Samuel Taylor, a sole trader who runs a small trading company, Tayloriana (distributing catering equipment) for help in producing year-end financial statements. He employs a part-time bookkeeper who has produced an extended trial balance for the business as at 31 March 20-5. Samuel is negotiating to enter into an existing partnership, Coleridge & Co, which operates in the same area of activity as his own. The existing partners of Coleridge & Co would like to see the latest profit figures of Samuel's business. You have been asked to assist in the preparation of a profit and loss account for the year ended 31 March 20-5.

The extended trial balance of Tayloriana as at 31 March 20-5 is set out on the next page.

Samuel Taylor has given you the following further information.

(a)   Stock has been counted on 31 March 20-5. The cost of stock calculated on a first in first out basis is £49,300. The selling price of the stock is estimated at £65,450.

(b)   After the year end, one of the debtors, whose year-end balance was £2,500, went into liquidation. The liquidator has stated that there will be no assets available to repay creditors. No provision for this bad debt has been made in the accounts and the balance is still included in year-end debtors.

REQUIRED

Draft and profit and loss account for Tayloriana for the year end 31 March 20-5 incorporating any adjustments which may be required as a result of the further information set out above.

EXTENDED TRIAL BALANCE name: Tayloriana date: 31 March 20-5

Description	Ledger balances Dr £	Ledger balances Cr £	Adjustments Dr £	Adjustments Cr £	Profit and loss Dr £	Profit and loss Cr £	Balance sheet Dr £	Balance sheet Cr £
Drawings	21,500						21,500	
Lighting and heating	1,760				1,760			
Purchases	162,430				162,430			
Sales		257,350				257,350		
Sales ledger control account	41,000						41,000	
Fixtures and fittings (cost)	28,000						28,000	
Motor vehicles (cost)	16,500						16,500	
Bad debts	540				540			
Returns outwards		7,460				7,460		
Capital 01/04/20-4		44,080						44,080
Stock 01/04/20-4	43,700				43,700			
Rent, rates and insurance	8,500		300	150	8,650			
Accumulated depreciation: fixtures and fittings		12,000		2,800				14,800
Accumulated depreciation: motor vehicles		6,300		4,100				10,400
Bank charges	320				320			
Cash at bank and in hand	1,800						1,800	
Purchase ledger control account		47,200						47,200
Depreciation: fixtures and fittings			2,800		2,800			
motor vehicles			4,100		4,100			
Carriage inwards	1,320				1,320			
Returns inwards	3,350				3,350			
Postage, stationery and telephone	2,910				2,910			
Wages	39,420				39,420			
Carriage outwards	850				850			
Prepayments			150				150	
Accruals				300				300
Discounts allowed	490				490			
Loss for the year						7,830	7,830	
	374,390	374,390	7,350	7,350	272,640	272,640	116,780	116,780

3 PARTNERSHIP FINAL ACCOUNTS

this chapter covers . . .

In the last chapter we looked at the accounts of a sole trader, ie one person in business. A partnership is also a common form of business unit. In this chapter we look at:

- the definition of a partnership

- the accounting requirements of the Partnership Act 1890

- the accounting requirements which may be incorporated into a partnership agreement

- the use of capital accounts and current accounts

- the appropriation of profits

- the layout of the capital section of the balance sheet

NVQ PERFORMANCE CRITERIA COVERED

unit 11: DRAFTING FINANCIAL STATEMENTS

element 2

draft limited company, sole trader and partnership year end financial statements

- financial statements are accurately drafted from the appropriate information

- subsequent adjustments are correctly implemented

- draft accounts comply with domestic standards and legislation and, where relevant, partnership agreement

- year end financial statements are presented for approval to the appropriate person in clear form

- confidentiality procedures are followed at all times

- the organisation's policies, regulations, procedures and timescales relating to financial statements are observed at all times

- discrepancies, unusual features or queries are identified and either resolved or referred to the appropriate person

DEFINITION OF A PARTNERSHIP

The Partnership Act of 1890 defines a partnership as:

the relation which subsists between persons carrying on a business in common with a view of profit

Normally, partnerships consist of between two and twenty partners (exceptions being large professional firms, eg solicitors and accountants). Partnerships are often larger businesses than sole traders because, as there is more than one owner, there is likely to be more capital. A partnership may be formed to set up a new business or it may be the logical growth of a sole trader taking in partners to increase the capital.

advantages and disadvantages

Partnerships are cheap and easy to set up; their **advantages** are:
- there is the possibility of increased capital
- individual partners may be able to specialise in particular areas of the business
- with more people running the business, there is cover for illness and holidays

The **disadvantages** are:
- as there is more than one owner, decisions may take longer because other partners may need to be consulted
- there may be disagreements amongst the partners
- each partner is liable in law for the dealings and business debts of the *whole* firm (unless it is a 'limited liability partnership' set up under the Limited Liability Partnerships Act, 2000)
- the retirement or death of one partner may adversely affect the running of the business

accounting requirements of a partnership

The accounting requirements of a partnership are:
- either to follow the rules set out in the Partnership Act 1890
- or – and more likely – for the partners to agree amongst themselves, by means of a partnership agreement (see page 69), to follow different accounting rules

Unless the partners agree otherwise, the Partnership Act 1890 states the following accounting rules:
- profits and losses are to be shared equally between the partners
- no partner is entitled to a salary

- partners are not entitled to receive interest on their capital
- interest is not to be charged on partners' drawings
- when a partner contributes more capital than agreed, he or she is entitled to receive interest at five per cent per annum on the excess

As noted above, the partners may well decide to follow different accounting rules – these will be set out in a partnership agreement (see the next page).

CONFIDENTIALITY PROCEDURES

All financial information relating to partnerships should be treated with confidentiality. In particular:

- details of the final accounts, eg net profit, should be disclosed to all partners at the same time (unless one partner has been authorised by the others to take responsibility for the financial aspects of the business)
- details of a particular partner's share of the profits, drawings and transactions involving capital should not be discussed with others; it is confidential information until it is shown in the final accounts of the partnership

The final accounts of partnerships have to be revealed to very few people – the Inland Revenue and lenders, for example. Apart from these, partners can keep their financial statements private within the confines of the partnership.

YEAR-END ACCOUNTS OF A PARTNERSHIP

A partnership prepares the same type of year-end accounts as a sole trader business:

- trading and profit and loss account
- balance sheet

The main difference is that, immediately after the profit and loss account, follows an **appropriation section** (often described as an appropriation account). This shows how the net profit from profit and loss account is shared amongst the partners.

example of sharing profits

Jan, Kay and Lil are partners sharing profits and losses equally; their profit and loss account for 2002 shows a net profit of £60,000. The appropriation of profits appears as:

JAN, KAY AND LIL
PROFIT AND LOSS APPROPRIATION ACCOUNT
for the year ended 31 December 2002

	£
Net profit	60,000
Share of profits:	
Jan	20,000
Kay	20,000
Lil	20,000
	60,000

The above is a simple appropriation of profits. A more complex appropriation account (see Case Study on page 72) deals with other accounting points from the partnership agreement (see next section).

PARTNERSHIP AGREEMENT

The accounting rules from the Partnership Act are often varied with the agreement of all partners, by means of a partnership agreement. In particular, a partnership agreement will usually cover the following:

- division of profits and losses between partners
- partners' salaries/commission
- whether interest is to be allowed on capital and at what rate
- whether interest is to be charged on partners' drawings, and at what rate

The money amounts involved for each of these points (where allowed by the partnership agreement) are shown in the partnership appropriation account (see Case Study on page 72).

division of profits and losses between partners

The Partnership Act states that, in the absence of an agreement to the contrary, profits and losses are to be shared equally. A partner's share of the profits is normally taken out of the business in the form of drawings. Clearly, if one partner has contributed much more capital than the other partner(s), it would be unfair to apply this clause from the Act. Consequently, many partnerships agree to share profits and losses on a different basis – often in the same proportions as they have contributed capital. Note that in an AAT assessment task if no mention is made of an agreed division of profits you should assume that the partners receive an equal share.

partners' salaries/commission

Although the Act says that no partner is entitled to a salary, it is quite usual in the partnership agreement for one or more partners to be paid a salary. The reason for doing this is that often in a partnership, one of the partners spends more time working in the partnership than the other(s). The agreement to pay a salary is in recognition of the work done. Note that partners' salaries are not shown as an expense in profit anf loss account; instead they appear in the partnership appropriation account (see Case Study on page 72).

Many professional partnerships, such as solicitors and accountants, have junior partners who receive a partnership salary because they work full-time in the business, but have not yet contributed any capital. In a partnership, there may not be a requirement to contribute capital, unless the partnership agreement states otherwise; however, most partners will eventually do so.

As an alternative to a salary, a partner might be paid a commission on sales. As with a salary, this is not shown as an expense in the profit and loss account, but appears in the partnership appropriation account.

interest allowed on capital

Many partnerships include a clause in their partnership agreement which allows interest to be paid on capital; the rate of interest will be stated also. This clause is used to compensate partners for the loss of use of their capital, ie it is not available to invest elsewhere. Often, interest is allowed on capital in partnerships where profits and losses are shared equally – it is one way of partly adjusting for different capital balances. As noted earlier, the Partnership Act does not permit interest to be paid on capital, so reference to it must be made in the partnership agreement.

When calculating interest on capital, it may be necessary to allow for part years. For example:

1 January 2002 capital balance	£20,000
1 July 2002 additional capital contributed	£4,000
the rate of interest allowed on capital	10% per annum
the partnership's financial year-end	31 December 2002

Interest allowed on capital is calculated as:

1 January - 30 June £20,000 x 10% (for 6 months)	£1,000
1 July - 31 December £24,000 x 10% (for 6 months)	£1,200
Interest allowed on capital for year	£2,200

interest charged on partners' drawings

In order to discourage partners from drawing out too much money from the business early in the financial year, the partnership agreement may stipulate that interest is to be charged on partners' drawings, and at what rate. This acts as a penalty against early withdrawal when the business may be short of cash. For example:

a partner's drawings for 2002	£24,000
withdrawal at the end of each quarter (31 March, 30 June, 30 September, 31 December)	£6,000
the rate of interest charged on partners' drawings	10% per annum
the partnership's financial year-end	31 December 2002

Interest charged is calculated as:

31 March: £6,000 x 10% x 9 months	£450
30 June: £6,000 x 10% x 6 months	£300
30 September: £6,000 x 10% x 3 months	£150
Interest charged on partner's drawings for year	£900

No interest is charged on the withdrawal on 31 December, because it is at the end of the financial year. The amount of interest charged on drawings for the year is shown in the partnership appropriation account (see Case Study on page 72), where it increases the profit to be shared amongst the partners.

other points – loans and interest

interest on loans to the partnership

If a partner makes a loan to the partnership, the rate of interest to be paid needs to be agreed, otherwise the rate specified in the Partnership Act 1890 applies – five per cent per annum.

Interest on loans is charged as an expense in the profit and loss account, and is not shown in the appropriation account.

interest on current accounts

The partnership agreement may state that interest is to be allowed at a specified rate on the credit balance of partners' current accounts (see below), and is to be charged on debit balances.

CAPITAL ACCOUNTS AND CURRENT ACCOUNTS

The important book-keeping difference between a sole trader and a partnership is that each partner usually has a capital account *and* a current account. The capital account is normally *fixed,* and only alters if a permanent increase or decrease in capital contributed by the partner takes place. The current account is *fluctuating* and it is to this account that:

- share of profits is credited
- share of loss is debited
- salary (if any), or commissions, are credited
- interest allowed on partners' capital is credited
- drawings and goods for own use are debited
- interest charged on partners' drawings is debited
- interest allowed on loans made by partners is credited

Thus, the current account is treated as a *working* account, while capital account remains fixed, except for capital introduced or withdrawn.

A partner's current account has the following layout:

Dr		**Partner Aye: Current Account**	Cr
	£		£
Drawings/goods for own use		Balance b/d	
Interest charged on drawings*		Share of net profit	
		Salary (or commissions)*	
		Interest allowed on capital*	
Balance c/d		Interest allowed on loans*	

* if these items are allowed by the partnership agreement

Note that whilst the normal balance on a partner's current account is credit, when the partner has drawn out more than his or her share of the profits, then the balance will be debit.

CASE STUDY

AYE AND BEE:
APPROPRIATION OF PARTNERSHIP PROFITS

As we have seen earlier in this chapter, the appropriation section (often described as the appropriation account) follows the profit and loss account and shows how net profit has been divided amongst the partners. This Case Study shows a partnership salary (not to be shown in profit and loss account), interest allowed on partners' capital, and interest charged on partners' drawings.

situation

Aye and Bee are in partnership sharing profits and losses 60 per cent and 40 per cent respectively. Net profit for the year ended 31 March 2002 is £42,000.

At 1 April 2001 (the start of the year), the partners have the following balances:

	Capital account £	Current account £
Aye	40,000	2,000 Cr
Bee	30,000	400 Cr

- There have been no changes to the capital accounts during the year; interest is allowed on partners' capitals at the rate of eight per cent per year.
- Bee is entitled to a salary of £16,000 per year.
- On 30 September 2001 (half-way through the financial year), partners' drawings were made: Aye £18,000, Bee £24,000; there were no other drawings. Interest is charged on partners' drawings at the rate of ten per cent per year.

solution

The appropriation of profits will be made as follows:

AYE AND BEE, IN PARTNERSHIP
PROFIT AND LOSS APPROPRIATION ACCOUNT
for the year ended 31 March 2002

	£	£
Net profit		42,000
Add interest charged on partners' drawings:		
Aye (£18,000 ÷ 2* x 10%)	900	
Bee (£24,000 ÷ 2* x 10%)	1,200	
* divided by two because interest is for 6 months		2,100
		44,100
Less appropriation of profits:		
Salary: Bee		16,000
Interest allowed on partners' capitals:		
Aye	3,200	
Bee	2,400	
		5,600
		22,500
Share of remaining profits:		
Aye (60%)	13,500	
Bee (40%)	9,000	
		22,500

Note that all of the available profit – after allowing for any salary, and interest charged and allowed – is shared amongst the partners, in the ratio in which they share profits and losses. The partners' current accounts for the year appear as follows:

Dr					Partners' Current Accounts			Cr
		Aye	Bee			Aye	Bee
2001/2		£	£	2001/2		£	£
31 Mar	Drawings	18,000	24,000	1 Apr	Balances b/d	2,000	400
31 Mar	Interest on drawings	900	1,200		Salary	–	16,000
31 Mar	Balance c/d	–	2,600	31 Mar	Interest on capital	3,200	2,400
				31 Mar	Share of profits	13,500	9,000
				31 Mar	Balance c/d	200	-
		18,900	27,800			18,900	27,800
2002/3				2002/3			
1 Apr	Balance b/d	200	–	1 Apr	Balance b/d	–	2,600

Note: The above layout for the partners' current accounts uses a normal 'T' account but in a side-by-side format with a column for each partner on both the debit and credit sides. As an alternative, separate current accounts can be produced for each partner.

From the current accounts we can see that Aye has drawn more out than the balance of the account; accordingly, at the end of the year, Aye has a debit balance of £200 on current account. By contrast, Bee has a credit balance of £2,600 on current account.

BALANCE SHEET

The balance sheet of a partnership must show the year-end balances on each partner's capital and current account. However, the transactions that have taken place on each account can be shown in summary form – in the same way that, in a sole trader's balance sheet, net profit for the year is added and drawings for the year are deducted.

The other sections of the balance sheet – fixed assets, current assets, current and long-term liabilities – are presented in the same way as for a sole trader.

The following is an example balance sheet layout for the 'Financed by' section (the other sections of the balance sheet are not shown). It details the capital and current accounts of the partnership of Aye and Bee (see Case Study above).

```
                      AYE AND BEE, IN PARTNERSHIP
                BALANCE SHEET (EXTRACT) as at 31 March 2002
        FINANCED BY                                      £          £
        Capital Accounts
          Aye                                         40,000
          Bee                                         30,000
                                                                 70,000
        Current Accounts
        Aye                                            (200)
        Bee                                            2,600
                                                                  2,400
                                                                 72,400
```

Note: Only the closing balances of the partners' current accounts have been shown here –
see the detailed double-entry accounts on the previous page. In an assessment task, be
guided by the requirements:

– either, show detailed double-entry accounts, carrying the balances into the balance
  sheet

– or, show detailed current accounts on the face of the balance sheet (see Case Study
  on page 78)

PARTNERSHIP FINAL ACCOUNTS FROM THE TRIAL BALANCE

Final accounts for a partnership can be prepared using the extended trial
balance method and will then be displayed in the conventional format, used
by accountants.

The procedures are exactly the same as for sole traders. The only differences
to note are that partners' capital and current accounts are shown in the
balance sheet. Transactions affecting the partners' current accounts – such as
share of profits, partners' salaries, drawings, etc – can be shown either in the
form of a double-entry 'T' account (see page 74 for an example), or directly
on the face of the balance sheet (see the following Case Study). Whichever
is done, it is the closing balances of the current accounts that are added in to
the 'financed by' section of the balance sheet.

CASE STUDY

EXE AND WYE:
PARTNERSHIP FINAL ACCOUNTS

situation

The extended trial balance for the partnership of Exe and Wye at 31 December 2002
is shown on the next page. All columns of the ETB have been completed ready for the
completion of final accounts in the conventional format.

Note that the ETB includes the following points:

- there are both accruals and prepayments
- provisions for depreciation have been made
- during the year the partners have taken goods for their own use – the figure for purchases has been reduced and the goods charged to each partner (note that the amounts of goods for own use have been shown separately on the ETB to show clearly the accounting treatment; they can be incorporated into the figure for drawings)
- the partners share profits and losses equally

solution

The final accounts of the partnership of Exe and Wye are shown in ETB format on the next page and in the conventional format used by accountants below and on page 78.

EXE AND WYE, IN PARTNERSHIP
TRADING AND PROFIT AND LOSS ACCOUNT
for the year ended 31 December 2002

	£	£	£
Sales			50,000
Opening stock (1 January 2002)		5,000	
Purchases	30,000		
Less Goods for own use	900		
		29,100	
		34,100	
Less Closing stock (31 December 2002)		10,000	
Cost of sales			24,100
Gross profit			25,900
Less overheads:			
Office expenses		5,600	
Vehicle expenses		4,300	
Provision for depreciation			
vehicles		4,000	
office equipment		1,000	
			14,900
Net profit			11,000
Share of profits:			
Exe			5,500
Wye			5,500
			11,000

EXTENDED TRIAL BALANCE — EXE AND WYE, IN PARTNERSHIP — 31 DECEMBER 2002

Description	Ledger balances		Adjustments		Profit and loss		Balance sheet	
	Dr £	Cr £	Dr £	Cr £	Dr £	Cr £	Dr £	Cr £
Stock at 1 Jan 2002	5,000				5,000			
Sales		50,000				50,000		
Purchases	30,000			900	29,100			
Vehicles	20,000						20,000	
Provision for depreciation: vehicles		8,000		4,000				12,000
Office equipment	5,000						5,000	
Provision for depreciation: office equipment		2,000		1,000				3,000
Office expenses	5,500		100		5,600			
Vehicle expenses	4,500			200	4,300			
Debtors	6,000						6,000	
Creditors		4,000						4,000
Value Added Tax		1,000						1,000
Bank	2,000						2,000	
Capital account: Exe		10,000						10,000
Capital account: Wye		10,000						10,000
Current account: Exe		3,000						3,000
Current account: Wye		500						500
Drawings: Exe	6,000						6,000	
Drawings: Wye	4,500						4,500	
Goods for own use: Exe			500				500	
Goods for own use: Wye			400				400	
Closing stock: Profit and loss				10,000		10,000		
Closing stock: Balance sheet			10,000				10,000	
Accruals				100				100
Prepayments			200				200	
Depreciation			5,000		5,000			
Net profit/loss: Exe					5,500			5,500
Net profit/loss: Wye					5,500			5,500
	88,500	88,500	16,200	16,200	60,000	60,000	54,600	54,600

EXE AND WYE, IN PARTNERSHIP
BALANCE SHEET
as at 31 December 2002

	£	£	£
Fixed Assets	Cost	Dep'n to date	Net
Vehicles	20,000	12,000	8,000
Office equipment	5,000	3,000	2,000
	25,000	15,000	10,000
Current Assets			
Stock		10,000	
Debtors		6,000	
Prepayments		200	
Bank		2,000	
		18,200	
Less Current Liabilities			
Creditors	4,000		
Accruals	100		
Value Added Tax	1,000		
		5,100	
Working Capital			13,100
NET ASSETS			23,100
FINANCED BY			
Capital Accounts			
Exe		10,000	
Wye		10,000	
			20,000

Current Accounts	EXE	WYE	
Opening balance	3,000	500	
Add: share of profit	5,500	5,500	
	8,500	6,000	
Less: drawings	6,000	4,500	
goods for own use*	500	400	
	2,000	1,100	
			3,100
			23,100

* goods for own use can be incorporated into the amount for drawings: it is shown here (and on the extended trial balance) separately so that the accounting treatment can be seen clearly.

- A partnership is formed when two or more (usually up to a maximum of twenty) people set up in business.

- The Partnership Act 1890 states certain accounting rules, principally that profits and losses must be shared equally.

- Many partnerships over-ride the accounting rules of the Act by making a partnership agreement which covers:

  - division of profits and losses between partners

  - partners' salaries/commissions

  - whether interest is to be allowed on capital, and at what rate

  - whether interest is to be charged on partners' drawings, and at what rate

- The usual way to account for partners' capital is to maintain a fixed capital account for each partner. This is complemented by a fluctuating current account which is used as a working account for share of profits, drawings, etc.

- The final accounts of partnerships are similar to those of sole traders, but incorporate:

  - an appropriation section, as a continuation of the profit and loss account, to show the share of profits and losses

  - individual capital and current accounts for each partner shown in the balance sheet

partnership	the relation which subsists between persons carrying on a business in common with a view of profit
Partnership Act 1890	legislation which includes the accounting rules of partnerships
partnership agreement	agreement between the partners which, amongst other things, often varies the accounting rules of the Partnership Act 1890
appropriation section	part of the profit and loss account which shows how the net profit is shared amongst the partners
capital account	account which records the amount of capital contributed by a partner; usually for a fixed amount, which only alters where a permanent increase or decrease takes place
current account	a fluctuating account to which is credited: share of profits, salary (if any), interest allowed on capital, and to which is debited: share of losses, drawings and interest charged on partner's drawings

STUDENT ACTIVITIES

3.1 If there is no partnership agreement then profits and losses will be:

(a) Shared in the same proportion as the capital contributions.

(b) Shared according to the amount of work completed by each partner.

(c) Shared equally.

(d) Shared as the partners think best.

3.2 When a partnership operates a system of fixed capital then any share of profit must be:

(a) Credited to the Capital account.

(b) Debited to the Capital account.

(c) Credited to the Current account.

(d) Debited to the Current account.

3.3 The correct double entry for the allocation of a partnership loss is:

(a) Debit Capital account.
Credit Profit and Loss appropriation account.

(b) Debit Profit and Loss appropriation account.
Credit Capital account.

(c) Debit Profit and Loss appropriation account.
Credit Current account.

(d) Debit Current account.
Credit Profit and Loss appropriation account.

3.4 Smith and Weston are in partnership paying partnership salaries of Smith £13,500 and Weston £8,500 per annum. Any residue profit is shared 60% Smith 40% Weston.

If the partnership makes a net profit of £120,000 in the year, what is Weston's share of the residue profit?

(a) £39,200

(b) £58,800

(c) £72,300

(d) £47,700

3.5 Define a partnership

3.6 State three provisions which are set out in the Partnership Act 1890 that will apply to a partnership where no partnership agreement exists.

3.7   Henry, Ian and Simon are in partnership together as a firm of Chartered Accountants. You work for the partnership as a trainee accountant, and you have been asked to assist in the preparation of their final accounts for the year to 30 June 20-2.

The partnership agreement gives each partner the following entitlements:

Partnership salaries

	£
Henry	12,000
Ian	15,000
Simon	10,000

Interest on Capital is to be paid at a rate of 8% per annum, based on the balance of the capital account at the beginning of the year. No interest is to be paid on partnership current accounts.

The balances for the Capital and Current accounts as at 1 July 20-1 were as follows:

	Capital Accounts	*Current Accounts*	
	£	£	
Henry	60,000	6,000	Cr
Ian	40,000	5,000	Cr
Simon	25,000	2,000	Dr

Cash drawings for the year amounted to:

	£
Henry	26,000
Ian	24,000
Simon	20,000

Interest on drawings is to be charged to each partner. For the year to 30 June 20-2 each partner is to be charged interest on drawings as calculated below:

	£
Henry	1,200
Ian	1,000
Simon	800

The partnership earned a profit of £70,000 for the year to 30 June 20-2.

The profit sharing ratios for the partnership are:

Henry	4/10
Ian	4/10
Simon	2/10

REQUIRED

Task 1
Prepare the partnership appropriation account for the year ended 30 June 20-2.

Task 2
Prepare the partners' current accounts for the year ended 30 June 20-2.

Task 3
List three disadvantages of a sole trader forming a partnership

3.8 Michael, Nigel and Elaine are in partnership together as a firm of solicitors. You have been asked to finalise the partnership accounts for the year ended 30 September 20-2.

You have been given the following information:

The profit for the year to 30 September 20-2 amounted to £212,240.

The partners are entitled to the following annual salaries.

	£
Michael	36,000
Nigel	32,000
Elaine	26,000

Interest on Capital is to be paid at a rate of 12% on the balance at the beginning of the year on the capital accounts. No interest is paid on Current accounts.

Cash drawings for the year amounted to:

	£
Michael	48,000
Nigel	37,000
Elaine	58,000

The balances on the capital and current accounts as at 1st October 20-1 were as follows:

	Capital Accounts £	Current Accounts £	
Michael	70,000	6,500	Cr
Nigel	50,000	1,450	Cr
Elaine	40,000	2,900	Dr

The profit sharing ratios in the partnership currently are:

Michael	4/10
Nigel	3/10
Elaine	3/10

REQUIRED

Task 1
Prepare the Partnership appropriation account for the year ended 30 September 20-2.

Task 2
Prepare the partners' current accounts for the year ended 30 September 20-2.

Task 3
List three advantages of forming a partnership.

3.9 Bossman and Stockwell trade as a partnership. Their partnership agreement provides for the following:

- Interest on fixed capital contributions at 10% per annum. No interest is to be charged on drawings or allowed or charged on current account balances.

- The partners are to receive the following annual salaries:
Bossman	£16,000
Stockwell	£14,000

- Profits and losses are to be shared as follows:
Bossman	70%
Stockwell	30%

The following trial balance has been extracted from the partnership books as at 31 May 20-1:

	Dr £	Cr £
Premises at cost	200,000	
Equipment at cost	125,000	
Provision for depreciation as at 31 May 20-1		
- Premises		20,000
- Equipment		79,000
Stock as at 1 June 20-0	28,690	
Purchases	250,900	
Sales		604,400
Discounts allowed	2,800	
Discounts received		7,500
Returns inwards	4,400	
Returns outwards		1,600
Wages and Salaries	164,400	
Carriage inwards	6,780	
General expenses	34,000	
Depreciation charges	30,000	
Trade debtors	64,600	
Trade creditors		40,700
Cash at bank and in hand	6,940	
Drawings:		
- Bossman	29,900	
- Stockwell	23,600	
Capital Accounts		
- Bossman		150,000
- Stockwell		70,000
Current Accounts		
- Bossman	1,080	
- Stockwell	110	
	973,200	973,200

Stock at the close of business on 31 May 20-1 has been valued at £32,770.

REQUIRED

Task 1

Prepare the trading, profit and loss and appropriation account for the year ended 31 May 20-1.

Task 2

Prepare the partnership balance sheet as at 31 May 20-1

Task 3

Explain how and why wages and salaries are treated differently from partners' salaries in the profit and loss account.

3.10 Richmond and Darlington are in partnership sharing profits and losses equally. On 31 May 20-1 the summary of the book-keeping is as follows:

	Dr	Cr
	£	£
Bank account		1,430
Business premises at cost	90,000	
Motor vehicles at cost	20,000	
Shop equipment and fittings at cost	16,000	
Provision for Depreciation 01.06.20-0		
Business premises		10,000
Motor vehicles		4,000
Shop equipment		3,400
Capital accounts		
Richmond		80,000
Darlington		60,000
Carriage inwards	4,280	
Carriage outwards	6,220	
Cash in hand	280	
Trade debtors	14,780	
Trade Creditors		18,650
Discounts allowed	5,240	
Discounts received		1,960
Drawings		
Richmond	22,000	
Darlington	29,600	
General expenses	8,950	
Insurance	7,230	
Purchases	140,900	
Sales		235,580
Returns inwards	4,580	
Returns outwards		2,140
Stock at 01.06.20-0	35,440	
Wages and Salaries	47,100	

Partners Current Accounts:

Richmond		18,670
Darlington		16,770
	452,600	452,600

Additional information

- For managing the business Darlington receives a partnership salary of £28,000 per annum. Richmond is involved with selling and he receives a 10% commission on net sales, instead of a partnership salary.

- Interest is to be allowed on partners fixed capital accounts at a rate of 12% per annum, but no interest is to be charged on partners drawings.

- Closing stock at 31 May 20-1 has been counted and valued at £39,240

- There is a prepayment on Insurance amounting to £580 as at 31 May 20-1

- Wages accrued at 31 May 20-1 totalled £2,600

- It is company policy to depreciate fixed assets at the following annual rates:

Business premises	2% on cost
Motor Vehicles	20% reduced balance method
Shop equipment	10% on cost

REQUIRED

Task 1
Prepare a trading, profit and loss and appropriation account for the year ended 31 May 20-1.

Task 2
Prepare a balance sheet as at 31 May 20-1.

Task 3
Explain the accounting treatment of sales commission receivable by Richmond.

4 CHANGES IN PARTNERSHIPS

this chapter covers . . .

In this chapter we continue our study of partnerships by looking at the principles involved and the accounting entries, for:

- admission of a new partner
- retirement of a partner
- death of a partner
- changes in profit-sharing ratios
- revaluation of assets
- dissolution of a partnership

Before we look at each of these, we need to consider the goodwill of the business, which features in most of the changes listed above.

NVQ PERFORMANCE CRITERIA COVERED

unit 11: DRAFTING FINANCIAL STATEMENTS

element 2

draft limited company, sole trader and partnership year end financial statements

- financial statements are accurately drafted from the appropriate information
- subsequent adjustments are correctly implemented
- draft accounts comply with domestic standards and legislation and, where relevant, partnership agreement
- year end financial statements are presented for approval to the appropriate person in clear form
- confidentiality procedures are followed at all times
- the organisation's policies, regulations, procedures and timescales relating to financial statements are observed at all times
- discrepancies, unusual features or queries are identified and either resolved or referred to the appropriate person

GOODWILL

The balance sheet of a partnership, like that of many businesses, rarely indicates the true 'going concern' value of the business: usually the recorded figures underestimate the worth of a business. There are two main reasons for this:

- **Prudence** – if there is any doubt about the value of assets, they are stated at the lowest possible figure.

- **Goodwill** – a going concern business will often have a value of goodwill, because of various factors, eg the trade that has been built up, the reputation of the business, the location of the business, the skill of the workforce, and the success at developing new products.

definition of goodwill

Goodwill can be defined formally in accounting terms as:

the difference between the value of a business as a whole, and the net value of its separate assets and liabilities.

For example, an existing business is bought for £500,000, with the separate assets and liabilities being worth £450,000 net; goodwill is, therefore, £50,000.

Thus goodwill has a value as an intangible fixed asset to the owner or owners of a going concern business, whether or not it is recorded on the balance sheet. As you will see in the sections which follow, a valuation has to be placed on goodwill when changes take place in a partnership.

valuation of goodwill

The valuation of goodwill is always subject to negotiation between the people concerned if, for instance, a partnership business is to be sold. It is, most commonly, based on the profits of the business – eg the average net profit over the last, say, three years and multiplied by an agreed figure, perhaps six times.

In a balance sheet, goodwill is shown as an intangible fixed asset. It is only recorded on the balance sheet when it has been purchased, eg a sole trader or a partnership purchasing goodwill when taking over another business. It should then:

- either, be depreciated (amortised) to profit and loss account over its estimated useful economic life (generally up to a maximum of 20 years)

- or, if the useful estimated economic life is deemed to be indefinite, the goodwill need not be amortised, provided that its continuing existence can be justified (by means of an annual 'impairment review')

We will now see how goodwill is used when changes are made to partnerships, eg the admission of a new partner or retirement of an existing partner. For these changes, a value for goodwill is agreed and this amount is temporarily debited to goodwill account, and credited to the partners' capital accounts in their profit-sharing ratio; after the change in the partnership, as you will see, the partners' capital accounts are debited and goodwill account is credited. Thus a 'nil' balance remains on goodwill account and, therefore, it is not recorded on the partnership balance sheet. This is a prudent approach, and is the method commonly followed when changes are made to partnerships.

ADMISSION OF A NEW PARTNER

A new partner – who can only be admitted with the consent of all existing partners – is normally charged a premium for goodwill. This is because the new partner will start to share in the profits of the business immediately and will benefit from the goodwill established by the existing partners. If the business was to be sold shortly after the admission of a new partner, a price will again be agreed for goodwill and this will be shared amongst all the partners (including the new partner).

To make allowance for this benefit it is necessary to make book-keeping adjustments in the partners' capital accounts. The most common way of doing this is to use a goodwill account which is opened by the old partners with the agreed valuation of goodwill and, immediately after the admission of the new partner, is closed by transfer to the partners' capital accounts, including that of the new partner.

The procedures on admission of a new partner are:

- **agree a valuation for goodwill**

- **old partners**
  - debit goodwill account with the amount of goodwill
  - credit partners' capital accounts (in their old profit-sharing ratio) with the amount of goodwill

- **old partners + new partner**
  - debit partners' capital accounts (in their new profit-sharing ratio) with the amount of goodwill
  - credit goodwill account with the amount of goodwill

The effect of this is to charge the new partner with a premium for goodwill.

CASE STUDY

AL AND BEN:
ADMISSION OF A NEW PARTNER

situation

Al and Ben are in partnership sharing profits and losses equally. Their balance sheet as at 31 December 2001 is as follows:

BALANCE SHEET OF AL AND BEN AS AT 31 DECEMBER 2001	
	£
Net assets	80,000
Capital accounts:	
Al	45,000
Ben	35,000
	80,000

On 1 January 2002 the partners agree to admit Col into the partnership, with a new profit-sharing ratio of 2:2:1. Goodwill has been agreed at a valuation of £25,000. Col will bring £20,000 of cash into the business as his capital, part of which represents a premium for goodwill.

solution

The accounting procedures on the admission of Col into the partnership are as follows:

- goodwill has been valued at £25,000

- old partners:
  - debit goodwill account £25,000
  - credit capital accounts (in their old profit-sharing ratio)
    - Al £12,500
    - Ben £12,500

- old partners + new partner

  - debit capital accounts (in their new profit-sharing ratio)
    - Al £10,000
    - Ben £10,000
    - Col £5,000
  - credit goodwill account £25,000

The capital accounts of the partners, after the above transactions have been recorded, appear as:

Dr				Partners' Capital Accounts				Cr
	Al	Ben	Col		Al	Ben	Col
	£	£	£		£	£	£
Goodwill written off	10,000	10,000	5,000	Balances b/d	45,000	35,000	-
Balances c/d	47,500	37,500	15,000	Goodwill created	12,500	12,500	-
				Bank	-	-	20,000
	57,500	47,500	20,000		57,500	47,500	20,000
				Balances b/d	47,500	37,500	15,000

The balance sheet, following the admission of Col, appears as:

BALANCE SHEET OF AL, BEN AND COL AS AT 1 JANUARY 2002

	£
Net assets (£80,000 + £20,000)	100,000
Capital accounts:	
Al (£45,000 + £12,500 - £10,000)	47,500
Ben (£35,000 + £12,500 - £10,000)	37,500
Col (£20,000 - £5,000)	15,000
	100,000

In this way, the new partner has paid the existing partners a premium of £5,000 for a one-fifth share of the profits of a business with a goodwill value of £25,000.

Although a goodwill account has been used, it has been fully utilised with adjusting entries made in the capital accounts of the partners, as follows:

Dr			Goodwill Account		Cr
		£			£
Al	goodwill created	12,500	Al	goodwill written off	10,000
Ben		12,500	Ben		10,000
			Col		5,000
		25,000			25,000

a note: goodwill – alternative treatment

As there is no remaining balance on goodwill account, it does not appear on the balance sheet. Whilst the write-off of goodwill is the most usual treatment in partnership accounts, it would be possible for goodwill account to be kept open with a debit balance, being the amount of the intangible fixed asset (in this example, for £25,000). The capital accounts would not, therefore, be debited with the goodwill written off (in this example, £10,000, £10,000 and £5,000). In assessments, the task will always state the accounting treatment of goodwill – invariably no account will remain open for goodwill, with all adjusting entries being passed through the partners' capital accounts.

RETIREMENT OF A PARTNER

When a partner retires it is necessary to calculate how much is due to the partner in respect of capital and profits. The partnership agreement normally details the procedures to be followed when a partner retires. The most common procedure requires goodwill to be valued and this operates in a similar way to the admission of a new partner, as follows:

- **agree a valuation for goodwill**
- **old partners**
  - debit goodwill account with the amount of goodwill
  - credit partners' capital accounts (in their old profit-sharing ratio) with the amount of goodwill
- **remaining partners**
  - debit partners' capital accounts (in their new profit-sharing ratio) with the amount of goodwill
  - credit goodwill account with the amount of goodwill

The effect of this is to credit the retiring partner with the amount of the goodwill built up whilst he or she was a partner. This amount, plus the retiring partner's capital and current account balances can then be paid out of the partnership bank account. (If there is insufficient money for this, it is quite usual for a retiring partner to leave some of the capital in the business as a loan, which is repaid over a period of time.)

CASE STUDY

JAN, KAY AND LIL: RETIREMENT OF A PARTNER

situation

Jan, Kay and Lil are in partnership sharing profit and losses in the ratio of 2:2:1 respectively. Partner Jan decides to retire on 31 December 2001 when the partnership balance sheet is as follows:

BALANCE SHEET OF JAN, KAY AND LIL AS AT 31 DECEMBER 2001	
	£
Net assets	100,000
Capital accounts:	
Jan	35,000
Kay	45,000
Lil	20,000
	100,000

Goodwill is agreed at a valuation of £30,000. Kay and Lil are to continue in partnership and will share profits and losses in the ratio of 2:1 respectively. Jan agrees to leave £20,000 of the amount due to her as a loan to the new partnership.

solution

The accounting procedures on the retirement of Jan from the partnership are as follows:

- goodwill has been valued at £30,000

- old partners:

    - debit goodwill account   £30,000

    - credit capital accounts (in their old profit-sharing ratio of 2:2:1)

Jan	£12,000
Kay	£12,000
Lil	£6,000

- remaining partners

    - debit capital accounts (in their new profit-sharing ratio of 2:1)

Kay	£20,000
Lil	£10,000

    - credit goodwill account   £30,000

The capital accounts of the partners, after the above transactions have been recorded, appear as:

Dr				**Partners' Capital Accounts**				Cr
	Jan	Kay	Lil		Jan	Kay	Lil
	£	£	£		£	£	£
Goodwill written off	–	20,000	10,000	Balances b/d	35,000	45,000	20,000
Loan account	20,000			Goodwill created	12,000	12,000	6,000
Bank	27,000						
Balances c/d	–	37,000	16,000				
	47,000	57,000	26,000		47,000	57,000	26,000
				Balances b/d	–	37,000	16,000

Note: After recording goodwill, the balance of Jan's capital account is £47,000 (ie £35,000 + £12,000, being her share of the goodwill). Of this, £20,000 will be retained in the business as a loan, and £27,000 will be paid to her from the partnership bank account.

The balance sheet, after the retirement of Jan, appears as follows:

BALANCE SHEET OF KAY AND LIL AS AT 1 JANUARY 2002

	£
Net assets (£100,000 - £27,000 paid to Jan)	73,000
Less Loan account of Jan	20,000
	53,000
Capital accounts:	
Kay (£45,000 + £12,000 - £20,000)	37,000
Lil (£20,000 + £6,000 - £10,000)	16,000
	53,000

The effect of this is that the remaining partners have bought out Jan's £12,000 share of the goodwill of the business, ie it has cost Kay £8,000, and Lil £4,000. If the business was to be sold later, Kay and Lil would share the goodwill obtained from the sale in their new profit-sharing ratio.

DEATH OF A PARTNER

The accounting procedures on the death of a partner are very similar to those for a partner's retirement. The only difference is that the amount due to the deceased partner is placed in an account called 'Executors (or Administrators) of X deceased' pending payment.

CHANGES IN PROFIT-SHARING RATIOS

It may be necessary, from time-to-time, to change the profit-sharing ratios of partners. A partner's share of profits might be increased because of an increase in capital in relation to the other partners, or because of a more active role in running the business. Equally, a share of profits may be decreased if a partner withdraws capital or spends less time in the business. Clearly, the agreement of all partners is needed to make changes, and the guidance of the partnership agreement should be followed.

Generally, a change in profit-sharing ratios involves establishing a figure for goodwill, even if the partnership is to continue with the same partners; this is to establish how much goodwill was built up while they shared profits in their old ratios. Each partner will, therefore, receive a value for the goodwill based on the old profit-sharing ratio.

CASE STUDY

COL AND DES:
CHANGES IN PROFIT-SHARING RATIOS

situation

Col and Des are in partnership sharing profits and losses equally. The balance sheet at 31 December 2001 is as follows:

BALANCE SHEET OF COL AND DES AS AT 31 DECEMBER 2001	
	£
Net assets	60,000
Capital accounts:	
Col	35,000
Des	25,000
	60,000

The partners agree that, as from 1 January 2002, Col will take a two-thirds share of the profits and losses, with Des taking one-third. It is agreed that goodwill shall be valued at £30,000.

solution

The accounting procedures on the change in the profit-sharing ratio are as follows:

• goodwill has been valued at £30,000

• old profit-sharing ratio:
  – debit goodwill account £30,000
  – credit capital accounts (in their old profit-sharing ratio of 1:1)

Col	£15,000
Des	£15,000

• new profit-sharing ratio:
  – debit capital accounts (in their new profit-sharing ratio of 2:1)

Col	£20,000
Des	£10,000

  – credit goodwill account £30,000

The capital accounts of the partners, after the above transactions have been recorded, appear as:

Dr			**Partners' Capital Accounts**		Cr
	Col	Des		Col	Des
	£	£		£	£
Goodwill written off	20,000	10,000	Balances b/d	35,000	25,000
Balances c/d	30,000	30,000	Goodwill created	15,000	15,000
	50,000	40,000		50,000	40,000
			Balances b/d	30,000	30,000

The balance sheet at 1 January 2002 appears as:

BALANCE SHEET OF COL AND DES AS AT 1 JANUARY 2002	
	£
Net assets	<u>60,000</u>
Capital accounts:	
Col (£35,000 + £15,000 − £20,000)	30,000
Des (£25,000 + £15,000 − £10,000)	<u>30,000</u>
	<u>60,000</u>

The effect is that Col has 'paid' Des £5,000 to increase his share of the profits from half to two-thirds. This may seem unfair but neither partner is worse off in the event of the business being sold, assuming that the business is sold for £90,000 (£60,000 assets + £30,000 goodwill). Before the change in the profit-sharing ratio they would have received:

Col £35,000 capital + £15,000 half-share of goodwill = £50,000
Des £25,000 capital + £15,000 half-share of goodwill = £40,000

After the change, they will receive:

Col £30,000 capital + £20,000 two-thirds share of goodwill = £50,000
Des £30,000 capital + £10,000 one-third share of goodwill = £40,000

As far as the realisation amounts are concerned, the position remains unchanged: it is only the profit-sharing ratios that will be different as from 1 January 2002. Also, any increase in goodwill above the £30,000 figure will be shared in the new ratio.

REVALUATION OF ASSETS

So far in this chapter we have looked at the adjustments made for goodwill in various changes made to partnerships. Goodwill, however, reflects only one aspect of a partner's interest in the business. For example, some of the assets may have appreciated in value, but adjustments may not have been made in the accounts; other assets may have fallen in value, while provisions for depreciation and/or bad debts may have been too much or too little. With a change in the personnel of a partnership, a **revaluation account** may be needed to correct any discrepancies in values. The accounting procedure is:

- **increase in the value of an asset**
  - debit asset account with the amount of the increase
  - credit revaluation account with the amount of the increase
- **reduction in the value of an asset**
  - debit revaluation account the amount of the reduction
  - credit asset account the amount of the reduction
- **increase in provision for depreciation/bad debts**
  - debit revaluation account with the amount of the increase
  - credit provision account with the amount of the increase

- **reduction in provision for depreciation/bad debts**
    - debit provision account with the amount of the reduction
    - credit revaluation account the amount of the reduction

After these adjustments have been recorded in the books of account, the balance of the revaluation account is divided among the partners in their profit-sharing ratios.

CASE STUDY

MAT, NIA AND OLLY: REVALUATION OF ASSETS

situation

Matt, Nia and Olly are in partnership sharing profits and losses equally. On 31 December 2001 their balance sheet is as follows:

BALANCE SHEET OF MATT, NIA AND OLLY AS AT 31 DECEMBER 2001			
	£	£	£
Fixed Assets	Cost	Dep'n to date	Net
Premises	100,000	-	100,000
Machinery	50,000	10,000	40,000
	150,000	10,000	140,000
Current Assets			
Stock		30,000	
Debtors		20,000	
Bank		5,000	
		55,000	
Less Current Liabilities			
Creditors		25,000	
Working Capital			30,000
NET ASSETS			170,000
FINANCED BY			
Capital accounts			
Matt			60,000
Nia			60,000
Olly			50,000
			170,000

Olly decides to retire at 31 December 2001; Matt and Nia are to continue the partnership and will share profits and losses equally. The following valuations are agreed:

Goodwill	£30,000
Premises	£150,000
Machinery	£30,000
Stock	£21,000

A provision for bad debts equal to five per cent of debtors is to be made.

Olly agrees that the money owing on retirement are to be retained in the business as a long-term loan.

solution

The revaluation account and adjusted balance sheet appear as follows:

Dr		**Revaluation Account**		Cr
	£			£
Provision for depreciation:		Goodwill		30,000
Machinery	10,000	Premises		50,000
Stock	9,000			
Provision for bad debts	1,000			
Surplus on revaluation c/d	60,000			
	80,000			80,000
Capital accounts:		Surplus on revaluation b/d		60,000
Matt (one-third)	20,000			
Nia (one-third)	20,000			
Olly (one-third)	20,000			
	60,000			60,000

Note that the amount of goodwill has been credited to revaluation account (and thus to the capital accounts); it will, later, be debited to the capital accounts of the two remaining partners at £15,000 each – in this way it will not feature on the balance sheet.

The capital accounts of the partners, after the above transactions have been recorded, appear as:

Dr				**Partners' Capital Accounts**				Cr
	Matt	Nia	Olly		Matt	Nia	Olly	
	£	£	£		£	£	£	
Goodwill written off	15,000	15,000	–	Balances b/d	60,000	60,000	50,000	
Loan account			70,000	Revaluation acc*				
Balances c/d	65,000	65,000	–	surplus	20,000	20,000	20,000	
	80,000	80,000	70,000		80,000	80,000	70,000	
				Balances b/d	65,000	65,000	–	

* Note that revaluation account includes goodwill created.

The balance sheet at 1 January 2002 appears on the next page:

BALANCE SHEET OF MATT AND NIA AS AT 1 JANUARY 2002

	£	£	£
Fixed Assets	Cost	Dep'n to date	Net
Premises	150,000	-	150,000
Machinery	50,000	20,000	30,000
	200,000	20,000	180,000
Current Assets			
Stock		21,000	
Debtors	20,000		
Less provision for bad debts	1,000		
		19,000	
Bank		5,000	
		45,000	
Less Current Liabilities			
Creditors		25,000	
Working Capital			20,000
			200,000
Less Long-term Liabilities			
Loan account of Olly (£50,000 + £20,000)			70,000
NET ASSETS			130,000
FINANCED BY			
Capital accounts			
Matt (£60,000 + £20,000 − £15,000)			65,000
Nia (£60,000 + £20,000 − £15,000)			65,000
			130,000

PARTNERSHIP CHANGES: SPLIT YEARS

Any of the changes in partnerships that we have looked at so far in this chapter may occur during the course of an accounting year, rather than at the end of it. For example, part-way through the year:

- the partners may decide to admit a new partner
- a partner might retire, or die
- the partners may decide to change their profit-sharing ratios

To avoid having to prepare final accounts at the date of the change, it is usual to continue the accounts until the normal year-end. Then, when profit for the year has been calculated, it is necessary to apportion the profit between the two parts of the financial year, ie to split the year into the period before the change, and the period after the change. This is often done by assuming that the profit for the year has been earned at an equal rate throughout the year. The apportionment is done by dividing the appropriation account between the two time periods.

CASE STUDY

RAJ AND SAM: SPLIT YEARS

situation

Raj and Sam are in partnership; their partnership agreement states:

- interest is allowed on partners' capital accounts at the rate of ten per cent per annum

- Sam receives a partnership salary of £18,000 per annum

- the balance of partnership profits and losses are shared between Raj and Sam in the ratio 2:1 respectively

At the beginning of the financial year, on 1 January 2001, the balances of the partners' capital accounts were:

Raj	£70,000
Sam	£50,000

During the year ended 31 December 2001, the net profit of the partnership was £50,500 before appropriations. The profit arose uniformly throughout the year.

On 1 October 2001, Raj and Sam admitted Tom as a partner. Tom introduced £40,000 in capital on this date.

The partnership agreement was amended on 1 October 2001 as follows:

- interest is allowed on partners' capital accounts at the rate of ten per cent per annum

- Sam and Tom are each to receive a partnership salary of £12,000 per annum

- the balance of partnership profits and losses are to be shared between Raj, Sam and Tom in the ratio of 2:2:1 respectively

solution

The appropriation account of the partnership for the year is shown on the next page.

PROFIT AND LOSS APPROPRIATION ACCOUNT OF RAJ, SAM AND TOM
FOR THE YEAR ENDED 31 DECEMBER 2001

	9 months to 30 September	3 months to 31 December	Total for year
	£	£	£
Net profit	37,875	12,625	50,500
Less appropriation of profits:			
Salaries:			
Sam £18,000 pa x 9 months	13,500	–	
£12,000 pa x 3 months		3,000	16,500
Tom £12,000 pa x 3 months		3,000	3,000
Interest on partners' capitals:			
Raj £70,000 @ 10% pa x 9 months	5,250	–	
£70,000 @ 10% pa x 3 months	–	1,750	7,000
Sam £50,000 @ 10% pa x 9 months	3,750	–	
£50,000 @ 10% pa x 3 months	–	1,250	5,000
Tom £40,000 @ 10% pa x 3 months	–	1,000	1,000
	*15,375	**2,625	18,000
Share of remaining profits:			
Raj	(2/3) 10,250	(2/5) 1,050	11,300
Sam	(1/3) 5,125	(2/5) 1,050	6,175
Tom	–	(1/5) 525	525
	15,375	2,625	18,000

*   Raj and Sam shared profits 2:1 respectively
** Raj, Sam and Tom shared profits 2:2:1 respectively

DISSOLUTION OF A PARTNERSHIP

There are various reasons why a partnership may come to an end:

- a partnership may be formed for a fixed term or for a specific purpose and, at the end of that term or when that purpose has been achieved, it is dissolved

- a partnership might be dissolved as a result of bankruptcy, or because a partner retires or dies and no new partners can be found to keep the firm going

- sales may fall due to changes in technology and product obsolescence, with the partners not feeling it is worthwhile to seek out and develop new products

- at the other end of the scale, the business might expand to such an extent that, in order to acquire extra capital needed for growth, the partnership may be dissolved and a limited company formed to take over its assets and liabilities.

Whatever the reason for dissolving the partnership, the accounts have to be closed. A **realisation account** is used to record the closing transactions, and this account shows the net gain or loss that is available for distribution among the partners. The Partnership Act 1890 requires that monies realised from the sale of assets are to be applied in the following order:

- firstly, in settlement of the firm's debts, other than those to partners

- then, in repayment of partners' loans

- then, in settlement of partners' capital and current accounts

steps to close the books of a partnership

1   Asset accounts (except for cash/bank) are closed by transfer to realisation account:
    – debit realisation account
    – credit asset accounts

2   Provisions accounts, eg depreciation, bad debts, are transferred to realisation account:
    – debit provision account
    – credit realisation account

3   As assets are sold, the proceeds are placed to cash/bank account, and the sum recorded in realisation account:
    – debit cash/bank account
    – credit realisation account

4   If a partner takes over any assets, the value is agreed and the amount is

deducted from the partner's capital account and transferred to realisation account:

– debit partner's capital account

– credit realisation account

5   As expenses of realisation are incurred, they are paid from cash/bank account and entered in realisation account:

– debit realisation account

– credit cash/bank account

6   Creditors are paid off:
     – debit creditors' accounts
     – credit cash/bank account

7   The balance of realisation account, after all assets have been sold and all creditors have been paid, represents the profit or loss on realisation, and is transferred to the partners' capital accounts in the proportion in which profits and losses are shared. If a profit has been made, the transactions are:

– debit realisation account

– credit partners' capital accounts

Where a loss has been made, the entries are reversed.

8   Partners' loans (if any) are repaid:

– debit partners' loan accounts

– credit cash/bank account

9   Partners' current accounts are transferred to capital accounts:

– debit partners' current accounts

– credit partners' capital accounts

If a partner has a debit balance on current account, the entries will be reversed.

10   If any partner now has a debit balance on capital account, he or she must pay in money from private funds to clear the balance:

– debit cash/bank account

– credit partner's capital account

11   The remaining cash and bank balances are used to repay the credit balances on partners' capital accounts:

– debit partners' capital accounts

– credit cash/bank account

DAN, EVE AND FAY:
DISSOLUTION OF A PARTNERSHIP

situation

Dan, Eve and Fay are in partnership, sharing profits and losses equally. As a result of falling sales they decide to dissolve the partnership as from 31 December 2002. The balance sheet at that date is shown below:

BALANCE SHEET OF DAN, EVE AND FAY AS AT 31 DECEMBER 2002			
	£	£	£
Fixed Assets	Cost	Dep'n to date	Net
Machinery	25,000	10,000	15,000
Delivery van	10,000	5,000	5,000
	35,000	15,000	20,000
Current Assets			
Stock		12,000	
Debtors		10,000	
Bank		3,000	
		25,000	
Less Current Liabilities			
Creditors		8,000	
Working Capital			17,000
NET ASSETS			37,000
FINANCED BY			
Capital accounts			
Dan			13,000
Eve			12,000
Fay			12,000
			37,000

The sale proceeds of the assets are machinery £12,000, stock £8,000, debtors £9,000. Dan is to take over the delivery van at an agreed valuation of £3,000. The expenses of realisation amount to £2,000.

solution

The realisation account, partners' capital accounts and bank account to record the dissolution of the partnership are shown on the next page:

Dr		Realisation Account		Cr
	£			£
Machinery	25,000	Provisions for depreciation:		
Delivery van	10,000	machinery		10,000
Stock	12,000	delivery van		5,000
Debtors	10,000	Bank: machinery		12,000
Bank: realisation expenses	2,000	Bank: stock		8,000
		Bank: debtors		9,000
		Dan's capital account: van		3,000
		Loss on realisation c/d		12,000
	59,000			59,000
Loss on realisation b/d	12,000	Capital accounts:		
		Dan (one-third)		4,000
		Eve (one-third)		4,000
		Fay (one-third)		4,000
	12,000			12,000

Dr		Partners' Capital Accounts					Cr
	Dan	Eve	Fay		Dan	Eve	Fay
	£	£	£		£	£	£
Realisation account:				Balances b/d	13,000	12,000	12,000
delivery van	3,000	-	-				
Realisation account:							
loss	4,000	4,000	4,000				
Bank	6,000	8,000	8,000				
	13,000	12,000	12,000		13,000	12,000	12,000

Dr		Bank Account		Cr
	£			£
Balance b/d	3,000	Realisation account: expenses		2,000
Machinery	12,000	Creditors		8,000
Stock	8,000	Capital accounts:		
Debtors	9,000	Dan		6,000
		Eve		8,000
		Fay		8,000
	32,000			32,000

As can be seen from the above accounts, the assets have been realised, the liabilities paid, and the balances due to the partners have been settled; the partnership has been dissolved.

THE RULE IN GARNER v MURRAY

When a partnership is dissolved, any partner with a debit balance remaining on capital account must pay in monies from private funds to clear the balance. However, if such a partner is insolvent, then the other partners must share the loss in the ratio of their *last agreed capital balances*, ie the balances of their capital accounts before the dissolution began.

This rule was established in the legal case of Garner v Murray (1904) and is a departure from other changes to partnerships where the ratio in which profits or losses are shared has been used.

CONFIDENTIALITY PROCEDURES

The financial details of changes to partnerships should always be treated with confidentiality. In particular:

- details of the amount of goodwill should be discussed only with existing or new partners; as it normally does not appear on the balance sheet, the valuation of goodwill is confidential

- new partners will expect details of the amount of capital they are bringing in to an existing partnership to be kept confidential, and also the premium paid for goodwill

- all partners, existing or new, will expect details of changes made to the ratios in which they share profits and losses to be kept confidential

- on dissolution of a partnership, partners will expect confidentiality in the realisation values of assets, and also the amount received by each partner

Very few details of partnerships need be revealed to other people; the Inland Revenue, lenders, and solicitors involved with the legal aspects are the only professionals outside the partnership who may need to have details of changes being made. Any disclosures should only be made with the prior approval of the partners.

- Goodwill is an intangible fixed asset.

- Goodwill should only be shown in the balance sheet when it has been purchased; it should then be:
  - either, amortised to profit and loss account over its estimated useful economic life
  - or, if the estimated useful economic life is deemed to be indefinite, the goodwill need not be amortised, provided that its continuing existence can be justified

- With partnerships, goodwill is normally calculated for transactions involving changes in the structure of the business to cover:
  - admission of a new partner
  - retirement of a partner
  - death of a partner
  - changes in profit-sharing ratios

  A goodwill account is normally created just before the change, and then deleted immediately after the change, ie it does not appear on the partnership balance sheet.

- When partnership changes take place part-way through the financial year, it is necessary to apportion the profit between the two parts of the financial year, usually by assuming that the profit has been earned at a uniform rate throughout the year.

- A revaluation account is used whenever assets are revalued prior to making changes to the personnel of the partnership.

- When a partnership is dissolved, a realisation account is used to record the sale proceeds of assets, and to calculate any profit or loss on realisation due to the partners.

goodwill	the difference between the value of a business as a whole, and the net value of its separate assets and liabilities
goodwill account	an account to which goodwill, an intangible fixed asset, is debited
premium for goodwill	amount charged to a new partner who joins an existing partnership
revaluation account	account used when assets are increased or decreased in value, eg when changes are made to a partnership
realisation account	account used when assets are realised, eg on the dissolution of a partnership

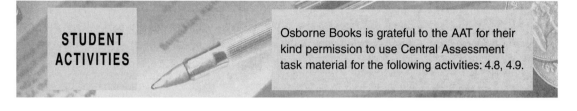

STUDENT
ACTIVITIES

Osborne Books is grateful to the AAT for their kind permission to use Central Assessment task material for the following activities: 4.8, 4.9.

4.1 John agrees to amalgamate his business with Tony's business. The net asset values shown on John's balance sheet total £420,000, but the value agreed for partnership purposes was £480,000.

Therefore goodwill can be calculated as:

(a) £900,000

(b) £60,000

(c) £120,000

(d) £30,000

4.2 Andrew and Barry are in partnership sharing profits in a ratio of 2:1 respectively. Colin is admitted to the partnership and the profit sharing ratios now become Andrew (2) Barry (2) and Colin (1). If goodwill at the time of Colin joining, is valued at £90,000 what will be the adjustments into Barry's capital account for Goodwill?

(a) Debit £36,000   Credit £30,000

(b) Debit £30,000   Credit £36,000

(c) Debit £36,000   Credit £36,000

(d) Debit £30,000   Credit £30,000

4.3 Matt Clive and Elaine are in partnership sharing profit on a 3:2:1 basis respectively. Sheila is to become a new partner in the business, and at the time of her joining, the new partnership profit sharing ratios will be Matt (4) Clive (3) Elaine (2) and Sheila (1). So that the new partnership can begin on an equal footing the business decides to revalue its fixed assets from £100,000 to £148,000. How much of this revaluation surplus will be received by Elaine?

(a) £4,800

(b) £14,800

(c) £24,667

(d) £8,000

4.4 Outline the rule established in Garner v Murray (1904).

4.5   Sam, Rick and Cameron are in partnership sharing profits in the ratio 4:2:2 respectively. Rick is to retire on 31 August 20-1 and is to be paid the amount due to him in cash.

The balance sheet drawn up immediately before Rick's retirement was as follows:

	£
Fixed assets	50,000
Current assets	10,000
Cash in hand	25,000
	85,000
Creditors	(10,000)
	75,000
Capital accounts:	
Sam	33,000
Rick	12,000
Cameron	30,000
	75,000

Goodwill is to be valued at £16,000 and fixed assets are to be revalued at £74,000 but no goodwill is to remain in the books after Rick's retirement.

In the new partnership Sam and Cameron are to share profits equally.

REQUIRED:

Task 1
The partners' capital accounts showing the amount Rick is to be paid upon retirement.

Task 2
The balance sheet immediately after Rick's departure from the business.

4.6   The partnership of Fame, Fortune and Fear has asked you to assist its book-keeper in the finalisation of its accounts for the year ended 31 March 20-2.

The following information is available:

The draft net profit of the business has been calculated as being £152,000, before taking into account any appropriations.

The original partners of the business are Fame and Fortune. They shared profits on an equal basis until 1 April 20-1 when Fear then joined them. Fear agreed to introduce £60,000 in cash on admission to the business. It was then agreed that the new profit sharing ratio would be:

Fame	3/8
Fortune	3/8
Fear	2/8

On 1 April 20-1 goodwill was valued at £80,000. No adjustment was made for goodwill at this time, but it is now the wish of the partners that goodwill is introduced against their opening capital accounts. (No goodwill account is to be maintained in the books of the partnership).

Partners salaries are as follows:

	£
Fame	20,000
Fortune	20,000
Fear	30,000

All partners receive interest of 15% per annum on their year-end balance on the capital accounts. No interest is to be paid on the current account balances.

The balance on capital and current accounts as at 1 April 20-1 were as follows:

	Capital Account	Current Account
	£	£
Fame	110,000	6,500
Fortune	90,000	7,800

In addition to the balance on the capital account Fortune has made a loan of £40,000 at a rate of 7.5% per annum. For the year to 31 March 20-2 no interest has been charged against the draft net profit figure. Any accrued interest receivable should be credited to Fortune 's current account.

Partners drawings were as follows:

	£
Fame	28,000
Fortune	32,000
Fear	24,000

REQUIRED

Task 1
Prepare the partners' Capital Accounts for the year ended 31 March 20-2, recording all the necessary entries for the admission of Fear to the partnership.

Task 2
Make the necessary adjustment against the draft net profit figure to introduce the accrued loan interest.

Task 3
Prepare the partnership appropriation account for the year ended 31 March 20-2.

Task 4
Prepare the partners' current accounts for the year ended 31 March 20-2.

4.7 Ernest, Harvey and Eileen are in partnership trading as a book shop called BooksRus. Most of the books are sold over the internet, although they also sell by retail outlet and via mail order. The partners have decided to close down the partnership and cease trading as from 31 March 20-2.

The partnership balance sheet as at 31 March 20-2 prior to any sell off was as follows:

FIXED ASSETS	£	£
Land and Buildings	280,000	
Fixtures, Furniture and Equipment	125,000	
Motor vehicles	40,000	445,000
CURRENT ASSETS		
Stock	35,000	
Debtors	12,000	
Cash at Bank	23,000	
	70,000	
CURRENT LIABILITIES		
Creditors	55,000	
NET CURRENT ASSETS		15,000
		460,000
Represented by:		
CAPITAL ACCOUNTS		
Ernest	180,000	
Harvey	120,000	
Eileen	100,000	400,000
CURRENT ACCOUNTS		
Ernest	25,000	
Harvey	15,000	
Eileen	20,000	60,000
		460,000

Ernest, Harvey and Eileen have always shared profits and losses on a 6:3:1 basis respectively. In the process of dissolution the assets were realised for the following cash amounts.

	£
Land and Buildings	350,000
Fixtures, Furniture and Equipment	85,000
Motor Vehicles	30,000
Stock	36,000
Debtors	9,000
Total proceeds	510,000

The creditors of BooksRus accepted a payment of £50,000 in settlement of debts totalling £55,000.

REQUIRED

Close off the books of account of the partnership, showing clearly the amounts due in cash to each respective partner.

4.8 You have been approached by a partnership, Barrow, Mark, Williams and James, to help finalise their accounts for the year to 30 June 20-4. A book-keeper working for the partnership has prepared a profit statement for the year. The net profit has been agreed at £40,000 after deduction of salaries and loan capital interest. You have been given a memo detailing the following information by the bookkeeper.

- Interest is payable on loans at a rate of 5% per annum; interest on capital is paid at the same rate, based on the year-end capital amounts. No interest is allowed on balance of current accounts.

- Drawings made for the year ending 30 June 20-4 were:
Barrow	£17,000
Mark	£20,000
Williams	£5,000
James	£13,000

- Mark is has a salary of £7,000 per annum, and James has a salary of £6,000 per annum.

- Barrow invested a further £10,000 capital into the partnership on 1 January 20-4. James invested a further £5,000 on 1 February 20-4.

- Barrow's loan account with the partnership stands at £6,000.

- The profits/losses are shared 3:4:2:1 by Barrow, Mark, Williams and James

- You have been supplied with the balance sheet of the partnership as at 30 June 20-3.

BALANCE SHEET OF BARROW, MARK, WILLIAMS AND JAMES AS AT 30 JUNE 20-3

	£	£
FIXED ASSETS		
Vehicles	19,000	
Fixtures and fittings	9,300	
		28,300
CURRENT ASSETS		
Stock	10,000	
Debtors	7,000	
Bank	13,000	
	30,000	
CURRENT LIABILITIES		
Creditors	9,000	
NET CURRENT ASSETS		21,000
		49,300
Represented by:		
CAPITAL ACCOUNTS		
Barrow	15,000	
Mark	15,000	
Williams	3,000	
James	5,000	
		38,000

CURRENT ACCOUNTS

Barrow	2,500
Mark	1,800
Williams	(1,000)
James	2,000
	5,300

LOAN ACCOUNT

Barrow	6,000
	49,300

Tasks

(a) Based on the above information, draw up an appropriation account for the partnership of Barrow, Mark, Williams and James for the year ended 30 June 20-4.

(b) Prepare the partners' current and capital accounts for the year ended 30 June 20-4.

(c) Explain the difference between an appropriation and an expense, illustrating your answer with reference to partners' capital and loans.

4.9   Samuel Taylor has a number of questions about his decision to enter into partnership with Coleridge & Co which he would like your help to answer. He has obtained the latest balance sheet of the partnership. The simplified balance sheet of the partnership Coleridge & Co as at 30 June 20-5 is set out below.

	£	£
FIXED ASSETS		240,000
NET WORKING CAPITAL		120,000
		360,000
PARTNERS' CAPITAL ACCOUNTS		
Wordsworth	138,000	
Quincey	65,000	
Southey	84,000	
		287,000
PARTNERS' CURRENT ACCOUNTS		
Wordsworth	35,000	
Quincey	18,000	
Southey	20,000	
		73,000
		360,000

The terms of the proposed entry of Samuel Taylor into the partnership are set out as follows:

1   On the entry of Samuel Taylor into the partnership, Wordsworth will retire. Samuel will pay £80,000 of capital in cash into the partnership.

2   Under the existing partnership agreement the three partners share profits in the following ratios.

Wordsworth   5/10

Quincey   3/10

Southey   2/10

When Samuel Taylor joins the partnership the new profit sharing ratio will be:

Quincey   4/10

Southey   3/10

Taylor   3/10

3   As part of the retirement arrangements the fixed assets of the old partnership will be revalued to £340,000. Goodwill has been estimated at £50,000 and the accounts will be adjusted to reflect this fact on the retirement of Wordsworth. Goodwill is to be eliminated in the books of the new partnership and so no goodwill account will be maintained.

4   The balance on the capital account of Wordsworth is to be transferred to a loan account and will be repaid in two years time.

Tasks

(a)   Make the necessary entries in the capital accounts of the partners to reflect the retirement of Wordsworth and the admission of Samuel Taylor into the partnership of Coleridge & Co in accordance with the provisions set out above, assuming that the entry was made on 30 June 20-5.

(b)   Samuel Taylor has asked the following question concerning his proposed entry into the partnership of Coleridge & Co.

"What is goodwill and why is it necessary to make an adjustment for goodwill on the retirement of a partner?"

How would you answer him?

5 INTRODUCTION TO LIMITED COMPANY ACCOUNTS

this chapter covers . . .

In this chapter we turn our attention to limited companies and look at:

- the advantages of forming a limited company

- the differences between a private limited company, a public limited company, and a company limited by guarantee

- the information contained in a company's Memorandum of Association and Articles of Association

- the differences between ordinary shares and preference shares

- the concept of reserves, and the difference between capital reserves and revenue reserves

- the appropriation section of a company's profit and loss account

- the layout of a company's balance sheet

NVQ PERFORMANCE CRITERIA COVERED

unit 11: DRAFTING FINANCIAL STATEMENTS

element 2

draft limited company, sole trader and partnership year end financial statements

- financial statements are accurately drafted from the appropriate information

- subsequent adjustments are correctly implemented

- year end financial statements are presented for approval to the appropriate person in clear form

- confidentiality procedures are followed at all times

- the organisation's policies, regulations, procedures and timescales relating to financial statements are observed at all times

- discrepancies, unusual features or queries are identified and either resolved or referred to the appropriate person

ADVANTAGES OF FORMING A LIMITED COMPANY

A limited company is a separate legal entity, owned by shareholders and managed by directors.

The limited company is often chosen as the legal status of a business for a number of reasons:

limited liability

The shareholders (members) of a company can only lose the amount of their investment, being the money paid already, together with any money unpaid on their shares (unpaid instalments on new share issues, for example). Thus, if the company became insolvent (went 'bust'), shareholders would have to pay any unpaid instalments to help pay the creditors. As this happens very rarely, shareholders are usually in a safe position: their personal assets, unless pledged as security to a lender (as in the case of a director/shareholder), are not available to the company's creditors.

separate legal entity

A limited company is a separate legal entity from its owners. Anyone taking legal action proceeds against the company and not the individual shareholders.

ability to raise finance

A limited company can raise substantial funds from outside sources by the issue of shares:

- for the larger public company – from the public and investing institutions on the Stock Exchange or similar markets
- for the smaller company – privately from venture capital companies, relatives and friends

Companies can also raise finance by means of debentures (see page 120).

membership

A member of a limited company is a person who owns at least one share in that company. The minimum number of members is two, but there is no upper limit. A member of a company is the same as a shareholder.

other factors

A limited company is usually a much larger business unit than a sole trader or partnership. This gives the company a higher standing and status in the business community, allowing it to benefit from economies of scale, and making it of sufficient size to employ specialists for functions such as production, marketing, finance and human resources.

THE COMPANIES ACT

Limited companies are regulated by the Companies Act 1985, as amended by the Companies Act 1989.

Under the terms of the 1985 Act there are two main types of limited company: the larger public limited company (abbreviated to 'Plc'), which is defined in the Act, and the smaller company, traditionally known as a private limited company (abbreviated to 'Ltd'), which is any other limited company. A further type of company is limited by guarantee.

public limited company (Plc)

A company may become a public limited company if it has:

- issued share capital of over £50,000

- at least two members (shareholders) and at least two directors

A public limited company may raise capital from the public on the Stock Exchange or similar markets – the new issues and privatisations of recent years are examples of this. A public limited company does not have to issue shares on the stock markets, and not all do so.

private limited company (Ltd)

The private limited company is the most common form of limited company. The term *private* is not set out in the Companies Act 1985, but it is a traditional description, and well describes the smaller company, often in family ownership. A private limited company has:

- no minimum requirement for issued share capital

- at least two members (shareholders) and at least one director

The shares are not traded publicly, but are transferable between individuals, although valuation will be more difficult for shares not quoted on the stock markets.

company limited by guarantee

A company limited by guarantee is not formed with share capital, but relies on the guarantee of its members to pay a stated amount in the event of the company's insolvency. Examples of such companies include charities, and artistic and educational organisations.

GOVERNING DOCUMENTS OF COMPANIES

There are a number of documents required by the Companies Act in the setting-up of a company. Two essential governing documents are the **Memorandum of Association** and the **Articles of Association**.

The **Memorandum of Association,** the constitution of the company, regulates the affairs of the company to the outside world and contains five main clauses:

1 the name of the company (together with the words 'public limited company' or 'limited', as appropriate)

2 capital of the company (the amount that can be issued in shares: the authorised share capital)

3 'objects' of the company, ie what activities the company can engage in; under the Companies Act the objects can be stated as being those of 'a general commercial company', ie the company can engage in any commercial activity

4 registered office of the company (not the address, but whether it is registered in England and Wales, or in Scotland)

5 a statement that the liability of the members is limited

The **Articles of Association** regulate the internal administration of the company, including the powers of directors and the holding of company meetings.

ACCOUNTING REQUIREMENTS OF THE COMPANIES ACT

The Companies Act 1985 (as amended by the Companies Act 1989) requires that companies produce sets of accounts. The Act seeks to protect the interests of shareholders, creditors, and lenders by requiring accounts to be presented in a standardised layout. This enables comparisons to be made with other companies so that users of accounts can understand and assess the progress being made. The Act also states the detailed information that must be disclosed.

For larger companies the accounts are audited by external auditors – this is a costly and time-consuming exercise (smaller and medium-sized companies are often exempt from audit). Nevertheless, the audit process enhances the reliability of the accounts for users.

The accounts must be sent to Companies House, where they are available for public inspection. The accounts are available to all shareholders, together with a report on the company's activities during the year.

In this chapter we will study the 'internal use' accounts, rather than being concerned with the detailed accounting requirements of the Companies Act. Chapter 6 will look at such 'published accounts', as they are often known.

Before we examine the financial statements in detail we will look first at the principal ways in which a company raises finance: shares. There are different types of shares which appear in a company's balance sheet as the company's share capital.

TYPES OF SHARES ISSUED BY LIMITED COMPANIES

The **authorised share capital** is stated in the Memorandum of Association and is the maximum share capital that the company is allowed to issue. The authorised share capital may not be the same as the **issued share capital**; under company law the issued capital cannot exceed the amount authorised. If a company which has issued the full extent of its authorised share capital wishes to make an increase, it must first pass the appropriate resolution at a general meeting of the shareholders.

The authorised share capital is shown on the balance sheet (or as a note to the accounts) 'for information', but is not added into the balance sheet total, as it may not be the same amount as the issued share capital. By contrast, the issued share capital – showing the classes and number of shares that have been issued – forms a part of the 'financed by' section of the balance sheet of a limited company.

The authorised and issued share capital may be divided into a number of classes or types of share; the main types are **ordinary shares** and, less commonly, **preference shares**.

ordinary (equity) shares

These are the most commonly issued class of share which carry the main 'risks and rewards' of the business: the risks are of losing part or all of the value of the shares if the business loses money or becomes insolvent; the rewards are that they take a share of the profits – in the form of **dividends** – after allowance has been made for all expenses of the business, including loan and debenture interest, taxation, and after preference dividends (if any). When a company makes large profits, it will have the ability to pay higher dividends to the ordinary shareholders; when losses are made, the ordinary shareholders may receive no dividend.

Companies rarely pay out all of their profits in the form of dividends; most retain some profits as reserves. These can always be used to enable a dividend to be paid in a year when the company makes little or no profit, always assuming that the company has sufficient cash in the bank to make the payment. Ordinary shareholders, in the event of the company becoming insolvent, will be the last to receive any repayment of their investment: other creditors will be paid off first.

Ordinary shares usually carry voting rights – thus shareholders have a say at the annual general meeting and at any other shareholders' meetings.

preference shares

Whereas ordinary share dividends will vary from year-to-year, preference shares usually carry a fixed percentage rate of dividend – for example, ten per cent of nominal value. Their dividends are paid in preference to those of ordinary shareholders; but they are only paid if the company makes profits. In the event of the company ceasing to trade, the preference shareholders will also receive repayment of capital before the ordinary shareholders.

Preference shares do not normally carry voting rights.

nominal and market values of shares

Each share has a **nominal value** – or face value – which is entered in the accounts. Shares may be issued with nominal values of 5p, 10p, 25p, 50p or £1, or indeed for any amount. Thus a company with an authorised share capital of £100,000 might state in its Memorandum of Association that this is divided up into:

100,000 ordinary shares of 50p each	£50,000
50,000 ten per cent preference shares of £1 each	£50,000
	£100,000

The nominal value usually bears little relationship to the market value. The market value is the price at which issued – or 'secondhand' – shares are traded. Share prices of a quoted public limited company may be listed in the *Financial Times*.

issue price

This is the price at which shares are issued to shareholders by the company – either when the company is being set up, or at a later date when it needs to raise more funds. The issue price is either **at par** (ie the nominal value), or above nominal value. In the latter case, the amount of the difference between issue price and nominal value is known as a **share premium** (see page 122): for example – nominal value £1.00; issue price £1.50; therefore share premium is 50p per share.

LOANS AND DEBENTURES

In addition to money provided by shareholders, who are the owners of the company, further funds can be obtained by borrowing in the form of loans or debentures:

- **Loans** are monies borrowed by companies from lenders – such as banks – on a medium or long-term basis. Generally repayments are made throughout the period of the loan, but can often be tailored to suit the needs of the borrower. Invariably lenders require security for loans so that, if the loan is not repaid, the lender has an asset – such as property – that can be sold.

   Smaller companies are sometimes also financed by directors' loans.

- **Debentures** are formal certificates issued by companies raising long-term finance from lenders and investors. Debenture certificates issued by large public limited companies are often traded on the Stock Exchange. Debentures are commonly secured against assets such as property that, in the event of the company ceasing to trade, could be sold and used to repay the debenture holders.

Loans and debentures usually carry fixed rates of interest that must be paid, just like other business overheads, whether a company makes profits or not. As loan and debenture interest is a business expense, this is shown in the profit and loss account along with all other overheads. In the event of the company ceasing to trade, loan and debenture-holders would be repaid before any shareholders.

TRADING AND PROFIT AND LOSS ACCOUNT

A limited company uses the same form of financial statements as a sole trader or partnership. However there are two overhead items commonly found in the profit and loss account of a limited company that are not found in those of other business types:

- **directors' remuneration** – ie amounts paid to directors; as directors are employed by the company, their pay appears amongst the overheads of the company

- **debenture interest** – as already noted, when debentures are issued by companies, the interest is shown as an overhead in the profit and loss account

A limited company follows the profit and loss account with an *appropriation section.* This shows how net profit has been distributed and includes:

- corporation tax – the tax payable on company profits
- dividends paid and proposed – on both ordinary and preference shares, including *interim dividends* (usually paid just over half-way through the financial year) and *final dividends* (proposed at the end of the year, and paid early in the next financial year)
- transfers to and from reserves – see below

The diagram on pages 124 and 125 shows an example of a limited company's trading and profit and loss account for internal use.

BALANCE SHEET

Balance sheets of limited companies follow the same layout as those we have seen earlier, but the capital section is more complex because of the different classes of shares that may be issued, and the various reserves. The diagram on pages 126 and 127 shows the internal use balance sheet of Orion Limited as an example (published accounts are covered in the next chapter).

RESERVES

A limited company rarely distributes all its profits to its shareholders. Instead, it will often keep part of the profits earned each year in the form of reserves. As the balance sheet of Orion Limited shows (page 127), there are two types of reserves:

- capital reserves, which are created as a result of a non-trading profit
- revenue reserves, which are retained profits from profit and loss account

capital reserves

Examples of capital reserves (which cannot be used to fund dividend payments) include:

- **Revaluation reserve.** This occurs when a fixed asset, most probably property, is revalued (in an upwards direction) in the balance sheet. The amount of the revaluation is placed in a revaluation reserve where it increases the value of the shareholders' investment in the company. Note, however, that this is purely a 'book' adjustment – no cash has changed hands.

  In the example on the next page a company revalues its property upwards by £250,000 from £500,000 to £750,000.

BALANCE SHEET (EXTRACTS)

	£
Before revaluation	
Fixed asset: property at cost	500,000
Share capital: ordinary shares of £1 each	500,000
After revaluation	
Fixed asset: property at revaluation	750,000
Share capital: ordinary shares of £1 each	500,000
Capital reserve: revaluation reserve	250,000
	750,000

- **Share premium account.** An established company may issue additional shares to the public at a higher amount than the nominal value. For example, Orion Ltd (page 127) seeks finance for further expansion by issuing additional ordinary shares. Although the shares have a nominal value of £1 each, because Orion is a well-established company, the shares are issued at £1.50 each. Of this amount, £1 is recorded in the issued share capital section, and the extra 50p is the share premium.

revenue reserves

Revenue reserves are profits generated from trading activities; they have been retained in the company to help build the company for the future. Revenue reserves include the balance of the appropriation section of the profit and loss account: this balance is commonly described as 'profit and loss account balance' or 'balance of retained profits'. Alternatively, a transfer may be made from the appropriation section to a named revenue reserve account, such as *general reserve*, or a revenue reserve for a specific purpose, such as *reserve for the replacement of machinery*. Transfers to or from these named revenue reserve accounts are made in the appropriation section of the profit and loss account.

reserves: profits not cash

It should be noted that reserves – both capital and revenue – are not cash funds to be used whenever the company needs money, but are in fact represented by assets shown on the balance sheet. The reserves record the fact that the assets belong to the shareholders via their ownership of the company.

EXAMPLE ACCOUNTS

On the next four pages are set out the trading and profit and loss account and balance sheet for Orion Limited, a private limited company. Note that these are the 'internal use' accounts – the detailed accounting requirements of the Companies Act are covered in Chapter 6.

Explanations of the financial statements are set out on the left-hand page.

ACCESSIBILITY AND CONFIDENTIALITY OF ACCOUNTS

accessibility

Limited company accounts are far more readily accessible to interested parties than the accounts of sole traders and partnerships:

– all limited companies must submit accounts to Companies House where they are available for public inspection

– a copy of the accounts is available to all shareholders, together with a report on the company's activities during the year

– the profit statements and balance sheets of larger public limited companies are commented on and discussed in the media

– the accounts of larger public limited companies are freely available to potential investors, lenders and other interested parties

confidentiality

Although company accounts are readily accessible, great care must be taken when they are being prepared. Confidentiality procedures must be observed at all times:

– during the preparation of year-end financial statements

– during the period after the accounts have been prepared but before they are sent to the shareholders and disclosed to the public

– for information that has been used in the preparation of the accounts but which is not required to be disclosed under the Companies Act (see also Chapter 6, which follows)

The **appropriation section** (or account) is the part of the profit and loss account which shows how net profit is distributed. It includes corporation tax, dividends paid and proposed, and transfers to and from reserves.

The **overheads** of a limited company include directors' remuneration and interest paid on debentures (if debentures have been issued).

The company has recorded a **net profit** of £43,000 in its profit and loss account – this is brought into the appropriation section.

Corporation tax, the tax that a company has to pay, based on its profits, is shown in the appropriation section. We shall not be studying the calculations for corporation tax in this book. It is, however, important to see how the tax is recorded in the financial statements.

The company has already paid **interim dividends** on the two classes of shares it has in issue (ordinary shares and preference shares); these would, most probably, have been paid just over half-way through the company's financial year. The company also proposes to pay a **final dividend** to its shareholders: these will be paid in the early part of the next financial year. Note that a dividend is often expressed as an amount per share, based on the nominal value, eg 5p per £1 nominal value share (which is the same as a five per cent dividend).

Added to **net profit** is a **balance** of £41,000. This represents profits of the company from previous years that have not been distributed as dividends. Note that the appropriation section shows a balance of retained profits at the year-end of £50,000. Such retained profits form a revenue reserve (see page122) of the company.

ORION LIMITED
TRADING AND PROFIT AND LOSS ACCOUNT
for the year ended 31 December 2002

	£	£
Sales		725,000
Opening stock	45,000	
Purchases	381,000	
	426,000	
Less closing stock	50,000	
Cost of Sales		376,000
Gross profit		349,000
Less overheads:		
Directors' remuneration	75,000	
Debenture interest	6,000	
Other overheads	225,000	
		306,000
Net profit for year before taxation		43,000
Less corporation tax		15,000
Profit for year after taxation		28,000
Less interim dividends paid		
ordinary shares	5,000	
preference shares	2,000	
final dividends proposed		
ordinary shares	10,000	
preference shares	2,000	
		19,000
Retained profit for year		9,000
Add balance of retained profits at beginning of year		41,000
Balance of retained profits at end of year		50,000

Limited company balance sheets usually distinguish between:

intangible fixed assets, which do not have material substance but belong to the company and have value, eg goodwill (the amount paid for the reputation and connections of a business that has been taken over), patents and trademarks; intangible fixed assets are depreciated (or amortised) in the same way as tangible fixed assets.

tangible fixed assets, which have material substance, such as premises, equipment, vehicles.

As well as the usual **current liabilities**, for limited companies, this section also contains the amount of proposed dividends (but not dividends that have been paid in the year) and the amount of corporation tax to be paid within the next twelve months. The amounts for both of these items are also included in the appropriation section of the profit and loss account.

Long-term liabilities are those that are due to be repaid more than twelve months from the date of the balance sheet, eg loans and debentures.

Authorised share capital is included on the balance sheet 'for information', but is not added into the balance sheet total, as it may not be the same amount as the issued share capital.

Issued share capital shows the classes and number of shares that have been issued. In this balance sheet, the shares are described as being fully paid, meaning that the company has received the full amount of the value of each share from the shareholders. Sometimes shares will be partly paid, eg ordinary shares of £1, but 75p paid. This means that the company can make a call on the shareholders to pay the extra 25p to make the shares fully paid.

Capital reserves are created as a result of non-trading profit.

Revenue reserves are retained profits from profit and loss account.

The total for **shareholders' funds** represents the stake of the shareholders in the company. It comprises share capital (ordinary and preference shares), plus reserves (capital and revenue reserves).

ORION LIMITED
Balance sheet as at 31 December 2002

Fixed Assets	Cost £	Dep'n to date £	Net £
Intangible			
Goodwill	50,000	20,000	30,000
Tangible			
Freehold land and buildings	180,000	20,000	160,000
Machinery	230,000	90,000	140,000
Fixtures and fittings	100,000	25,000	75,000
	560,000	155,000	405,000

Current Assets		
Stock	50,000	
Debtors	38,000	
Bank	22,000	
Cash	2,000	
	112,000	

Less Current Liabilities		
Creditors	30,000	
Proposed dividends	12,000	
Corporation tax	15,000	
	57,000	
Working Capital*		55,000
		460,000

Less Long-term Liabilities	
10% debentures	60,000
NET ASSETS	400,000

FINANCED BY
Authorised Share Capital

100,000 10% preference shares of £1 each	100,000
600,000 ordinary shares of £1 each	600,000
	700,000

Issued Share Capital

40,000 10% preference shares of £1 each, fully paid	40,000
300,000 ordinary shares of £1 each, fully paid	300,000
	340,000

Capital Reserve

Share premium account	10,000

Revenue Reserve

Profit and loss account	50,000
SHAREHOLDERS' FUNDS	400,000

* working capital is often referred to as 'net current assets'

CHAPTER SUMMARY

- A limited company has a separate legal entity from its owners.

- A company is regulated by the Companies Act 1985 (as amended by the Companies Act 1989), and is owned by shareholders and managed by directors.

- A limited company may be either a public limited company or a private limited company.

- The liability of shareholders is limited to any money unpaid on their shares.

- The main types of shares that may be issued by companies are ordinary shares and preference shares.

- Borrowings in the form of loans and debentures are a further source of finance.

- The final accounts of a company include an appropriation section, which follows the profit and loss account.

- The balance sheet of a limited company is similar to that of sole traders and partnerships but the capital and reserves section reflects the ownership of the company by its shareholders:
  - a statement of the authorised and issued share capital
  - details of capital reserves and revenue reserves

KEY TERMS

limited company — a separate legal entity owned by shareholders and managed by directors

limited liability — shareholders of a company are liable for company debts only to the extent of any money unpaid on their shares

shareholder — person who owns at least one share in a limited company; a shareholder is also a member of a company

public limited company — a company, registered as a plc, with an issued share capital of over £50,000 and at least two members and at least two directors; it may raise funds on the stock markets

private limited company — any limited company with share capital other than a public limited company

Memorandum of Association — the document setting out the constitution of the company, which regulates the affairs of the company to the outside world

Articles of Association — the document regulating the internal administration of the company

ordinary shares	commonly issued type of shares which take a share in the profits of the company but which also carry the main risks
preference shares	shares which carry a fixed rate of dividend paid, subject to sufficient profits, in preference to ordinary shareholders; in event of repayment of capital, rank before the ordinary shareholders
debentures	issued by companies raising long-term finance; debenture interest is an overhead in profit and loss account
nominal value	the face value of the shares entered in the accounts
issue price	the price at which shares are issued to shareholders by the company
market value	the price at which shares are traded
directors' remuneration	amounts paid to directors as employees of the company; an overhead in profit and loss account
appropriation section	the part of profit and loss account which shows how net profit is distributed, and includes corporation tax, dividends paid and proposed, and transfers to and from reserves
dividends	amounts paid to shareholders from the profit of the company; an interim dividend is paid just over half-way through a financial year; a final dividend is paid early in the following year
authorised share capital	amount of share capital authorised by the company's Memorandum of Association
issued share capital	the classes and number of shares that have been issued by the company; cannot exceed the authorised share capital
reserves	profits retained by the company; two main types: – capital reserves, created as a result of a non-trading profit – revenue reserves, retained profits from profit and loss account
revaluation reserve	capital reserve created by the upwards revaluation of a fixed asset, most usually property; cannot be used to fund dividend payments
share premium account	capital reserve created by the issue of shares at a price higher than nominal value, the excess being credited to share premium; cannot be used to fund dividend payments

STUDENT ACTIVITIES

5.1 In limited company financial statements, directors salaries are:

    (a)   Debited to the profit and loss appropriation account.

    (b)   Debited to the profit and loss account.

    (c)   Credited to the profit and loss appropriation account.

    (d)   Credited to the profit and loss account.

5.2 The authorised share capital of a limited company is:

    (a)   The amount of shares issued to shareholders.

    (b)   The amount paid for shares by the shareholders.

    (c)   The maximum amount of shares that can be issued.

    (d)   The minimum amount of shares that can be issued.

5.3 Which of these items would not appear in the appropriation account of a limited company?

    (a)   Debenture interest payable.

    (b)   Ordinary dividend proposed.

    (c)   Interim preference dividend paid.

    (d)   The retained profit for the year.

5.4 What are the main differences between preference shares and ordinary shares?

5.5 List four differences between a profit and loss account of a limited company and that of a sole trader business.

5.6   The following trial balance has been extracted from the books of account of Gretton plc as at 31 March 20-2

	Dr	Cr
	£000	*£000*
Administrative expenses	210	
Called up share capital (ordinary shares of £1 fully paid)		600
Debtors	670	
Cash at bank and in hand	15	
Share Premium		240
Distribution costs	420	
Rent, Rates and Insurance	487	
Plant and machinery		
At cost	950	
Accumulated depreciation (at 1 April 20-1)		220
Profit and loss (at 1 April 20-1)		182
Purchases	960	
Stock (at 1 April 20-1)	140	
Trade creditors		260
Sales Turnover		2,350
	3,852	3,852

Additional information

- Stock at 31 March 20-2 was valued at £180,000.
- The corporation tax charged based on the profits for the year is estimated to be £32,000.
- A final ordinary dividend of 10p per share is proposed.
- It is company policy to depreciate the plant and machinery based on an annual rate of 10% on cost.

REQUIRED

Prepare the company's profit and loss account for the year ended 31 March 20-2 and a balance sheet as at that date.

5.7 Hickson PLC prepares its accounts to 30 September each year. At 30th September 20-2 its trial balance was as follows:

	Dr	Cr
	£	£
Equipment at cost	140,000	
Depreciation to 01.10.20-1		20,000
Fixtures and Fittings at Cost	40,000	
Depreciation to 01.10.20-1		10,000
Motor Vehicles at Cost	80,000	
Depreciation to 01.10.20-1		30,000
Stock at 01.10.20-1	25,000	
Purchases	125,000	
Sales		280,000
Wages and Salaries	40,000	
Directors fees	29,000	
Printing, Telephone and stationery	7,000	
General expenses	6,000	
Rent Rates and Insurance	11,000	
Trade Debtors	26,000	
Trade Creditors		14,000
Cash at bank	5,000	
Cash in Hand	1,000	
Ordinary Shares 25p each		80,000
10% Preference Shares £1 each		30,000
Share Premium Account		6,000
Profit and Loss Account		15,000
8% Debenture Loan		50,000
	535,000	535,000

Additional information

- Closing stock is valued at £49,000

- The interest on the debenture loan needs to be accrued for, for the whole year.

- Depreciation of the fixed assets is to be provided for as follows:
Equipment	10% on cost
Fixtures & Fittings	15% on cost
Motor vehicles	25% Reducing balance method

- The directors now propose to pay the following dividends:
  All of the preference dividend for the year
  An ordinary dividend of 2p per share

- Provision of £8,000 corporation tax is to be made.

REQUIRED

Prepare the financial statements of Hickson PLC for the year ended 30 September 20-2.

5.8 The following list of balances has been extracted from the books of Grayson plc as at 31 December 20-2:

	Dr £	Cr £
Sales		2,640,300
Administration expenses	120,180	
Selling and distribution costs	116,320	
Wages and Salaries	112,800	
Directors Salaries and Fees	87,200	
Interest paid on loan stock	10,000	
Postage and Telephone	7,900	
Bank Loan Account		50,000
Purchases	2,089,600	
Stock at 01.01.20-2	318,500	
Cash at bank	20,640	
Trade debtors	415,800	
Provision for doubtful debts at 01.01.20-2		10,074
Bad debts	8,900	
Creditors		428,250
10% loan stock		200,000
Motor Expenses	12,280	
Bank charges and loan interest	7,720	
Office Equipment at NBV	110,060	
Vehicles at NBV	235,000	
50p Ordinary shares		200,000
Profit and loss account at 01.01.20-2		144,276
	3,672,900	3,672,900

Additional information

- Provide for £10,000 loan stock interest which is payable on 01.01.20-3.

- Provide for administration expenses paid in advance at 31.12.20-2 £12,200 and distribution costs of £21,300 owing at 31.12.20-2 .

- Provision for doubtful debts is to be maintained at 3% of debtors.

- Stock at 31.12.20-2 is £340,600.

- Provide for corporation tax of £45,000 payable on 01.10.20-3.

- The directors recommend a dividend of 15 pence per share.

- Depreciation on the fixed assets has already been calculated for the year and charged to administration costs and distribution costs accordingly.

REQUIRED

Prepare the financial statements of Grayson plc for the year ended 31 December 20-2.

6 PUBLISHED ACCOUNTS OF LIMITED COMPANIES

this chapter covers . . .

- the financial statements required by the Companies Act

- the reasons for, and the layout of, published accounts

- interpretation of the auditors' report

- the accounting policies followed by a particular company

- bonus issues and rights issues of shares

Towards the end of the Chapter (page 157) we see how an extended trial balance for a company is converted into the layout of published accounts.

NVQ PERFORMANCE CRITERIA COVERED

unit 11: DRAFTING FINANCIAL STATEMENTS
element 2
draft limited company, sole trader and partnership year end financial statements

- financial statements are accurately drafted from the appropriate information

- subsequent adjustments are correctly implemented

- draft accounts comply with domestic standards and legislation and, where relevant, partnership agreement

- year end financial statements are presented for approval to the appropriate person in clear form

- confidentiality procedures are followed at all times

- the organisation's policies, regulations, procedures and timescales relating to financial statements are observed at all times

- discrepancies, unusual features or queries are identified and either resolved or referred to the appropriate person

INTRODUCTION

All limited companies have shareholders. Each shareholder owns a part of the company and, although they do not take part in the day-to-day running of the company (unless they are also directors), they are entitled to know the financial results of the company.

Every limited company, whether public or private, is required by law to produce financial statements, which are also available for anyone to inspect if they so wish. We need to distinguish between the *statutory accounts* and the *report and accounts*. The **statutory accounts** are those which are required to be produced under company law, and a copy of these is filed with the Registrar of Companies. Smaller companies – see page 154 – can file abbreviated accounts.

The **report and accounts** – often referred to as the **corporate report** – is available to every shareholder and contains:

- directors' report
- auditors' report (where required)
- profit and loss account
- balance sheet
- cash flow statement (where required)
- notes to the accounts, including a statement of the company's accounting policies

Company law not only requires the production of financial statements, but also states the detailed information that must be disclosed. The legal requirements are detailed in the relevant sections of the Companies Act 1985 (as amended by the Companies Act 1989).

STATEMENTS REQUIRED BY THE COMPANIES ACT

The financial statements required by the Companies Act are:

- profit and loss account
- balance sheet
- directors' report
- auditors' report
- consolidated accounts, where appropriate (see Chapter 11)

When producing financial statements, companies also have to take note of the requirements of the accounting standards (SSAPs and FRSs). Of particular note is FRS 1, which requires larger limited companies to include a cash flow statement (see Chapter 9) as part of the published accounts.

The reporting procedures of smaller companies allow for simpler and less detailed disclosure requirements (see pages 154-155).

PROFIT AND LOSS ACCOUNT

The published profit and loss account does not, by law, have to detail every single overhead incurred by the company – to do so would be to disclose important management information to competitors. Instead, the main items are summarised; however, the Companies Act requires that certain items must be detailed either in the profit and loss account itself, or in separate notes to the accounts (see page 146).

The profit and loss account must follow one of two standard formats set out in the Act, and the example on the next page shows the one that is most commonly used by trading companies, and is adapted to take note of the requirements of FRS 3 – see below and page 224. (The other format is appropriate for manufacturing companies.) Specimen figures have been shown – the presentation is in vertical style.

As mentioned above, much of the detail shown in profit and loss account is summarised. For example:

- turnover incorporates the figures for sales and sales returns
- cost of sales includes opening stock, purchases, purchases returns, carriage inwards and closing stock
- distribution costs include warehouse costs, post and packing, delivery drivers' wages, running costs of vehicles, depreciation of vehicles, etc
- administrative expenses include office costs, rent and rates, heating and lighting, depreciation of office equipment, etc.

A recent profit and loss account for The Body Shop International PLC is shown on page 138. This gives the consolidated (or group) profit and loss account, together with the figures for the previous year. Group accounts are covered in Chapter 11.

continuing and discontinued operations

Limited company profit and loss accounts are also required (by FRS 3 *Reporting financial performance*) to show the financial results of any changes to the structure of the company, eg the purchase of another company, or the disposal of a section of the business. To this end the profit and loss account must distinguish between (continued on page 138):

XYZ PLC
Profit and Loss Account for the year ended 31 December 2002

	£000s	£000s
Turnover		
Continuing operations	22,000	
Acquisitions	3,000	
	25,000	
Discontinued operations	2,000	27,000
Cost of sales		16,500
Gross profit		10,500
Distribution costs		4,250
Administrative expenses		4,000
Operating profit		
Continuing operations	2,000	
Acquisitions	200	
	2,200	
Discontinued operations	50	2,250
Profit on disposal of discontinued operations		250
		2,500
Other operating income		250
Income from shares in group undertakings		–
Income from participating interests		–
Income from other fixed asset investments		100
Other interest receivable and similar income		–
Amounts written off investments		–
Profit on ordinary activities before interest		2,850
Interest payable and similar charges		200
Profit on ordinary activities before taxation		2,650
Tax on profit on ordinary activities		725
Profit on ordinary activities after taxation		1,925
Extraordinary items		–
Profit for the financial year		1,925
Dividends		1,125
Retained profit for the financial year		800

42 | Consolidated Profit and Loss Account For the 52 weeks ended 26 February 2000

	Note	2000 £m	1999 £m
Turnover	2	330.1	303.7
Cost of sales		(130.9)	(127.7)
Gross profit		199.2	176.0
Operating expenses – excluding exceptional costs	3	(166.2)	(151.4)
– exceptional costs	3	–	(4.5)
Operating profit	2, 3	33.0	20.1
Restructuring costs	4	(2.7)	(16.6)
		30.3	3.5
Interest payable (net)	5	(1.5)	(0.1)
Profit on ordinary activities before taxation		28.8	3.4
Taxation on profit on ordinary activities	7	(10.4)	(8.0)
Profit/(loss) for the financial year	8	18.4	(4.6)
Dividends paid and proposed	9	(10.9)	(10.9)
Retained profit/(loss)	20	7.5	(15.5)
Basic earnings per ordinary share	10	9.6p	(2.4p)
Earnings per ordinary share before exceptional and restructuring costs	10	10.7p	7.0p
Diluted earnings per ordinary share	10	9.6p	(2.4p)
Profit before taxation, goodwill amortisation, restructuring and exceptional costs		33.1	25.0

All amounts relate to continuing activities

A statement of the movement in reserves can be found in Note 20

Profit and loss account of The Body Shop International PLC
(note that, for comparison, figures for both the current year and last year are shown)

continued from page 136 . . .

- results of continuing operations, ie from those parts of the business that have been kept throughout the year
- results of acquisitions, ie from businesses bought during the year
- results of discontinued operations, ie from parts of the business that have been sold or terminated during the year
- exceptional items (see below) of which the following are to be disclosed:

- – profits or losses on the sale or termination of an operation
- – costs of fundamental reorganisation
- – profits or losses on the disposal of fixed assets
- extraordinary items (see below)

The objective of these requirements is to give more information to users of accounts.

non-recurring profits and losses

FRS 3 distinguishes between three categories of non-recurring profits and losses:

Exceptional items are defined as 'material items which derive from events or transactions that fall within the ordinary activities of the reporting entity and which individually or, if of a similar type, in aggregate, need to be disclosed by virtue of their size or incidence if the financial statements are to give a true and fair view'.

Extraordinary items are defined as 'material items possessing a high degree of abnormality which arise from events or transactions that fall outside the ordinary activities of the reporting entity and which are not expected to recur'. As extraordinary items are recorded in profit and loss account 'below the line' – ie after profit on ordinary activities – FRS 3 requires virtually all one-off transactions to be classified as exceptional items and shown 'above the line'.

Prior period adjustments are defined as 'material adjustments applicable to prior periods arising from changes in accounting policies or from the correction of fundamental errors'.

Any such adjustments are accounted for by restating the figures for the prior period and by adjusting the opening balance of retained profits for the current year.

statement of total recognised gains and losses

FRS 3 requires that a statement of total recognised gains and losses is included in the year-end financial statements and is given the same prominence as profit and loss account and balance sheet. As its name implies, it shows total recognised gains and losses – from profit and loss account, together with *unrealised* profits (for example, the revaluation of fixed assets) – to record the total movement in shareholders' funds for the accounting period.

The statement starts with the figure of profit for the financial year (from profit and loss account before deduction of dividends) and then adjusts for unrealised gains and losses, differences arising from changes in foreign currency exchange rates, and prior period adjustments. An example is given below:

XYZ PLC	
Statement of Total Recognised Gains and Losses	
for the year ended 31 December 2002	
	£000s
Profit for the financial year	2,650
Unrealised surplus on revaluation of properties	1,000
Total recognised gains	3,650
Prior year adjustment	(100)
Total gains and losses for year	3,550

other notes required by FRS 3

As well as the accounting requirements of FRS 3 described above, the standard requires two notes to the accounts to be shown:

– the reconciliation of movements in shareholders' funds
– the note of historical cost profit and losses

These two notes are described fully in Chapter 8, pages 224-226.

BALANCE SHEET

The Companies Act 1985 sets out the standard formats for balance sheets. The example below is presented in the layout most commonly used. As with the profit and loss account, extra detail is often shown in the notes to the balance sheet (see page 146).

The layout of the balance sheet follows that which we have used for limited companies in the previous chapter. However, some of the terms used need further explanation:

• **intangible fixed assets** – those assets which do not have material substance but belong to the company, eg goodwill (the amount paid for the reputation and connections of a business that has been taken over), patents and trademarks

• **tangible fixed assets** – those assets which have material substance, such as premises, equipment, vehicles

• **investments** – shares held in other companies, or government securities: classed as fixed asset investments if there is the intention to hold them for a long time, and as current asset investments where they are likely to be sold within twelve months of the balance sheet date

- **creditors: amounts falling due within one year** – the term used in company balance sheets to mean current liabilities, ie amounts that are due to be paid within twelve months of the balance sheet date
- **creditors: amounts falling due after more than one year** – the term used to mean long-term liabilities, ie amounts that are due to be paid more than twelve months from the balance sheet date, eg loans and debentures
- **provisions for liabilities and charges** – an estimate of possible liabilities to be paid in the future: see FRS 12 for provisions (page 218), and FRS 19 for deferred tax (page 212).

XYZ PLC
Balance Sheet as at 31 December 2002

	£000s	£000s
Fixed assets		
Intangible assets		50
Tangible assets		6,750
Investments		1,000
		7,800
Current assets		
Stock	1,190	
Debtors	1,600	
Investments	–	
Cash at bank and in hand	10	
	2,800	
Creditors: amounts falling due within one year	1,800	
Net current assets		1,000
Total assets *less* current liabilities		8,800
Creditors: amounts falling due after more than one year		1,500
Provisions for liabilities and charges		100
		7,200
Capital and reserves		
Called up share capital		2,800
Share premium		400
Revaluation reserve		1,500
Profit and loss account		2,500
		7,200

A recent balance sheet for The Body Shop International PLC is shown on page 142. This gives the consolidated (or group) balance sheet, together with the figures for the previous year; group accounts are covered in Chapter 11.

43| Balance Sheets At 26 February 2000

	Note	Group 26 Feb 2000 £m	Group 27 Feb 1999 £m	Company 26 Feb 2000 £m	Company 27 Feb 1999 £m
Fixed assets					
Intangible assets	11	31.5	13.1	–	–
Tangible assets	12	68.4	71.3	39.9	47.0
Investments	13	4.8	3.4	87.9	57.6
		104.7	87.8	127.8	104.6
Current assets					
Stocks	14	44.7	38.6	25.6	23.5
Debtors	15	51.9	40.3	63.0	51.1
Cash at bank and in hand		19.2	34.0	9.8	21.0
		115.8	112.9	98.4	95.6
Creditors: amounts falling due within one year	16	96.4	82.6	83.2	66.5
Net current assets		19.4	30.3	15.2	29.1
Total assets less current liabilities		124.1	118.1	143.0	133.7
Creditors: amounts falling due after more than one year	17	1.7	2.1	–	–
Provisions for liabilities and charges					
Deferred taxation	18	0.7	1.7	1.6	1.9
		121.7	114.3	141.4	131.8
Capital and reserves					
Called up share capital	19	9.7	9.7	9.7	9.7
Share premium account	20	42.8	42.8	42.8	42.8
Profit and loss account	20	68.9	61.8	88.9	79.3
Shareholders' funds (all equity)		121.4	114.3	141.4	131.8
Minority equity interests		0.3	–	–	–
		121.7	114.3	141.4	131.8

These financial statements were approved by the Board on 25 April 2000 and signed on its behalf by:

TG RODDICK
Director

Balance sheet of The Body Shop International PLC

(note that both the 'group' and 'company' balance sheets are shown – see also consolidated accounts, covered in Chapter 11)

44 | Consolidated Cash Flow Statement For the 52 weeks ended 26 February 2000

	Note	£m	2000 £m	£m	1999 £m
Net cash inflow from operating activities	21a		31.4		50.0
Returns on investments and servicing of finance					
Interest received		0.7		1.3	
Interest paid		(2.2)	(1.5)	(1.4)	(0.1)
Taxation			(9.6)		(13.7)
Capital expenditure and financial investment					
Purchase of tangible fixed assets		(14.2)		(12.0)	
Purchase of other investments		(1.4)		(1.4)	
Sale of tangible fixed assets		1.8	(13.8)	1.1	(12.3)
Acquisitions and disposals					
Cash consideration	22	(26.5)		(16.1)	
Cash acquired		–		1.7	
Cash received on disposal of manufacturing		8.0	(18.5)	–	(14.4)
Equity dividends paid			(10.9)		(10.9)
Cash outflow before use of liquid resources and financing			(22.9)		(1.4)
Management of liquid resources					
Short term deposits			6.6		5.1
Financing					
Syndicated loans		8.8		7.1	
Loan repayments		(1.0)	7.8	(1.0)	6.1
(Decrease)/increase in cash	21b		(8.5)		9.8

Cash flow statement of The Body Shop International PLC

DIRECTORS' REPORT

The report contains details of the following:

- review of the activities of the company over the past year and of likely developments in the future, including research and development activity
- directors' names and their shareholdings
- proposed dividends
- significant differences between the book value and market value of land and buildings
- political and charitable contributions
- policy on employment of disabled people
- health and safety at work of employees
- action taken on employee involvement and consultation
- policy on payment of creditors

CASH FLOW STATEMENTS

All but the smaller limited companies must include, as part of their published accounts, a cash flow statement, which we will look at in detail in Chapter 9. Such a statement shows where the funds (money) have come from during the course of a financial year, and how such funds have been used. The statement also provides a direct link between the previous year's balance sheet and the current one. A recent cash flow statement for The Body Shop International PLC is shown on page 143.

AUDITORS' REPORT

Larger companies must have their accounts audited by external auditors, who are appointed by the shareholders to check the accounts. The auditors' report, which is printed in the published accounts, is the culmination of their work. The three main sections of the auditors' report are:

- **respective responsibilities of directors and auditors** – the directors are responsible for preparing the accounts, while the auditors are responsible for forming an opinion on the accounts
- **basis of opinion** – the framework of Auditing Standards (issued by the Auditing Practices Board) within which the audit was conducted, other assessments, and the way in which the audit was planned and performed
- **opinion** – the auditors' view of the company's accounts

An *'unqualified'* auditors' opinion will read as follows:

> *'In our opinion the financial statements give a true and fair view of the state of affairs of the Company at .... 20.., and of the profit, and cash flows of the Company for the year then ended, and have been properly prepared in accordance with the Companies Act 1985.'*

A *'qualified'* auditors' report will raise points that the auditors consider have not been dealt with correctly in the accounts. Where such points are not too serious, the auditors will use phrases such as 'except for ...' or 'subject to ... the financial statements give a true and fair view'. Much more serious is where the auditors' statement says that the accounts 'do not show a true and fair view' or 'we are unable to form an opinion ...'. These indicate a major disagreement between the company and the auditors, and a person involved with the company – such as an investor or creditor – should take serious note.

Note that smaller private companies are exempt from audit requirements if their turnover (sales) for the year is below a certain figure.

ACCOUNTING POLICIES

The Companies Act requires companies to include a statement of their accounting policies in the published accounts. FRS 18 *Accounting policies* (see page 177) defines accounting policies as 'those principles, bases, conventions, rules and practices applied by an entity that specify how the effects of transactions and other events are to be reflected in its financial statements through

* recognising
* selecting measurement bases for, and
* presenting

assets, liabilities, gains, losses and changes to shareholders' funds'.

The objective of FRS 18 is to ensure that:

* entities adopt the most appropriate accounting policies in order to give a true and fair view
* accounting policies adopted are reviewed regularly to ensure that they remain appropriate, and changes are made as necessary
* information is disclosed in the financial statements to enable users to understand the accounting policies adopted and their implementation

When selecting accounting policies, the four criteria from Statement of Principles of relevance, reliability, comparability and understandability (see diagram in Chapter 1 on page 24) need to be considered.

Estimation techniques – such as straight-line and reducing balance depreciation methods, discounting of expected cash flows, and provisions for bad debts – are not accounting policies but, instead, are ways in which money amounts are arrived at under accounting policies. An accounting policy may say 'we depreciate computers over five years', but an estimation technique – eg straight-line depreciation – is used to calculate the money amounts shown in the financial statements.

An extract from the accounting policies of The Body Shop International PLC is shown on the next page.

NOTES TO THE ACCOUNTS

The Companies Act 1985, as well as requiring the presentation of financial statements in a particular layout, also requires additional information to be provided. These *notes to the accounts* include:

- disclosure of accounting policies (see previous section)
- details of authorised and allotted share capital
- movements on fixed assets
- details of listed investments
- movements on reserves
- provision for deferred tax
- analysis of indebtedness
- details of charges and contingent liabilities
- details of interest or similar charges on loans and overdrafts
- basis of computation of UK Corporation Tax and details of tax charge
- directors' emoluments including Chairman's emoluments where necessary
- auditor's remuneration

We will look at each of these in turn.

details of authorised and allotted share capital

These details include:

- where appropriate, the different classes of shares (eg ordinary, preference), the number of shares and the total nominal value
- the amount of share capital allotted and called up
- details of any changes made during the year

An example (at 31 December 2002) is shown on page 148.

46 | Notes to the Accounts For the 52 weeks ended 26 February 2000

1 Accounting Policies

The financial statements have been prepared under the historical cost convention and in accordance with applicable accounting standards. Under the Companies Act 1985, the Company has taken advantage of the exemption from presenting its own profit and loss account.

Accounts are prepared to the Saturday nearest to the end of February in each year. On that basis the 2001 Accounts will be prepared for a 53 week period ending 3 March 2001. The principal accounting policies are:

Basis of consolidation

The consolidated accounts incorporate the financial statements of The Body Shop International PLC and all of its subsidiary undertakings made up to 26 February 2000. The Group uses the acquisition method of accounting to consolidate the results of subsidiary undertakings and the results of subsidiary undertakings are included from the date of acquisition to the date of disposal. The holding company's accounting policies have been applied consistently in dealing with items which are considered material in relation to the consolidated accounts.

Goodwill

Goodwill arising on the acquisition of a subsidiary or business is the difference between the consideration paid and the fair value of the assets and liabilities acquired. Goodwill arising on acquisitions prior to 27 February 1999 was set off directly against reserves and has not been reinstated on implementation of FRS10.

Positive goodwill arising on acquisitions from 1 March 1998 is capitalised, classified as an asset on the balance sheet and amortised on a straight line basis over its useful economic life up to a presumed maximum of 15 years. It will be reviewed for impairment at the end of the first full financial year following the acquisition and in other periods if events or changes indicate that the carrying value may not be recoverable. Any goodwill previously eliminated to reserves will be charged/credited to the profit and loss account upon disposal of the related business.

Valuation of investments

Investments held as fixed assets are stated at cost less any provision for a permanent diminution in value.

Depreciation

Depreciation is provided to write off the cost, less estimated residual values, of all tangible fixed assets, except for freehold land, over their expected useful lives.

It is calculated using the following rates:
Freehold buildings – Over 50 years
Leasehold property – Over the period of the respective leases
Plant and equipment – Over 3 to 10 years.

Stocks

Stocks are valued at the lower of cost and net realisable value.

Cost is calculated as follows:
Raw materials – Cost of purchase on first-in first-out basis
Work in progress and finished goods – Cost of raw materials and labour together with attributable overheads.

Net realisable value is based on estimated selling price less further costs to completion and disposal.

Extract from the accounting policies of The Body Shop International PLC

	£000s
Authorised share capital	
3,000,000 ordinary shares of £1 each	3,000
500,000 6% preference shares of £1 each	500
	3,500
Issued share capital	
2,500,000 ordinary shares of £1 each, fully paid	2,500
300,000 6% preference shares of £1 each, fully paid	300
	2,800

movements on fixed assets (tangible & intangible)

This section of the notes requires the company to:

- disclose amounts of cost or valuation
  - at the beginning of the year
  - at the end of the year
- disclose the amount of depreciation (or amortisation of intangibles, such as goodwill)
  - at the beginning of the year
  - at the end of the year
- give details of changes during the year
  - acquisitions
  - disposals
  - revaluations (giving the date and basis of valuation)
  - depreciation (or amortisation)

An example (at 31 December 2002) is shown on the opposite page.

details of listed investments

Listed investments are those that are quoted on a stock exchange. Investments to be held for the foreseeable future are treated as fixed assets; short-term investments are treated as current assets. The notes will show:

- the cost price, together with any additions or disposals during the year
- the market value where it differs from the carrying value (ie book value)

An example (at 31 December 2002) is shown on page 150.

INTANGIBLE FIXED ASSETS

	Goodwill
	£000s
Cost at 1 Jan and 31 Dec 2002	100
Amortisation	
at 1 Jan 2002	40
charge for year	10
at 31 Dec 2002	50
Net book value:	
at 1 Jan 2002	60
at 31 Dec 2002	50

TANGIBLE FIXED ASSETS

	Freehold land and buildings	*Plant and machinery*	*Total*
	£000s	*£000s*	*£000s*
Cost or valuation:			
at 1 Jan 2002	5,200	1,000	6,200
Additions	–	200	200
Revaluations	1,000	–	1,000
Disposals	–	(100)	(100)
at 31 Dec 2002	6,200	1,100	7,300
Depreciation:			
at 1 Jan 2002	200	500	700
Charge for year	90	110	200
Revaluation	(290)	–	(290)
Disposals	–	(60)	(60)
at 31 Dec 2002	–	550	550
Net book value:			
at 1 Jan 2002	5,000	500	5,800
at 31 Dec 2002	6,200	550	6,750

- Included in freehold land and buildings is land valued at £700,000 which is not depreciated.

- The freehold land and buildings were valued on the basis of open market values on 31 December 2002 by Petham & Co, Chartered Surveyors.

Listed investments	£000s
Cost:	
at 1 Jan 2002	950
Additions	100
Disposals	(50)
at 31 Dec 2002	1,000
Valuation:	
market value	1,232

movements on reserves

Notes in the accounts for reserves (eg profit and loss account, revaluation reserve, share premium account) show

- opening balance, movements and closing balance
- changes in provisions for liabilities and charges, disclosed in the same way (see provision for deferred tax, below)

An example (at 31 December 2002) is shown below.

Reserves	£000s
Profit and loss account:	
at 1 Jan 2002	1,700
Retained profit for year	800
at 31 Dec 2002	2,500
Revaluation reserve:	
at 1 Jan 2002	500
Revaluation surplus	1,000
at 31 Dec 2002	1,500

provision for deferred tax

Deferred tax (see page 212) is a potential liability that may have to be paid to the Inland Revenue. A deferred tax account is included in the balance sheet under the heading 'provisions for liabilities and charges'. The notes will show the opening balance, movements and the closing balance.

An example (at 31 December 2002) is shown on the next page.

Provisions for liabilities and charges	£000s
Deferred taxation:	
at 1 Jan 2002	75
Transfer from profit and loss account	25
Transfer to profit and loss account	(–)
at 31 Dec 2002	100

analysis of indebtedness

Indebtedness in all forms – eg trade creditors, bank loans, overdrafts, debentures, taxation, social security costs, etc – is split between amounts due within one year and amounts due in more than one year (the balance sheet layout – see page 141 – shows this).

Notes to the accounts disclose amounts due for each form of indebtedness:

- for creditors falling due after five years, the notes must state in respect of each item shown the total amounts of debts which

    - are repayable, other than by instalments, more than five years after the end of the financial year

    - are repayable by instalments, any of which fall due after the five-year period, with the total amount of the instalments falling due after the end of that time also stated

- the terms of repayment and the rates of interest are normally to be stated for debts falling due after five years

- where creditors are secured, there must be stated the total amount of debts for which security has been given and an indication of the nature of those securities

- for debentures issued during the financial year, details should be given which include the amount of money raised by the issue

- FRS 4, *Capital instruments*, requires additional information to be given in the notes – see page 217

An example (at 31 December 2002) is shown on the next page.

Creditors: amounts falling due within one year	£000s
Bank overdraft	20
Trade creditors	630
Corporation tax	700
Social security costs	50
Proposed final dividend	400
	1,800

The bank overdraft is secured by a floating charge on the assets of the company

Creditors: amounts falling due after more than one year	
10% debentures repayable in 2012	1,500

The debentures are secured by a fixed charge on the freehold property

details of charges and contingent liabilities

- for liabilities and charges show
  - opening balance
  - movements
  - closing balance
- provision for deferred tax (see page 150, and page 212) is to be disclosed separately
- contingent liabilities should be disclosed as a note to the accounts with an estimate of the financial effect, its legal nature and details of any security
- FRS 12, *Provisions, contingent liabilities and contingent assets*, sets out the principles of accounting for these items – see page 218
- an example (at 31 December 2002) is shown below:

Contingent liabilities

A customer has commenced an action against the company in respect of faulty goods supplied. Legal proceedings are due to commence in March 2003; if the action is successful it has been estimated that the liability is £15,000. The company has been advised by its lawyers that it is possible, but not probable, that the action will be successful. Accordingly no provision for any liability has been made in this year's accounts.

interest or similar charges on loans and overdrafts

Separate disclosure is required of interest and other charges on

- bank loans and overdrafts

- other loans

An example (for year to 31 December 2002) is shown below.

Interest payable and similar charges	£000s
Bank loans and overdrafts	50
Other loans	150
	200

basis of computation of UK Corporation Tax and details of tax charge

The notes will disclose the total charge for tax on profit on ordinary activities distinguishing between major components such as:

- UK corporation tax

- deferred tax

- foreign tax

FRS 16, *Current tax,* discusses corporation tax in more detail – see page 211. An example (at 31 December 2002) is shown below.

Taxation on profit on ordinary activities	£000s
UK corporation tax at 30%	700
Deferred tax	25
	725

directors' emoluments

The notes should show the total of directors' emoluments (note that the term 'emoluments' includes salaries, fees and bonuses, allowances which are taxed, and the value of benefits in kind).

The notes should also disclose the highest paid director's emoluments (only required to be shown for listed companies, and where total directors' emoluments exceed £200,000 per year).

Look at the example (for year to 31 December 2002) shown on the next page.

Directors' emoluments	£000s
Emoluments	<u>250</u>
The amount is respect of the highest paid director is:	
Emoluments	<u>95</u>

auditors' remuneration

These notes disclose the amount of auditors' remuneration, including expenses. An example (for year to 31 December 2002) is shown below.

	£000s
Auditors' remuneration	<u>15</u>

SMALL AND MEDIUM-SIZED COMPANIES

The Companies Act allows small and medium-sized *private* companies to file modified accounts with the Registrar of Companies. However, accounts must still be prepared in full form for presentation to their members. A company qualifies to be treated as small or medium-sized if it satisfies any two or more of the following conditions:

	small	*medium*
• turnover (sales) does not exceed	£2.8m	£11.2m
• assets do not exceed	£1.4m	£5.6m
• average number of employees does not exceed	50	250

small companies

A small company need not file a profit and loss account. The directors' report can be abbreviated and details of directors' emoluments need not be disclosed. The balance sheet can list only the main asset and liability headings, with notes to the accounts reduced to include only details of accounting policies, share capital, indebtedness, and figures for the previous year.

For taxation purposes, the Inland Revenue accepts a simple profit and loss account which is used to calculate the amount of corporation tax due.

medium-sized companies

Concessions for medium-sized companies are more limited: details of sales turnover and the make-up of cost of sales need not be given; instead, the profit and loss account starts with the figure for gross profit. In all other respects, a full set of accounts must be filed.

Note: the above concessions apply only to private limited companies; public limited companies of all sizes must file full accounts.

BONUS ISSUES AND RIGHTS ISSUES

Limited companies – and particularly plcs – quite often increase their capital by means of either **bonus issues** or **rights issues** of shares. Whilst both of these have the effect of increasing the number of shares in issue, they have quite different effects on the structure of the company balance sheet.

bonus issues

A bonus issue is made when a company issues free shares to existing shareholders; it does this by using reserves that have built up and capitalising them (ie they are turned into permanent share capital). The bonus issue is distributed on the basis of existing shareholdings – for example, one bonus share for every two shares already held.

With a bonus issue no cash flows in or out of the company. The shareholders are no better off: with more shares in issue the stock market price per share will fall in proportion to the bonus issue, ie the company's net assets are now spread among a greater number of shares.

Bonus issues are made in order to acknowledge the fact that reserves belong to shareholders. Often a build-up of reserves occurs because a company hasn't the cash to pay dividends, so a bonus issue is a way of passing the reserves to shareholders.

Note that capital or revenue reserves can be used for bonus issues. If there is a choice, then capital reserves are used first – this is because it is one of the few uses of a capital reserve, which cannot be used to fund the payment of dividends.

rights issues

A rights issue is used by a company seeking to raise further finance through the issue of shares. Instead of going to the considerable expense of offering additional shares to the public, it is cheaper to offer shares to existing shareholders at a favourable price (usually a little below the current market price). As with a bonus issue the extra shares are offered in proportion to the shareholders' existing holding. The shareholder may take up the rights by subscribing for the shares offered; alternatively the rights can often be sold on the stock market.

SEVERN PLC AND WYE PLC: BONUS ISSUES AND RIGHTS ISSUES

situation

The following are the summary balance sheets of Severn plc and Wye plc:

	Severn	Wye
	£	£
Fixed assets	300,000	300,000
Current assets (including bank)	100,000	100,000
	400,000	400,000
Ordinary shares of £1 each	200,000	200,000
Reserves (capital and revenue)	200,000	200,000
	400,000	400,000

Severn is planning a one-for-two bonus issue.

Wye is seeking finance for a capital expenditure programme through a one-for-two rights issue at a price of £1.80 per share (the current market price is £2.10).

solution

After the issues, the balance sheets appear as:

	Severn	Wye
	£	£
Fixed assets	300,000	300,000
Current assets (including bank)	100,000	280,000
	400,000	580,000
Ordinary shares of £1 each	300,000	300,000
Share premium account (capital reserve)	–	80,000
Reserves	100,000	200,000
	400,000	580,000

The changes are:

Severn   Reserves are reduced by £100,000, whilst share capital is increased by the same amount; the ordinary share capital is now more in balance with fixed assets; no cash has been received.

Wye   The bank balance has increased by £180,000, being 100,000 shares (assuming that all shareholders took up their rights) at £1.80; share capital has increased by £100,000, whilst 80p per share is the share premium, ie £80,000 in total. The company now has the money to finance its capital expenditure programme. There are also significant reserves which could be used for a bonus issue in the future.

tutorial note – preparing for assessment

In the AAT Central Assessment for the Unit covered by this book you will often be presented with a completed extended trial balance of a limited company. Some points of further information will also be given to you.

You will then be required to produce a profit and loss account and/or a balance sheet using the figures from the extended trial balance and incorporating the further information. A specimen layout of the financial statement(s) is normally provided in the answer booklet.

In the Case Study which follows we will see how the profit and loss account and balance sheet are prepared in published accounts format from the figures given in an extended trial balance

CASE STUDY

WYVERN OFFICE PRODUCTS LTD: PREPARING THE ACCOUNTS FROM AN ETB

situation

You have been asked to assist in the preparation of the financial statements of Wyvern Office Products Limited for the year ended 31 December 2002. The company sells office equipment and supplies to businesses and individuals through its shops and warehouses.

You have been provided with the extended trial balance of Wyvern Office Products Limited as at 31 December 2002 as shown on page 158.

The following information is available to you:

- the authorised share capital of the businesses, all of which has been issued, consists of ordinary shares with a nominal value of £1

- depreciation has been calculated on the fixed assets of the business and has already been transferred into the balances for distribution costs and administration expenses shown on the extended trial balance

- the corporation tax charge for the year has been calculated as £215,000

- the company paid an interim dividend of 6p per share during the year but has not provided for a proposed final dividend of 10p per share

continued on page 159

EXTENDED TRIAL BALANCE — **WYVERN OFFICE PRODUCTS LIMITED** — **31 DECEMBER 2002**

Description	Trial balance Dr £000	Trial balance Cr £000	Adjustments Dr £000	Adjustments Cr £000	Profit and loss Dr £000	Profit and loss Cr £000	Balance sheet Dr £000	Balance sheet Cr £000
Sales		10,641				10,641		
Purchases	7,028				7,028			
Returns inwards	65				65			
Returns outwards		48				48		
Stock	2,220		2,533	2,533	2,220	2,533	2,533	
Distribution costs	1,524		176		1,700			
Administration expenses	1,103		308		1,411			
Accruals				67				67
Prepayments			24				24	
Interest	80				80			
Land – cost	510						510	
Buildings – cost	1,490						1,490	
Fixtures and fittings – cost	275						275	
Vehicles – cost	316						316	
Office equipment – cost	294						294	
Investments	1,850						1,850	
Buildings – accumulated depn		407		298				705
Fixtures and fittings – accumulated depn		142		55				197
Vehicles – accumulated depn		124		48				172
Office equipment – accumulated depn		107		30				137
Trade debtors	1,592						1,592	
Provision for bad debts		70		10				80
Bank	44						44	
Trade creditors		2,051						2,051
10% Debentures		1,600						1,600
Interim dividend	120				120			
Share capital		2,000						2,000
Share premium		750						750
Profit and loss account		571						571
Profit					598			598
	18,511	18,511	3,041	3,041	13,222	13,222	8,928	8,928

- interest on the 10% debentures has been paid for the first six months of the year only

From the extended trial balance, and the information provided above, you are to draft a profit and loss account for the year ended 31 December 2002 and a balance sheet as at that date.

Notes:

- journal entries are not required for any necessary adjustments to the figures in the extended trial balance
- ignore the effect of any of the adjustments to the tax charge for the year
- show workings relevant to the figures appearing in the financial statements

solution

Note the profit and loss account and balance sheet are presented in a suitable form for publication; however, the full notes to the accounts have not been given.

WYVERN OFFICE PRODUCTS LIMITED
Profit and Loss Account for the year ended 31 December 2002

	£000
Turnover	
Continuing operations	10,576
Cost of sales	6,667
Gross profit	3,909
Distribution costs	(1,700)
Administration expenses	(1,411)
Operating profit	
Continuing operations	798
Interest payable and similar charges	(160)
Profit on ordinary activities before taxation	638
Tax on profit on ordinary activities	(215)
Profit on ordinary activities after taxation	423
Dividends	(320)
Retained profit for the financial year	103

Balance Sheet as at 31 December 2002

	£000	£000
Fixed assets		
Tangible assets		1,674
Investments		1,850
		3,524
Current assets		
Stock	2,533	
Debtors	1,536	
Cash at bank and in hand	44	
	4,113	
Creditors: amounts falling due within one year	(2,613)	
Net current assets		1,500
Total assets *less* current liabilities		5,024
Creditors: amounts falling due after more than one year		(1,600)
		3,424
Capital and reserves		
Called up share capital		2,000
Share premium		750
Profit and loss account		674
		3,424

tutorial notes

(All figures £000)

1 Sales (turnover) 10,641 *less* returns inwards 65 = 10,576

2 Calculation of cost of sales:

Opening stock	2,220
Purchases	7,028
less Returns outwards	48
	9,200
less Closing stock	2,533
Cost of sales	6,667

3 Interest payable:

80 + 80 (half-year's interest on 10% debentures accrued) = 160

4   Dividends:

Interim dividend paid	120
Final dividend proposed	200
	320

5   Fixed Assets:

	Cost	Accumulated depreciation	Net book value
Land	510	–	510
Buildings	1,490	705	785
Fixtures and fittings	275	197	78
Vehicles	316	172	144
Office equipment	294	137	157
	2,885	1,211	1,674

6   Debtors:

Trade debtors	1,592
less Provision for doubtful debts	80
	1,512
Prepayments	24
	1,536

7   Creditors: amounts falling due within one year

Trade creditors	2,051
Corporation tax payable	215
Dividends proposed (see above)	200
Accruals (67 + interest 80)	147
	2,613

8   Profit and loss account:

at 1 Jan 2002	571
Retained profit for the year	103
at 31 Dec 2002	674

It is important, when working from an extended trial balance, to pick up the adjustments (here for interest accrual, corporation tax and proposed dividends) and to amend, or list, the figures in the ETB. Then focus on the profit and loss account – remembering that the profit figure will be different (because of adjustments) from that shown in the ETB. Finally, focus on the balance sheet – remembering that the total figure shown will be nothing like that of the ETB totals (because the conventional layout is considerably different from the ETB).

CONFIDENTIALITY PROCEDURES

The published accounts of limited companies are readily available to shareholders and interested parties either from the company itself or from Companies House (www.companieshouse.gov.uk). Nevertheless, as noted in this chapter, only certain information has to be disclosed in the published accounts.

For those involved in the preparation of the accounts, confidentiality procedures must be observed at all times:

– during the preparation of published accounts

– during the period after the accounts have been prepared but before they are sent to the shareholders, filed at Companies House, and disclosed to the public

– for detailed information that is needed in the preparation of the accounts but is not required to be disclosed under the Companies Acts

CHAPTER SUMMARY

- The Companies Act 1985 (as amended by the Companies Act 1989) requires a considerable amount of detail to be disclosed in the published accounts of limited companies.

- The Act requires all limited companies to produce:
  - a profit and loss account
  - a balance sheet
  - a directors' report
  - an auditors' report
  - consolidated accounts (where appropriate)

- The Act lays down formats for profit and loss account and balance sheet.

- Besides the requirements of the Companies Act, companies must also abide by the Statements of Standard Accounting Practice (SSAPs) and Financial Reporting Standards (FRSs), as laid down by the Accounting Standards Board.

- Most companies also include in their published accounts a cash flow statement which shows where the funds (money) has come from during the course of the financial year, and how it has been used.

- For larger companies, external auditors report to the shareholders on the state of affairs of the company.

- The directors establish the accounting policies which the company will follow.

- Bonus issues and rights issues increase the number of shares in issue – only the latter brings in cash to the company.

statutory accounts	financial statements required by law, a copy of which is filed at Companies House, where it can be inspected
report and accounts	the corporate report of the company which is available to every shareholder
summary financial statement	a shorter version of the statutory accounts which, by agreement with individual shareholders, can be sent in place of the report and accounts
exceptional items	'material items which derive from events or transactions that fall within the ordinary activities of the reporting entity and which individually or, if of a similar type, in aggregate, need to be disclosed by virtue of their size or incidence if the financial statements are to give a true and fair view' (FRS 3)
extraordinary items	'material items possessing a high degree of abnormality which arise from events or transactions that fall outside the ordinary activities of the reporting entity and which are not expected to recur' (FRS 3)
prior period adjustments	'material adjustments applicable to prior periods arising from changes in accounting policies or from the correction of fundamental errors' (FRS 3)
auditors' report	gives the auditors' opinion on the company's financial statements as to whether they give a true and fair view of the state of affairs of the company
accounting policies	the specific accounting principles, bases, conventions, rules and practices that the directors of a company choose to follow
bonus issue	the capitalisation of reserves – either capital or revenue – in the form of free shares issued to existing shareholders in proportion to their holdings; no cash flows into the company
rights issue	the raising of cash by offering shares to existing shareholders, in proportion to their holdings, at a favourable price

**STUDENT
ACTIVITIES**

Osborne Books is grateful to the AAT for their kind permission to use Central Assessment task material for the following activities: 6.10, 6.11.

6.1 Which of the following statements is not required by the Companies Act?

(a)   Profit and Loss Account

(b)   Auditors Report

(c)   Directors Report

(d)   Chairman's statement

6.2 Which one of the following is not a non-recurring profit and loss, as defined by FRS3 'Reporting Financial Performance'?

(a)   Exceptional items

(b)   Extraordinary items

(c)   Post balance sheet events

(d)   Prior period adjustments

6.3 According to the Companies Act 1985 which of the following features is applicable to a medium sized company?

(a)   Turnover of £15M

(b)   Turnover of £10M

(c)   Assets of £8M

(d)   Average number of employees 300

6.4 Which of the following transactions does not involve the movement of cash?

(a)   A bonus issue of shares

(b)   A rights issue of shares

(c)   The redemption of shares

(d)   An issue of non-cumulative preference shares

6.5 Briefly outline the benefits to a company's shareholders when a business produces a statement of total recognised gains and losses as part of its corporate report.

6.6 List four items that need to be included in a Directors report.

6.7 The following trial balance has been extracted from the books of account of Proudlock PLC as at 31 March 20-2.

	£000	£000
Administration Expenses	240	
Called up Capital £1 Ordinary Shares		700
Debtors	600	
Cash in Bank	75	
Accruals		15
Share Premium account		200
Distribution costs	500	
Other Creditors		80
Fixed Asset Investments	600	
Plant Machinery at cost	1,000	
Accumulated Depreciation as at 31.03.20-2		500
Profit and Loss Account b/f		210
Purchases	1,200	
Stock at 01.04.20-1	160	
Trade Creditors		300
Sales		2,295
Dividends Received		75
	4,375	4,375

Additional information

- Stock at 31 March 20-2 was valued at £180,000.

- Corporation tax charge based on the profits for the year is estimated to be £65,000.

- A final ordinary dividend of 40 pence per share is proposed.

Students should note that depreciation has already been provided for in the list of balances above and allocated to administration expenses and distribution costs accordingly.

REQUIRED

Task 1

Prepare journal entries for the adjustments listed above under 'additional information'.

Task 2

In so far as the information permits, prepare the company's published profit and loss account for the year to 31 March 20-2 and a balance sheet as at that date in accordance with the Companies Act 1985 and FRS3 (revised).

Note – A statement of accounting policies is NOT required and no formal notes should be submitted, but where relevant, working notes should be attached to your answer.

6.8 The following information has been extracted from the books of Broadfoot PLC for the year to 31 March 20-2.

	Dr £000	Cr £000
Administrative expenses	185	
Called up share capital (ordinary shares of £1 each)		200
Cash at bank and in hand	15	
Accruals		90
Distribution costs	240	
Land and buildings: at cost	210	
accumulated depreciation (at 1 April 20-1)		48
Plant and machinery: at cost	125	
accumulated depreciation (at 1 April 20-1)		75
Profit and loss account (at 1 April 20-1)		350
Purchases	470	
Sales		1,300
Stock (at 1 April 20-1)	150	
Trade creditors		60
Trade debtors	728	
	2,123	2,123

Additional information

- Stock at 31 March 20-2 was valued at £250,000.

- Buildings and plant and machinery are depreciated on a straight-line basis (assuming no residual value) at the following rates:

On cost:	%
Buildings	5
Plant and machinery	20

Land at cost was £110,000. Land is not depreciated.

There were no purchases or sales of fixed assets during the year to 31 March 20-2.

The depreciation charges for the year to 31 March 20-2 are to be apportioned as follows:

	%
Cost of sales	60
Distribution costs	20
Administrative expenses	20

- Corporation tax for the year to 31 March 20-2 (based on profits for that year at a rate of 35%) is estimated to be £135,000.

- The directors propose to pay a dividend of 150p per share.

REQUIRED

Task 1

Prepare journal entries for the adjustments listed above under 'additional information'.

Task 2

As far as the information permits, prepared Broadfoot plc's profit and loss account for the year to 31 March 20-2 and a balance sheet as at that date in accordance with the minimum disclosure requirements of the Companies Act 1985, FRS3 (revised) and related statements of standard accounting practice. (Note: A statement of accounting policies is *not* required and no formal notes should be submitted, but where relevant, working notes should be attached to your answer).

6.9   The following list of balances was extracted from the books of Grandware PLC on 31 December 20-2

	£
Sales	2,640,300
Administration expenses	220,180
Selling and distribution costs	216,320
Interest paid on loan stock	10,000
Dividends received	2,100
Share Premium Account	40,000
Purchases	2,089,600
Stocks at 01.01.20-2	318,500
Cash at bank	20,640
Trade debtors	415,800
Provision for doubtful debts at 01.01.20-2	10,074
Bad debts	8,900
Creditors	428,250
10% loan stock	200,000
Long-term investments in listed companies	20,000
Office equipment	110,060
Vehicles	235,000
£1 ordinary shares	200,000
Profit and loss account at 01.01.20-2	144,276

Notes:

• Accrue for the 6 months £10,000 loan stock interest due, which is payable 01.01.20-3.

• Provide for administration expenses of £12,200 paid in advance at 31.12.20-2 and distribution costs of £21,300 owing at 31.12.20-2.

• Provision for doubtful debts is to be maintained at 3% of debtors.

- Stocks at 31.12.20-2 were valued at £340,600.

- Provide for corporation tax £45,000 which is payable 31.12.20-3.

- The directors recommend a dividend of 28 pence per share.

- Depreciation on tangible fixed assets has already been allocated for the year and apportioned to the respective expense accounts in the list of balances provided.

REQUIRED

Task 1

Prepare journal entries for the adjustments listed above under 'notes'.

Task 2

Prepare for presentation to the shareholders a profit and loss account for the year ended 31 December 20-2 and a balance sheet as at that date, which comply, in so far as the information given allows, with the requirements of the Companies Act 1985 and FRS3 (revised).

Formal notes are not required but working notes should be attached to your answer.

6.10 You are working as assistant to the Financial Director of Da Vinci Group plc, a trading conglomerate. The group has a number of trading subsidiaries which will be consolidated into the financial statements of the group. The group's reporting year end has arrived and the Financial Director is co-ordinating the production of financial statements for the group.

The Financial Director has asked you to assist the book-keeper of one of the subsidiaries of the group, Poussin Ltd, in drafting the financial statements of the company at the year end. Poussin Ltd is a trading company which sells and distributes paints to wholesalers. The book-keeper has produced an extended trial balance, which includes some of the normal year end adjustments, and has gathered some further information which you may require to complete the task.

The extended trial balance of Poussin Ltd is shown opposite.

The following further information is provided:

1 The authorised share capital of the company is as follows:

2,000,000 ordinary shares of £1.00 each

500,000 7.6 per cent preference shares of £1.00 each

The ordinary share capital and preference share capital in the extended trial balance is fully paid. There were no movements on the share premium account during the year.

2 The land has been valued by a qualified chartered surveyor during the year. The market value of the land is £800,000. The revaluation is to be incorporated into the final financial statements.

3 It is proposed that the preference dividend should be provided for at the year end and that a final dividend of 6.5p per ordinary share relating to the current year should be provided for in the financial statements. An interim ordinary share dividend of 8.2p per share was paid in the year.

EXTENDED TRIAL BALANCE name: Poussin Ltd date: 31 December 20-1

Description	Ledger balances Dr £	Ledger balances Cr £	Adjustments Dr £	Adjustments Cr £	Profit and loss Dr £	Profit and loss Cr £	Balance sheet Dr £	Balance sheet Cr £
Purchases	8,201,311				8,201,311			
Salaries and wages	1,835,308				1,835,308			
Salesmens' commission	603,681				603,681			
Motor expenses	853,762				853,762			
Sales		15,184,365				15,184,365		
Rates	122,457			37,505	84,952			
Light and heat	104,804		21,557		126,361			
Carriage inwards	125,219				125,219			
Advertising	565,494		27,721		593,215			
Stock	1,486,955		2,009,480	2,009,480	1,486,955	2,009,480	2,009,480	
Trade debtors	3,656,391						3,656,391	
Provision for doubtful debts		49,296		23,134				72,430
Cash in hand	2,935						2,935	
Cash at bank		43,465						43,465
Trade creditors		850,753						850,753
Land (cost)	600,000						600,000	
Buildings (cost)	721,583						721,583	
Fixtures and fittings (cost)	387,054						387,054	
Motor vehicles (cost)	920,726						920,726	
Office equipment (cost)	138,967						138,967	
Buildings (acc. dep.)		157,321		14,432				171,753
Fixtures and fittings (acc. dep.)		172,941		38,705				211,646
Motor vehicles (acc. dep.)		408,528		159,665				568,193
Office equipment (acc. dep.)		35,922		19,165				55,087
Depreciation (motor vehicles)			159,665		159,665			
Depreciation (fixtures and fittings)			38,705		38,705			
Depreciation (office equipment)			19,165		19,165			
Depreciation (buildings)			14,432		14,432			
Returns inwards	325,431				325,431			
Interim dividend	49,200				49,200			
Increase in provision for doubtful debts			23,134		23,134			
General expenses	86,514				86,514			
Discount allowed	74,187				74,187			
Returns outwards		186,653				186,653		
Insurance	21,937				21,937			
Profit and loss account		714,681						714,681
Development costs	351,572						351,572	
Accruals				49,278				49,278
Prepayments			37,505				37,505	
12 per cent Debentures		2,400,000						2,400,000
Ordinary share capital		600,000						600,000
7.6 per cent Preference share capital		200,000						200,000
Share premium		231,563						231,563
Profit					2,657,364			2,657,364
	21,235,488	21,235,488	2,351,364	2,351,364	17,380,498	17,380,498	8,826,213	8,826,213

NB The figures are actual figures and are not rounded to the nearest thousand.

4 The debenture interest has not yet been paid or provided for in the trial balance. The debentures are secured against the land and buildings and are due for repayment in the year 20-9.

5 The corporation tax charge for the year has been calculated as £735,157. The rate of corporation tax for the year is 35 per cent.

6 Directors' remuneration of £252,157 is included in the salaries and wages figure in the extended trial balance. The salary of the Sales Director is £86,521. The other directors work on general administration.

7 Audit fees of £36,573 relating to the audit of the year end accounts have yet to be provided for.

8 Stock which was valued at cost and included in the year end accounts at £147,213 was sold after the year end for £60,948. The auditors have asked that the stock be included in the year end accounts at a value of £60,948.

9 Additions to fixed assets in the year were as follows:

	£
Fixtures and fittings	37,415
Motor vehicles	209,325
Office equipment	12,465

Disposals in the year were as follows:

	Cost	Accumulated Depreciation
	£	£
Fixtures and fittings	15,513	10,622
Motor vehicles	183,921	57,462
Office equipment	9,460	5,587

The additions and disposals have all been entered in the ledger accounts in the extended trial balance.

10 The company is currently engaged in a legal case involving some faulty paints sold to a customer. The customer is seeking damages for losses sustained as a result of the use of the defective paint amounting to £365,938. The lawyers of Poussin Ltd claim that the company has a very good defence against such a claim and that, in their opinion, it is unlikely that the damages will have to be paid.

11 The development costs included in the extended trial balance relate to costs sustained by the company in developing a new concept paint product with a manufacturer of household paints. The costs relate to the company's share of development costs specific to the product. The company is reasonably certain that the product will be viable given market research and projections of future revenue and expects to generate revenue from the project within two years. The company has sufficient resources to complete the project.

12 All operations of the company are continuing operations.

13 For the purposes of published financial statements, the following allocation of expenses is to be made:

	Distribution Costs	Administrative Expenses
Motor expenses	80 per cent	20 per cent
Motor depreciation	80	20
General expenses	80	20
Rates	75	25
Building depreciation	75	25
Light & heat	75	25
Insurance	75	25
Office equipment depreciation	60	40
Fixtures and fittings depreciation	100	-

The salaries and wages costs (including the directors' remuneration) are made up of £1,092,135 relating to the sales department and £491,016 relating to other administrative staff.

REQUIRED

Task 1

Make any adjustments to the balances in the extended trial balance which you feel to be necessary as a result of the further information provided. Set out your adjustments in the form of journal entries. (Ignore any effect of these adjustments on the tax charge for the year as given above).

Task 2

(a) Draft a profit and loss account for the year ended 31 December 20-1 and a balance sheet as at that date in a form suitable for publication in accordance with the Companies Act 1985 as supplemented by FRS 3 'Reporting Financial Performance'. (Students are NOT required to prepare a statement of total recognised gains and losses or the reconciliation of movements in shareholders' funds required under FRS 3).

(b) Provide suitable notes to the accounts, in so far as the information given above allows, for the following accounting items:

1 tangible fixed assets

2 share capital

6.11   You have been assigned to assist in the preparation of the financial statements of Dowango Ltd for the year ended 31 March 20-6. The company is a cash and carry operation that trades from a large warehouse on an industrial estate. You have been provided with the extended trial balance of Dowango Ltd on 31 March 20-6 which is set out on the following page.

You have been given the following further information:

1   The authorised and issued share capital of the business consists of ordinary shares with a nominal value of £1.

2   The company has paid an interim dividend of 4p per share during the year but has not provided for the final dividend of 6p per share.

3   Depreciation has been calculated on all of the fixed assets of the business and has already been entered on a monthly basis into the distribution expenses and administration costs ledger balances as shown on the extended trial balance.

4   The tax charge for the year has been calculated as £211,000.

5   Interest on the long-term loan has been paid for six months of the year. No adjustment has been made for the interest due for the final six months of the year. Interest is charged on the loan at a rate of 10 per cent per annum.

6   An advertising campaign was undertaken during the year at a cost of £19,000. No invoices have yet been received for this campaign and no adjustment for this expense has been made in the extended trial balance.

7   The investments consist of shares in a retail company that were purchased with a view to resale at a profit. Dowango Ltd owns 2 per cent of the share capital of the company. At the end of the year a valuation of the shares was obtained with a view to selling the shares in the forthcoming year. The shares were valued at £56,000.

REQUIRED

Task 1

Make any adjustments you feel to be necessary to the balances in the extended trial balance as a result of the matters set out in the further information above. Set out your adjustments in the form of journal entries. Narratives are not required.

Task 2

Draft a profit and loss account for the year ended 31 March 20-6 and a balance sheet as at that date in accordance with the Companies Act 1985 as supplemented by FRS 3 'Reporting Financial Performance.'

(You are **NOT** required to prepare a statement of total recognised gains and losses or the reconciliation of movements in shareholders' funds required under FRS 3).

EXTENDED TRIAL BALANCE name: Dowango Ltd date: 31 March 20-6

Description	Ledger balances Dr £000	Ledger balances Cr £000	Adjustments Dr £000	Adjustments Cr £000	Profit and loss Dr £000	Profit and loss Cr £000	Balance sheet Dr £000	Balance sheet Cr £000
Land (cost)	431						431	
Buildings (cost)	512						512	
Fixtures and fittings (cost)	389						389	
Motor vehicles (cost)	341						341	
Office equipment - (cost)	105						105	
Buildings - (acc. dep.)		184						184
Fixtures and fittings - (acc. dep.)		181						181
Motor vehicles - (acc. dep.)		204						204
Office equipment - (acc. dep.)		56						56
Stock	298		365	365	298	365	365	
Investments	64						64	
Debtors	619						619	
Provision for doubtful debts		27						27
Prepayments			21				21	
Cash in hand	3						3	
Cash at bank		157						157
Creditors		331						331
Accruals				41				41
Sales		5,391				5,391		
Purchases	2,988				2,988			
Returns inwards	39				39			
Returns outwards		31				31		
Carriage inwards	20				20			
Distribution expenses	1,092		23	11	1,104			
Administrative costs	701		18	10	709			
Interest charges	15				15			
Interim dividend	20				20			
Share capital		500						500
Profit and loss account		275						275
Long term loan		300						300
Profit					594			594
	7,637	7,637	427	427	5,787	5,787	2,850	2,850

7 ACCOUNTING FOR ASSETS

this chapter covers . . .

In this chapter we focus on the accounting standards (SSAPs and FRSs) that impact on the way in which assets are accounted for in both profit and loss account and balance sheet. We look first of all at the selection of accounting policies (FRS 18), and then consider the importance of reporting the commercial substance of transactions in financial statements (FRS 5). We then focus on the fixed assets, to cover:

- goodwill, intangible assets, and impairment of fixed assets (FRSs 10 and 11)

- fixed assets (FRS 15)

- investment properties (SSAP 19)

- hire purchase and leasing (SSAP 21)

- research and development expenditure (SSAP 13)

- government grants (SSAP 4)

For current assets we look at accounting for stocks (SSAP 9).

NVQ PERFORMANCE CRITERIA COVERED

unit 11: DRAFTING FINANCIAL STATEMENTS

element 2

draft limited company, sole trader and partnership year end financial statements

- financial statements are accurately drafted from the appropriate information

- subsequent adjustments are correctly implemented

- draft accounts comply with domestic standards and legislation and, where relevant, partnership agreement

- year end financial statements are presented for approval to the appropriate person in clear form

- confidentiality procedures are followed at all times

- the organisation's policies, regulations, procedures and timescales relating to financial statements are observed at all times

- discrepancies, unusual features or queries are identified and either resolved or referred to the appropriate person

HOW TO STUDY THE ACCOUNTING STANDARDS

As we have seen in earlier chapters, accounting standards – in the form of Statements of Standard Accounting Practice (SSAPs) and Financial Reporting Standards (FRSs) – play a major role in the presentation and detail of financial statements.

The NVQ Unit *Drafting Financial Statements* requires knowledge of a large number of standards – in this book we have attempted, as far as possible, to group standards together where they relate to particular topics. Accordingly, this chapter focuses on those standards that relate to assets. The next chapter looks at the standards covering liabilities and profit and loss account; Chapter 11 deals with consolidated accounts, so the standards which cover group accounts (and also associated companies) are covered there. The cash flow statement is detailed in an accounting standard (FRS 1) and this is detailed in Chapter 9. A few standards do not fit readily to such groupings and so these have been included at what seems to be the most logical place. We believe that this 'grouping' approach is preferable to explaining the standards in their numerical order, which results in a long 'list' where often unrelated topics follow one another.

the accounting standards

The table below shows the current accounting standards, together with their titles and the page in this book where each is covered. Note that the index also shows page numbers for the various standards.

---

coverage of accounting standards

SSAP 4	Accounting for government grants	page 194
SSAP 5	Accounting for value added tax	page 215
SSAP 9	Stocks and long-term contracts	page 196
SSAP 13	Accounting for research and development	page 192
SSAP 17	Accounting for post balance sheet events	page 222
SSAP 19	Accounting for investment properties	page 185
SSAP 20	Foreign currency translation	page 230
SSAP 21	Accounting for leases and hire purchase contracts	page 187
SSAP 25	Segmental reporting	page 229
FRS 1	Cash flow statements	page 241

continued . . .

organising your study of accounting standards

In this textbook we cover the aspects of each accounting standard that are assessable under *Drafting Financial Statements*. Note, however, that some standards cover more detailed issues that are not assessable. The texts of all current standards are available from the Accounting Standards Board.

For learning the key points of accounting standards, it is strongly recommended that you use a system of index cards: put the number and name of each standard on the top of an index card and then outline the key points of the standards on the cards, using bullet point format. The set of index cards (don't use very small cards!) then forms a useful learning and revision aid which can be carried around and easily referred to at almost any time.

It is also important to keep up-to-date with any changes to accounting standards – use accountancy magazines and web sites. The Accounting Standards Board's web site (www.asb.org.uk) is especially useful for this purpose.

FRS 18 – ACCOUNTING POLICIES

FRS 18 defines accounting policies as *'those principles, bases, conventions, rules and practices applied by an entity that specify how the effects of transactions and other events are to be reflected in its financial statements through*

- *recognising*
- *selecting measurement bases for, and*
- *presenting*

assets, liabilities, gains, losses and changes to shareholders' funds'.

An entity should adopt accounting policies most appropriate to its particular circumstances for the purpose of giving a true and fair view. Two accounting concepts – going concern, and accruals (see page 29) – play an important part in the selection and application of accounting policies.

In the choice of accounting policies an entity must consider the objectives of

- **relevance** – the financial information is useful to users of accounts
- **reliability** – the financial information can be depended upon by users
- **comparability** – financial information can be compared with that from previous accounting periods
- **understandability** – users can understand the financial information provided

Once selected, accounting policies are to be reviewed regularly to ensure that they remain appropriate, and are changed when necessary.

In the financial statements, an entity must disclose sufficient information to enable users to understand the accounting policies adopted and how they have been implemented.

FRS 5 – REPORTING THE SUBSTANCE OF TRANSACTIONS

FRS 5 requires that transactions should be treated in the financial statements in accordance with their underlying **commercial substance** (reality), rather than their technical **legal form** – a case of 'substance over form'.

In most cases, commercial substance and legal form are the same: if a company buys a property it is shown as a fixed asset in the balance sheet because the company owns it. However a number of techniques – often connected with financing – have been devised that enable a business to receive economic benefits from an asset without showing it on the balance sheet. An example of this is a finance lease (see page 188), where the user of an asset, such as a machine or vehicle, is not the legal owner but, nevertheless, benefits from the asset. FRS 5 identifies three common features of transactions where commercial substance and legal form may differ:

- where the beneficiary of an asset is not the legal owner of the asset

- where a transaction is one of a series of similar transactions – the whole series will need to be considered in order to determine the commercial substance

- where there is an option – for example for the original owner to repurchase – which is likely to be exercised

CASE STUDY

WYVERN TOYS LIMITED: SUBSTANCE OVER FORM

situation

Wyvern Toys Limited is coming towards the end of its financial year at 31 December 2002. Unfortunately trade has been poor in the run-up to Christmas and the company has £50,000 too much stock in its warehouse. The Managing Director, Alexandra Foster, has come up with an idea to improve the look of the company's year-end balance sheet. What she proposes is that the company should 'do a deal' with a nearby business, Mercia Retail Limited, to:

- sell £50,000 of stock to Mercia Retail for cash in December

- enter into a repurchase agreement to buy the stock back for £55,000 by the end of January 2003 unless Mercia has already sold them at a higher price

As Alexandra explains: 'This is a 'win-win' situation; we reduce our stock figure for the balance sheet and improve our bank balance – that should keep the bank happy! For Mercia Retail, they earn £5,000 'interest' on their money in a month! It won't affect their balance sheet as I know that their year-end is 30 June. We've done business with Mercia Retail before and I've spoken to their MD who is pleased to help us. What do you think?'

How should this transaction be recorded in the financial statements of Wyvern Toys Limited?

solution

Under the circumstances of this sale and repurchase agreement, Wyvern Toys has the option to buy back the goods, provided they have not already been sold by Mercia Retail. As it seems that the option is likely to be exercised, the transaction should be treated as a loan instead of being classed as a sale of goods. Accordingly, Wyvern Toys must keep the stock on its balance sheet and record the money from Mercia Retail as a loan (in the current liabilities section of its balance sheet, as the loan is repayable in January 2003).

The commercial substance of the transaction is that it is a loan instead of the legal form of a sale of goods: under FRS 5 'substance over form' prevails and it will be recorded as a loan. Users of the financial statements will have a clearer view of the state of the business.

FRS 10 – GOODWILL AND INTANGIBLE ASSETS

goodwill

The value of a well-established and profitable business is often greater than the value of the separate assets and liabilities which comprise the business. This is because, if the business were to be sold, a buyer would be prepared to pay above the value of the tangible assets and liabilities to acquire the existing products, customers, reputation, etc: this extra amount paid is for the **goodwill** of the business.

Goodwill may be defined as the difference between the value of a business as a whole and the aggregate (total) of the fair value of its separate net assets. For example, an existing business is bought for £500,000, with the net assets being worth £400,000; goodwill is, therefore, £100,000. Note that:

- goodwill can be either positive, where the value is greater than the net assets (as above), or negative, where the value is less than the net assets

- fair value is, effectively, the price at which assets and liabilities would be sold for on the open market (see FRS 7 *Fair values in acquisition accounting*, on page 314, for a formal definition).

- goodwill is an asset but it cannot be sold separately from the business as a whole

FRS 10 distinguishes between:

- **purchased goodwill**, which is the amount of goodwill arising on the purchase of a business

- **non-purchased goodwill,** which is goodwill other than that which has been purchased; for example, the owner of a business says that she has built up goodwill since setting up the business – this is non-purchased (or internally generated) goodwill

Only purchased goodwill can be recognised in accounting statements. The accounting treatment is to capitalise (ie record) it on the balance sheet as an intangible fixed asset (note that negative goodwill is shown in the assets section – below positive goodwill – and is deducted) and then

- either, amortised (depreciated) through profit and loss account over its estimated useful economic life (generally up to a maximum of 20 years)

- or, if its estimated useful economic life is considered to be indefinite, the goodwill need not be amortised

Note that FRS 10 presumes that goodwill does not have a useful economic life of more than 20 years; however, the Standard accepts that there may be arguments for a life which is greater than 20 years. A business, or other entity, would need to disclose, as a note to the accounts, why it believed the useful economic life exceeded 20 years.

intangible assets

Intangible assets are fixed assets that do not have physical substance but which are identifiable and are controlled by an entity through custody or legal rights. Examples include licences, quotas, patents, copyrights, franchises and trade marks.

The accounting treatment for intangible assets is the same as that for goodwill:

- they should be recognised in the financial statements by capitalising them on the balance sheet as fixed assets at cost price
- when intangible assets are acquired as part of a takeover of another business, they should be capitalised separately from goodwill if their fair value can be measured reliably; where such value cannot be measured reliably, the intangible assets can be subsumed (included) into goodwill
- they should be amortised through profit and loss account over the assets' useful economic life; where this is considered to be indefinite, the assets need not be amortised
- as with goodwill, FRS 10 presumes that intangible assets do not have a useful economic life of more than 20 years; however the Standard accepts that there may be arguments for a life which is greater than 20 years, or even indefinite (in which case the business, or other entity, needs to disclose why it believes this to be the case)

FRS 11 – IMPAIRMENT OF FIXED ASSETS AND GOODWILL

objectives

The objectives of FRS 11 are to ensure that:

- fixed assets and goodwill are recorded in the financial statements at no more than their recoverable amount
- any resulting impairment loss is measured and recognised on a consistent basis
- sufficient information is disclosed for users of accounts to understand the impact of impairment on the financial performance of the organisation

The standard defines impairment as 'a reduction in the recoverable amount of a fixed asset or goodwill below its carrying amount'. (The 'carrying amount' is the cost of the asset less depreciation to date.)

The principle of the standard is that fixed assets (excluding investment properties) and goodwill need be reviewed for impairment only when there is evidence that impairment has taken place. Therefore a review may not be required every year (except for goodwill and other intangibles with an indefinite or over 20-year life – see FRS 10), but is only needed when something happens to the asset or economic circumstances change.

indicators of impairment

FRS 11 gives a number of indicators of impairment:

* persistent operating losses or negative cash flows from operations
* a significant fall in the asset's market value
* physical damage to, or obsolescence of, the asset
* an adverse change in the company's competitive or regulatory environment
* a significant reorganisation
* a loss of key employees
* a significant increase in market interest rates or other market rates of return

the impairment review

Steps to carry out an impairment review are as follows (see also the Case Study, below):

STEP 1   What is the asset's carrying amount (net book value, ie cost less depreciation to date)?

STEP 2   What is the asset's recoverable amount? See the diagram below.

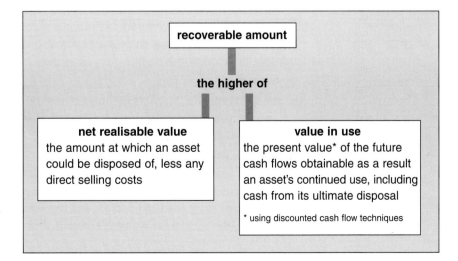

STEP 3   If carrying value is greater than recoverable amount, then the asset is impaired and should be written down to its recoverable amount. The amount of the impairment is written down as an expense in profit and loss account (unless it arises on a previously revalued fixed asset when it is normally taken to the statement of total recognised gains and losses).

<table>
<tr><td>

CASE STUDY

</td><td>

INITIAL TRAINING PLC: THE IMPAIRMENT REVIEW

situation

Initial Training plc is a large training organisation providing government-sponsored 'return-to-work' courses.

You are helping to prepare the company's year-end accounts and have been asked by your boss, the company accountant, to carry out an impairment review on fixed assets held at the training centre at Rowcester. Today you have obtained details of the two photocopiers in the print room at Rowcester:

• **Machine 1** is six years old and is a relatively slow photocopier based on old technology. The cost of this machine was £8,000 and depreciation to date (the year-end) is £4,800, giving it a net book value of £3,200. Since the arrival of the other photocopier, this machine has been relegated to 'standby' use.

• **Machine 2** is only a few months old. It is a digital copier incorporating the latest technology. It is very fast and versatile, and has the capacity to meet the needs of the entire training centre. It cost £15,000 and depreciation to the end of the financial year will be £1,500, giving it a net book value of £13,500. This machine is much preferred by the staff who use it as a first choice.

solution

The impairment review you carry out is as follows:

Machine 1

• Carrying value (ie net book value): £3,200

• The company accountant has given you the following information to enable you to calculate the recoverable amount:

the higher of

– net realisable value: £1,000 resale value of machine on the secondhand market

– value in use: £2,000 being the present value of the future benefits from continued use as a standby machine

Therefore the recoverable amount is £2,000.

• As carrying value (£3,200) is greater than the machine's recoverable amount (£2,000), the asset is impaired. Accordingly, the amount of the impairment (£1,200) is to be shown as an overhead in profit and loss account, and the value of the machine will be shown on the company's balance sheet at the recoverable amount of £2,000.

</td></tr>
</table>

Machine 2

- Carrying value (ie net book value): £13,500

- You are given the following information to enable you to calculate the recoverable amount:

the higher of

- net realisable value: £10,000 resale value of machine on the secondhand market

- value in use: £55,000 being the present value of the future benefits from continued use as the main machine

Therefore recoverable amount is £55,000.

- As carrying value (£13,500) is less than the machine's recoverable amount (£55,000), the asset is not impaired and does not need to be written down. Accordingly, the machine will be shown in the year-end accounts at cost price less depreciation to date.

FRS 15 – TANGIBLE FIXED ASSETS

This standard sets out the principles of accounting for tangible fixed assets:

- initial measurement
- valuation
- depreciation

Note that investment properties are covered by SSAP 19 (see below).

initial measurement

Tangible fixed assets are initially measured at cost (ie purchase price, less any trade discounts). Note that:

- included in cost (ie capitalised) can be other costs which are *directly attributable* to bringing the asset into working condition, eg installation costs, legal fees, finance costs

- where finance costs are capitalised the policy of capitalisation should be applied consistently to all tangible fixed assets when finance costs are incurred

valuation

Revaluation of tangible fixed assets is not compulsory, but where a policy of revaluation is implemented . . .

- all assets of the same class are to be revalued

- valuations are to be kept up-to-date by undertaking full valuations every five years, with at least one interim valuation during year 3

(where there is thought to be a material change in value, interim valuations in years 1, 2 and 4 should be undertaken)

- valuations are normally undertaken by qualified external valuers (eg Chartered Surveyors), interim valuations can be conducted by qualified external or internal valuers

- all gains are to be recorded in the statement of total recognised gains and losses (unless they reverse losses previously charged to profit and loss account – in which case the gain is credited to profit and loss account)

- losses are normally charged to profit and loss account

Also note that:

- properties of a non-specialist nature are valued on the basis of existing use value.

- tangible fixed assets other than properties are valued at either market value, or depreciated replacement cost (ie replacement cost less deduction for proportion of useful economic life used)

depreciation

The objective of depreciation is to reflect in operating profit the cost of the use of the tangible fixed assets in the period.

All tangible fixed assets having a known useful economic life are to be depreciated (the most common exception is land).

Note that:

- non-depreciation of fixed assets is usually ruled out on the grounds that

  - residual values are normally assumed to be negligible

  - maintenance alone will not normally extend an asset's life indefinitely

- under exceptional circumstances a long useful economic life, or high residual value, can give rise to immaterial depreciation

- when depreciation is not charged on grounds of immateriality, and where the estimated useful economic life exceeds 50 years, annual impairment reviews are required

- any acceptable depreciation method can be used to spread the cost of the asset over its estimated useful economic life: two of the more common methods are straight-line and reducing balance

- where fixed assets are revalued, depreciation is based on the revalued amount

SSAP 19 – ACCOUNTING FOR INVESTMENT PROPERTIES

An investment property is defined by the standard as

'an interest in land and/or buildings:

(a) *in respect of which construction work and development have been completed;*

and

(b) *which is held for its investment potential, any rental income being negotiated at arm's length.'*

Thus a property owned and occupied by an entity for its own purpose is not an investment property, nor is a property let to and occupied by another group company.

SSAP 19 states that it is the current value of investment properties, and changes in that current value, that are of prime importance – rather than a calculation of systematic annual depreciation. As a consequence, a different accounting treatment is used:

- Investment properties are not depreciated on the basis of FRS 15, except for leasehold properties – which are depreciated at least over the period during which the unexpired term of the lease is 20 years or less.

- Investment properties are shown in the fixed assets section of the balance sheet at their open market value, with the name or qualification of the valuer being disclosed together with the valuation bases used.

- The valuation need not be made by a professional valuer who can, in fact, be an employee of the entity. The exception to this is where investment properties represent a substantial proportion of the total assets of a major enterprise (such as a company listed on a stock market): here a professional external valuer should be used at least every five years.

- Changes in the value of investment properties should not be taken to profit and loss account but should be disclosed as a movement on an *investment revaluation reserve*, shown in the balance sheet, and reported through the statement of total recognised gains and losses.

- If investment revaluation reserve has a debit balance representing unrealised losses (ie the value of investment properties has fallen) and the losses are considered to be permanent, then the full amount can be charged to profit and loss account. A debit balance which is considered to be temporary is allowed to remain.

WYVERN CARS LIMITED: ACCOUNTING FOR INVESTMENT PROPERTIES

situation

Wyvern Cars Limited is a 'niche' manufacturer of hand-built sports cars. On 1 January 2001 it buys an office block near to the works for £2m. The office block will not be used by Wyvern Cars, but is to be held as an investment property.

During the next few years the valuation of the office block at 31 December (the financial year-end of Wyvern Cars) is as follows:

31 December 2001	£2.4m
31 December 2002	£2.2m
31 December 2003	£1.9m*

* the professional valuers used by Wyvern Cars consider this fall to be temporary

Show how the investment property will be shown in the balance sheets of Wyvern Cars.

solution

Year-ended 31 December 2001

Fixed assets	£m
Investment property at cost	2.0
Revaluation	0.4
	2.4

Capital and reserves	
Investment revaluation reserve:	
Revaluation in year	0.4
	0.4

- The increase in valuation is credited to revaluation reserve (ie is not credited to profit and loss account).

- The £0.4m revaluation is reported through the statement of total recognised gains and losses.

Year-ended 31 December 2002

Fixed assets	£m
Investment property at revaluation	2.4
Revaluation	(0.2)
	2.2

Capital and reserves	
Investment revaluation reserve:	
Balance at start of year	0.4
Revaluation in year	(0.2)
Balance at end of year	0.2

- The decrease in valuation is debited to revaluation reserve (ie is not debited to profit and loss account).

- The £0.2m decrease in valuation is reported through the statement of total recognised gains and losses.

Year-ended 31 December 2003

Fixed assets	£m
Investment property at revaluation	2.2
Revaluation	(0.3)
	1.9
Capital and reserves	
Investment revaluation reserve:	
Balance at start of year	0.2
Revaluation in year	(0.3)
Balance at end of year	(0.1)

- The decrease in valuation is debited to revaluation reserve.

- As the decrease in valuation is considered to be temporary, then the £0.1m negative balance on the investment revaluation reserve can remain.

- The £0.3m decrease in valuation is reported through the statement of total recognised gains and losses.

- If the decrease in valuation was considered to be permanent then:

  - revaluation reserve would be debited with £0.2m, being the amount remaining in the account

  - profit and loss account would be debited with £0.1m

  - the £0.2m decrease in investment revaluation reserve would be reported through the statement of total recognised gains and losses

SSAP 21 – LEASES AND HIRE PURCHASE CONTRACTS

Leasing and hire purchase contracts are means by which companies obtain the right to use or purchase fixed assets, such as machinery or vehicles. The lessee (under a leasing contract), or the hirer (under a hire purchase contract), makes agreed payments for a period of time to a lessor or vendor (often a finance company). There is normally no provision in a lease contract for legal title to the leased asset to pass to the lessee. By contrast, under a hire purchase contract, which has similar features to a lease, the hirer may acquire legal title by exercising an option to purchase the asset.

SSAP 21 sets out the accounting treatment where fixed assets are obtained for use by a business under:

- an **operating lease** (a short-term lease, where there is no transfer of the risks and rewards of ownership to the lessee)

- a **finance lease** (a long-term lease, under which substantially all of the risks and rewards of ownership are transferred to the lessee)
- a **hire purchase agreement** (under which the hirer has the use of the asset while paying for it by instalments over an agreed period of time)

A simple example illustrates the difference between these: hiring a van for the weekend to move some furniture is an operating lease; a business that leases a van under a four or five year contract does so under a finance lease; under a four or five year hire purchase contract the business will own the van (subject to the terms of the contract).

In more technical terms, a finance lease is when, at the inception of the lease, the present value of the minimum lease payments amounts to substantially all (normally 90 per cent or more) of the asset's fair value. As such, the lessee enjoys substantially all of the risks and rewards of ownership – apart from legal title. An operating lease, by contrast, involves the lessee paying a rental for the use of the asset for a time period which is normally substantially less than its total useful economic life; also, the lessor retains the risks and rewards of ownership of the asset and is responsible for the costs of repairs and maintenance.

With an operating lease, the rental payments are shown as an overhead in the profit and loss account of the lessee.

With a finance lease and hire purchase agreement:

- the cost of the fixed asset (excluding interest) is capitalised on the balance sheet of the lessee or hirer, as if they were the purchaser of the asset outright (this is the application of 'substance over form' – see FRS 5, page 177)
- the asset is depreciated over its estimated useful economic life, with depreciation charged to profit and loss account
- interest payable to the finance company is shown as an overhead in profit and loss account
- the amount due to the finance company for the capital amount (ie excluding interest) is shown as a liability on the balance sheet, and is split between long-term liabilities and current liabilities, as appropriate

CASE STUDY

WYVERN ENGINEERING LIMITED: ACCOUNTING FOR LEASING

situation

Wyvern Engineering Limited is leasing two machines for use in its business:

1   A **portable compressor** is leased from The Hire Shop as and when it is needed at a cost of £100 per week; usage was as follows:

2001	5 weeks
2002	3 weeks
2003	6 weeks
2004	10 weeks

When the machine is not being used, Wyvern Engineering returns it to The Hire Shop where it is available for hire by other customers. The estimated useful economic life of the machine is six years.

2   A **pressing machine** is leased from Mercia Finance plc from 1 January 2001. The details are:

cost price of machine	£10,000
leasing period	4 years
estimated useful economic life	4 years
leasing payments	£3,500 per year (payable monthly on 1st of each month in advance)

Explain how these two leases will be recorded in the accounts of the lessee. Show relevant extracts from the profit and loss account and balance sheet for the years ending 31 December 2001, 2002, 2003 and 2004.

solution

1   The **portable compressor** is being leased under an operating lease because

- the lessee is renting the machine for a period which is substantially less than its total useful economic life

- the lessor retains the risks and rewards of ownership of the asset and is responsible for the costs of repairs and maintenance

The only accounting entries will be a charge to profit and loss account of the lease rentals payable in each financial year.

2   The **pressing machine** is being leased under a finance lease because

- the present value of the leasing payments amounts to substantially all of the asset's fair value, ie *£14,000 (£3,500 x 4 years), compared with £10,000

- substantially all of the risks and rewards of ownership are transferred to the lessee

The accounting entries are shown below.

* For simplicity, the £14,000 has not been discounted; at a 10% discount rate the present value would be approximately £12,000 – well above the 90% or more of the asset's fair value set by SSAP 21.

accounting entries: operating lease for the portable compressor

Debit profit and loss account with lease rentals, ie

	£
	£
2001	500
2002	300
2003	600
2004	1,000

accounting entries: finance lease for the pressing machine

The first step is to apportion the leasing payments between finance charges and capital payments. With total leasing payments of £14,000 and the cost price of the machine at £10,000, the finance charges and capital payments are as follows:

	leasing payment	finance charge	capital payment
	£	£	£
2001	3,500	1,000	2,500
2002	3,500	1,000	2,500
2003	3,500	1,000	2,500
2004	3,500	1,000	2,500
	14,000	4,000	10,000

Note that the finance charge has been calculated here using the straight-line method. This is acceptable under SSAP 21, as are other methods which weight the finance charge more to the early years of the contract.

Depreciation on the machine (using the straight-line method) will be:

$$\frac{£10,000}{4 \text{ years}} = £2,500 \text{ per year}$$

profit and loss account extracts

£

2001

Operating lease rental	500
Finance charge under finance lease	1,000
Depreciation of machinery	2,500
	4,000

2002

Operating lease rental	300
Finance charge under finance lease	1,000
Depreciation of machinery	2,500
	3,800

2003

Operating lease rental	600
Finance charge under finance lease	1,000
Depreciation of machinery	2,500
	4,100

2004

Operating lease rental	1,000
Finance charge under finance lease	1,000
Depreciation of machinery	2,500
	4,500

balance sheet extracts

Note: only the finance lease appears on the balance sheet.

2001 £

Fixed assets

Machinery under finance lease at cost	10,000
Less depreciation to date	2,500
	7,500

Liabilities

Current – obligations under finance lease	*2,500
Long-term – obligations under finance lease	5,000
	7,500

* next year's payments are a current liability

2002 £

Fixed assets

Machinery under finance lease at cost	10,000
Less depreciation to date	5,000
	5,000

Liabilities

Current – obligations under finance lease	2,500
Long-term – obligations under finance lease	2,500
	5,000

2003 £

Fixed assets

Machinery under finance lease at cost	10,000
Less depreciation to date	7,500
	2,500

Liabilities

Current – obligations under finance lease	2,500

2004 – this balance sheet will show neither asset nor liability, as the leasing contract will terminate on 31 December 2004.

SSAP 13 - ACCOUNTING FOR RESEARCH AND DEVELOPMENT

The accounting treatment of research and development expenditure can lead to the creation of an intangible fixed asset when it is not fully written off to the profit and loss account in the year in which it is incurred. SSAP 13 sets out three categories of research and development expenditure:

- **pure (or basic) research** – experimental or theoretical work undertaken primarily to acquire new scientific or technical knowledge for its own sake rather than directed towards any specific aim or application
- **applied research** – original or critical investigation undertaken in order to gain new scientific or technical knowledge and directed towards a specific practical aim or objective
- **development** – use of scientific or technical knowledge in order to produce new or substantially improved products, services, or systems prior to the commencement of commercial production or commercial applications, or to improving substantially those already produced or installed

SSAP 13 requires that expenditure on pure and applied research is to be written off as revenue expenditure to profit and loss account in the year in which it is incurred. However, capital expenditure on fixed assets – such as a new research laboratory – is to be recorded as fixed assets and depreciated over the useful lives of the assets.

Development expenditure should, generally, be written off to profit and loss account as it is incurred. It may, however, be *capitalised* and treated as an intangible fixed asset if it relates to an ultimately profitable project. The criteria for this are:

- there is a clearly defined project
- the related expenditure is separately identifiable
- the outcome of such a project has been assessed with reasonable certainty as to
  - its technical feasibility, and
  - its ultimate commercial viability, taking into account factors such as likely market conditions (including competing products), public opinion, consumer and environmental legislation
- estimated future profits are reasonably expected to exceed past and future development costs
- adequate resources are available to complete the project

Provided that all these criteria can be satisfied, the development expenditure can be capitalised as an intangible fixed asset and recorded on the balance sheet. The intangible asset will then be amortised (depreciated down to zero) in proportion to sales of the product as they materialise.

CASE STUDY

POMONA AGROCHEMICAL COMPANY: RESEARCH AND DEVELOPMENT COSTS

situation

Pomona Agrochemical Company has the following account in its book-keeping system:

Dr			Research and Development Expenditure Account		Cr
2002		£	2002		£
24 Mar	Bank (research)	24,000			
18 Nov	Bank (development)	40,000			

The development costs have been incurred in respect of a new agricultural chemical, WACL X123. This product has been on sale since 1 January 2003 and sales in the first few weeks look very promising.

It is now February 2003 and you are preparing the company's accounts for the financial year ended 31 December 2002. How will you deal with the research and development expenditure?

solution

research expenditure

The research expenditure of £24,000 will be charged as an overhead in the profit and loss account for the year ended 31 December 2002.

development expenditure

The development expenditure of £40,000 should be charged to profit and loss account unless it meets the criteria set out in SSAP 13. Here, the development of the new chemical does appear to be a clearly defined project, for which the related expenditure is separately identifiable, and for which the outcome is technically feasible and has commercial viability. Thus, the development expenditure can be capitalised and shown on Pomona's balance sheet as an intangible fixed asset with a value of £40,000 at 31 December 2002.

As the new chemical is now in production, the asset must now be amortised over its expected life, so the question for the following year's accounts (2003) will be to decide how long sales of the product will last – this will determine the amount of amortisation to be shown in the profit and loss account for the year ended 31 December 2003, and the reduced value of the intangible fixed asset for the year-end balance sheet.

SSAP 4 – ACCOUNTING FOR GOVERNMENT GRANTS

Various types of grants are available to businesses and other entities from government departments and similar bodies, whether local, national or international (including grants from the European Union).

revenue grants

These are grants which contribute to profit and loss account expenditure. Examples include grants towards the training costs of employees, grants towards the costs of employing particular categories of employees (such as those who have just left school, or those who have previously been unemployed), grants towards the rent and rates of premises in order to encourage businesses to establish in certain areas.

The accounting treatment of revenue grants is that they should be credited to profit and loss account in the same period as the expenditure to which they contribute was incurred. This fits in with the accounting concept of matching (accruals).

capital grants

These grants contribute to the cost of capital expenditure (eg premises, machinery, equipment). The accounting treatment is that such grants should be credited to profit and loss account over the expected useful economic lives of the assets to which they relate. The usual way of dealing with this is to treat the amount of the grant as a deferred credit, a portion of which will be credited to profit and loss account each year. The part of the grant that has not yet been transferred to profit and loss account shows on the balance sheet as deferred income – either under the heading of creditors, or under a separate liability heading for 'accruals and deferred income' (see Case Study, below).

disclosure in financial statements

For government grants the following information should be disclosed:

- the accounting policy adopted for government grants

- the effects of government grants on the results for the period and/or the financial position of the enterprise

- any potential liability to repay grants (see also FRS 12, *Provisions, contingent liabilities and contingent assets* – page 218)

- if appropriate, the material effects of government assistance, other than grants, on the financial statements

MEREFORD MANUFACTURING LIMITED: ACCOUNTING FOR GRANTS

situation

In January 2001 Mereford Manufacturing Limited re-equips its factory with computer-controlled machinery at a cost of £250,000. The Wyvern Development Agency, a government-sponsored body charged with the task of developing business in its area, gives a 20 per cent grant towards the cost of Mereford's new machinery. The grant is paid in February 2001. The useful economic life of the machinery is expected to be five years, after which it will have a scrap value of £10,000.

The expected profit of Mereford, before accounting for depreciation on the new machinery, is expected to be £100,000 each year for the next five years.

Show how the grant will be treated in the financial statements of Mereford for each of the five years ending 31 December 2001 - 2005.

solution

Depreciation on new machinery (using the straight-line method) is

$$\frac{£250,000 - £10,000}{5 \text{ years}} = £48,000 \text{ per year}$$

Profit and loss account (extracts)

	2001	2002	2003	2004	2005
	£000	£000	£000	£000	£000
Profit before depreciation	100	100	100	100	100
Grant*	10	10	10	10	10
Depreciation	(48)	(48)	(48)	(48)	(48)
Profit	62	62	62	62	62

* £250,000 x 20% = £50,000 ÷ 5 years = £10,000 per year

Balance sheet (extracts)

	2001	2002	2003	2004	2005
Fixed assets	£000	£000	£000	£000	£000
Machinery at cost	250	250	250	250	250
Less depreciation to date	48	96	144	192	240
Net book value	202	154	106	58	10
Deferred income**					
Government grant – deferred credit	40	30	20	10	–

** shown either under the heading of creditors, or under a separate liability heading for 'accruals and deferred income'.

SSAP 9 – STOCKS AND LONG-TERM CONTRACTS

Note that for the NVQ Unit *Drafting Financial Statements*, the valuation of long-term contracts is not assessable.

Businesses often have stocks of goods in various forms:

• stocks of raw materials, for use in a manufacturing process

• stocks of work-in-progress (partly manufactured goods)

• stocks of finished goods, made by the business and ready for resale to customers

• stocks of finished goods, which have been bought in by the business for resale

The principle of stock valuation, as set out in SSAP 9, is that stocks should be valued at 'the lower of cost and net realisable value'. This valuation applies the prudence concept and is illustrated by the following diagram:

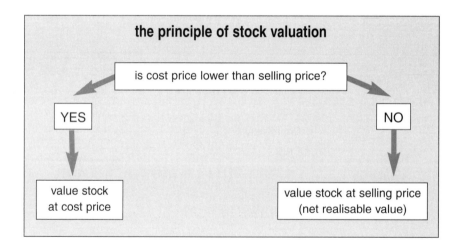

Thus two different stock values are compared:

• cost, including additional costs to bring the product or service to its present location and condition

• net realisable value (the expected selling price less any further costs such as selling and distribution)

The lower of these two values is taken, and *different items or groups of stock are compared separately*. These principles are illustrated in the two Case Studies which follow.

STOCK VALUATION
THE CLOTHING STORE

situation

The Clothing Store bought in a range of 'designer' beachwear in the Spring, with each item costing £15 and retailing for £30. Most of the stock is sold but, by Autumn, ten items remain unsold. These are put on the 'bargain rail' at £18 each. On 31 December, at the end of the store's financial year, five items remain unsold. At what price will they be included in the year-end stock valuation?

Twelve months later, three items still remain unsold and have been reduced further to £10 each. At what price will they now be valued in the year-end stock valuation?

solution

- At 31 December, the five items will be valued at a cost of £15 each,

  ie 5 x £15 = £75.

- Twelve months later, the three items remaining unsold will be valued at a net realisable value of £10 each, ie 3 x £10 = £30.

Important note: Stock is never valued at selling price when selling price is above cost price. The reason for this is that selling price includes profit, and to value stock in this way would recognise the profit in the accounts before it has been realised.

STOCK VALUATION
PAINT AND WALLPAPER SUPPLIES

situation

The year-end stocks for the two main groups of stock held by the business Paint and Wallpaper Supplies are found to be:

	Cost	Net Realisable Value
	£	£
Paints	2,500	2,300
Wallpapers	5,000	7,500
	7,500	9,800

Which of the following stock valuations do you think is correct?

(a)   £7,500

(b)   £9,800

(c)   £7,300

(d)   £10,000

solution

Stock valuation (c) is correct, because it has taken the 'lower of cost and net realisable value' for each *group* of stock, ie

Paints (at net realisable value)	£2,300
Wallpapers (at cost)	£5,000
	£7,300

You will also note that this valuation is the lowest of the four possible choices, indicating that stock valuation follows the *prudence concept.*

commonly used stock valuation methods

Businesses use different methods to calculate the cost price of stock. Three commonly used methods are:

- **FIFO** (first in, first out) – this method assumes that the first stocks acquired are the first to be used, so that the valuation of stock on hand at any time consists of the most recently acquired stock.

- **LIFO*** (last in, first out) – here it is assumed that the last stocks acquired are the first to be used, so that the stock on hand is made up of earlier purchases.

- **AVCO** (average cost) – here the average cost of items held at the beginning of the period is calculated; as new stocks are acquired a new average cost is calculated (usually based on a weighted average, using the number of units bought as the weighting).

* Note that SSAP 9 discourages the use of LIFO because it usually does not provide an up-to-date valuation (being based on older stock); however, the Companies Act 1985 does permit the use of LIFO.

The use of a particular method does not necessarily correspond with the method of physical distribution adopted in a firm's stores. For example, in a car factory, one car battery of type X is the same as another, and no-one will be concerned if the storekeeper issues one from the latest batch received, even if the FIFO system has been adopted. However, perishable goods are always physically handled on the basis of first in, first out, even if the accounting stock records use another method.

Having chosen a suitable stock valuation method, a business would continue to use that method unless there were good reasons for making the change. This is in line with the consistency concept of accounting.

closing stock valuation for a manufacturer

The principles of SSAP 9 are applied to a manufacturer, who may hold three types of stock at the year-end:

- raw materials

- work-in-progress
- finished goods

For **raw materials,** the comparison is made between cost (which can be found using techniques such as FIFO, LIFO, or AVCO) and net realisable value.

For stocks of both **work-in-progress** and **finished goods**, SSAP 9 requires that the cost valuation includes expenditure not only on direct materials but also on direct labour, direct expenses and production overheads. Thus for work-in-progress and finished goods, 'cost' comprises:

- direct materials
- direct labour
- direct expenses
- production overheads (to bring the product to its present location or condition)
- other overheads, if any, attributable to bringing the product or service to its present location and condition

Such 'cost' is then compared with net realisable value, and the lower figure is taken as the stock valuation (remember that different items or groups of stock are compared separately).

CASE STUDY

STOCK VALUATION: XYZ MANUFACTURING

situation

XYZ Manufacturing started in business on 1 July 2001 producing security devices for doors and windows. During the first year 2,000 units were sold and at the end of the year, on 30 June 2002, there were 200 finished units in stock and 20 units which were exactly half-finished as regards direct materials, direct labour and production overheads.

Costs for the first year were:

	£
Direct materials used	18,785
Direct labour	13,260
Production overheads	8,840
Non-production overheads	4,420
TOTAL COST FOR YEAR	45,305

At 30 June 2002 it was estimated that the net realisable value of each completed security device was £35. At the same date, the company holds stocks of raw materials as follows:

	cost £	net realisable value £
Material X	1,400	1,480
Material Y	400	360
Material Z	260	280

Calculate the stock valuation at 30 June 2002 for:

- raw materials
- work-in-progress
- finished goods

solution

RAW MATERIALS

Using the SSAP 9 rule of 'the lower of cost and net realisable value' the total value is:

	£	
Material X	1,400	(cost)
Material Y	360	(net realisable value)
Material Z	260	(cost)
	2,020	

WORK-IN-PROGRESS

To calculate the value of work-in-progress and finished goods we need to know the production cost, ie direct materials, direct labour and production overheads. This is:

	£
Direct materials used	18,785
Direct labour	13,260
Production overheads	8,840
PRODUCTION COST FOR YEAR	40,885

All these costs must be included because they have been incurred in bringing the product to its present location or condition. Non-production overheads are not included because they are not directly related to production. Thus, a production cost of £40,885 has produced:

Units sold	2,000
Closing stock of completed units	200

calculation continued . . .

Closing stock of work-in-progress –

20 units exactly half-finished equals

10 completed units	10
PRODUCTION FOR YEAR	2,210

The **cost per unit** is: $\dfrac{£40,885}{2,210}$ = **£18.50 per unit**

The 20 half-finished units have a cost of (20 ÷ 2) x £18.50 = **£185**. They have a net realisable value of (20 ÷ 2) x £35 = £350. The value of work-in-progress will, therefore, be shown in the accounts as £185, which is the lower of cost and net realisable value.

FINISHED GOODS

The completed units in stock at the end of the year have a production cost of 200 x £18.50 = £3,700, compared with a net realisable value of 200 x £35 = £7,000. Applying the rule of lower of cost and net realisable value, finished goods stock will be valued at **£3,700**.

CONFIDENTIALITY PROCEDURES

It is a requirement of the Companies Act for directors of companies – other than most small or medium-sized companies – to disclose whether the accounts have been prepared in accordance with applicable accounting standards, particulars of any material departure from the standards and the reasons for the departure. Whilst this information is readily available to users of accounts, for those involved in the preparation of the accounts, confidentiality procedures must be observed at all times:

– regarding any discussion about accounting standards with the directors

– regarding how the standards have been applied to a particular set of financial statements

– concerning any figures used but not disclosed in the accounts; for example, the calculation of stock valuations at cost price and net realisable value, or the calculation of amortisation of goodwill

– concerning any investigations to determine whether to treat an item in one way rather than another; for example, confidential information about the development of a new product, the outcome of which will determine whether costs are to be capitalised on the balance sheet or, alternatively, written off to profit and loss account

CHAPTER SUMMARY

- Accounting standards comprise SSAPs and FRSs.

- **FRS 18** 'Accounting policies' sets out the principles of selecting accounting policies. The accounting concepts of going concern and accruals play an important part in the selection and application of policies.

- **FRS 5** 'Reporting the substance of transactions' requires that business transactions should be treated in the financial statements in accordance with their underlying commercial substance, rather than their technical legal form, ie 'substance over form'.

- **FRS 10** 'Goodwill and intangible assets' covers the recognition of purchased goodwill and intangible assets in financial statements. The usual accounting treatment is for amortisation through profit and loss account over the asset's estimated useful economic life.

- **FRS 11** 'Impairment of fixed assets and goodwill' requires an impairment review to be carried out when there is evidence that impairment has taken place. The standard gives a number of indicators of impairment.

- **FRS 15** 'Tangible fixed assets' sets out the principles of accounting for tangible fixed assets:
  - initial measurement
  - valuation
  - depreciation

- **SSAP 19** 'Accounting for investment properties' requires investment properties to be shown on the balance sheet at their open market value. Changes in value are reported through an investment revaluation reserve.

- **SSAP 21** 'Leases and hire purchase contracts' sets out the accounting treatment for
  - operating leases
  - finance leases
  - hire purchase agreement

- **SSAP 13** 'Accounting for research and development' requires that
  - research expenditure is written off as revenue expenditure to profit and loss account in the year in which it is incurred
  - development expenditure should generally be written off to profit and loss account as it is incurred, but may be capitalised and treated as an intangible fixed asset if certain criteria are met

- **SSAP 4** 'Accounting for government grants' distinguishes between revenue grants and capital grants:
  - revenue grants are to be credited to profit and loss account in the same

period as the expenditure to which they contribute was incurred

- capital grants are to be credited to profit and loss account over the expected useful economic lives of the assets to which they relate; this is usually accounted for by treating the grant as a deferred credit, a portion of which will be credited to profit and loss account each year

• **SSAP 9** 'Stocks and long-term contracts' requires that stock is normally valued at the lower of cost and net realisable value. Stock valuation methods include:

- FIFO (first in, first out)

- LIFO (last in, first out)

- AVCO (average cost, based on a weighted average)

KEY TERMS

SSAP	Statement of Standard Accounting Practice; part of the rules of accounting
FRS	Financial Reporting Standard; part of the rules of accounting
accounting policies	those principles, bases, conventions, rules and practices applied by an entity that specify how the effects of transactions and other events are to be reflected in its financial statements
goodwill	the difference between the value of a business as a whole and the aggregate (total) of the fair value of its separate net assets
intangible assets	fixed assets that do not have physical substance but which are identifiable and are controlled by an entity through custody or legal rights
amortisation	technique of writing down intangible assets through profit and loss account
impairment	a reduction in the recoverable amount of fixed assets or goodwill below its carrying amount
depreciation	the objective of depreciation is to reflect in operating profit the cost of the use of the tangible fixed assets in the period
investment property	an interest in land and/or buildings:
	(a) in respect of which construction work and development have been completed; and

(b) where it is held for its investment potential, any rental income being negotiated at arm's length

operating lease

a short-term lease, where there is no transfer of the risks and rewards of ownership to the lessee

finance lease

a long-term lease, under which substantially all of the risks and rewards of ownership are transferred to the lessee

hire purchase

agreement under which the hirer has the use of the asset while paying for it by instalments over an agreed period of time

pure research

experimental or theoretical work undertaken primarily to acquire new scientific or technical knowledge for its own sake rather than directed towards any specific aim or application

applied research

original or critical investigation undertaken in order to gain new scientific or technical knowledge and directed towards a specific practical aim or objective

development expenditure

use of scientific or technical knowledge in order to produce new or substantially improved products, services, or systems prior to the commencement of commercial production or commercial applications, or to improving substantially those already produced or installed

revenue grants

grants which contribute to profit and loss account expenditure

capital grants

grants which contribute to the cost of capital expenditure

first in, first out (FIFO)

stock valuation method which assumes that the first stocks acquired are the first to be used

last in, first out (LIFO)

stock valuation method which assumes that the last stocks acquired are the first to be used

average cost (AVCO)

stock valuation method which calculates an average cost (based on a weighted average) whenever new stocks are acquired

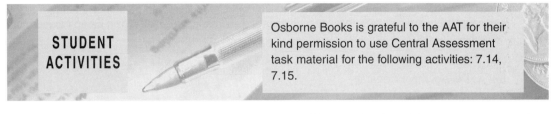

STUDENT
ACTIVITIES

Osborne Books is grateful to the AAT for their kind permission to use Central Assessment task material for the following activities: 7.14, 7.15.

7.1 Which of the following statements, according to SSAP 9 *Stock and long term contracts*, best describes the valuation of stock at the end of the financial year?

(a) The lower of cost and net realisable value

(b) The higher of cost and net realisable value

(c) All stock should be valued at historic cost

(d) All stock should be valued at net realisable value

7.2 Joe Yates runs a Garage buying and selling cars. At the end of his financial year he has the following cars in stock. What is the correct valuation to be recorded according to SSAP 9?

	Cost £	Net realisable value £
Vauxhall Vectra	2,800	3,500
Landrover Discovery	10,000	15,000
Nissan Primera	3,400	2,600
Ford Focus	6,000	7,500
Volkswagon Polo	1,200	500

(a) £23,400

(b) £21,900

(c) £30,600

(d) £29,100

7.3 The Betterland Company purchased a freehold warehouse on 1st January 20-0 for £250,000. The Directors decided to depreciate the warehouse over its anticipated economic life of 50 years. At 1st January 20-5, the building is valued at £345,000, and the directors decide to incorporate this valuation into the books of account from this date.

1 What is the amount to be transferred to the asset revaluation account?

(a) £120,000

(b) £100,000

(c) £125,000

(d) £250,000

2 Assuming that the assets life still has 46 years to run as from the 1st January 20-5, what would be the depreciation charge from the 31st December 20-5 onwards?

(a) £5,000

(b) £10,000

(c) £7,500

(d) £2,500

7.4 In certain circumstances Research and Development expenditure can be deferred to later periods and carried forward on a business balance sheet as an intangible asset. Which broad category best describes this deferral process?

(a) Basic research
(b) Development research
(c) Applied research
(d) Basic, Applied and Development research

7.5 During 20-3 The Hassan Trading Company Ltd acquired another business for £180,000 in cash and in exchange for 50,000 £1 ordinary shares valued at £2.50 each.

The fair value of separable net assets of the company acquired at the date of purchase was:

	£
Land and Buildings	100,000
Plant and Equipment	60,000
Stock	35,000
Debtors	25,000
	220,000

All liabilities were discharged by the previous owner.

What is the correct valuation for goodwill?

(a) £10,000
(b) £60,000
(c) £85,000
(d) £165,000

7.6 Machin Ltd has three assets in use

	Net book Value	Net realisable Value	Value in use
	£	£	£
Compressor	8,000	12,000	10,000
Fork lift truck	20,000	18,000	19,000
Dumper truck	10,000	7,000	13,000

The recoverable amounts of these three assets are:

	£
Compresssor	14,000
Fork lift truck	17,500
Dumper truck	12,000

Which of the above assets is impaired and needs to be written down as indicated?

(a) Compressor written down by £2,000
(b) Fork lift truck written down by £2,000
(c) Fork lift truck written down by £2,500
(d) Dumper truck written down by £3,000

7.7   Briefly explain the accounting treatment available to companies, when dealing with capital and revenue based grants. Your answer should make specific reference to SSAP 4.

7.8   Briefly outline the three broad classifications for research and development expenditure. Your answer should make specific reference to SSAP 13.

7.9   What are the main differences between an operating lease and a finance lease, as defined by SSAP 21?

7.10 Briefly explain the difference in accounting treatment, between an owner occupied freehold property, and that of a freehold investment property. You should make specific reference to FRS 15 and SSAP 19.

7.11 On 1 January 20-0, Makeshift Enterprises PLC purchased a freehold property, Castle Hamlets at a cost of £400,000, which it intended to hold as an investment property.

In subsequent years, the valuation of the property was as follows:

At 31 December	20-1	20-2	20-3
	£000	£000	£000
	440	460	380

The valuation made in 20-3 is assumed to be a permanent valuation at that time.

Task 1

Show how the property and the revaluation surpluses and deficits would be recorded in the books of account and the financial statements for the years to 31st December 20-0 to 20-3.

Task 2

How would the accounts and book-keeping differ if we had been told that the valuation made on 31 December 20-3 was a temporary one?

7.12 Chemco Plc has its own research and development department, the breakdown of costs for the year to 31st December 20-3 are as follows:

(a)   Project Xchem was started in July 20-3, researching into the possibility that an arm patch could be used to cure the common cold. Some minor testing had been completed but the results had proved to be disappointing and no real benefits recorded. It was unlikely that the project would continue in the foreseeable future and the costs to date amounted to £295,000.

(b)   Project Zchem had also started this year, investigating the possibility of producing insulin in tablet form to help sufferers of diabetes. Results to date had proved to be most encouraging, and matters were progressing at a pace. Production is due to start next year (20-4) and demand for this type of product initially, is likely to be very high and lucrative. The product has already been patented and its planned selling price is likely to yield a high level of profit, until competition can enter the market in 20-9. Costs for the year to date amounted to £435,000.

The company has sufficient finance and resources to complete both projects.

Task

How should the total research and development expenditure be dealt with in the financial statements for 20-3 and subsequent years (if appropriate)?

7.13 Sampson PLC has recently acquired a new business – Delia Ltd. The purchase consideration has led the business to account for purchased goodwill.

The directors are keen to know more about what it is.

Task 1
Define purchased goodwill.

Task 2
List five aspects of Delia Ltd which may give rise to goodwill.

Task 3
Account for the difference in prescribed accounting practice for purchased and non-purchased goodwill. Your answer should make reference to FRS10 – *Goodwill and intangible assets*.

7.14 Answer the following questions which the directors of Poussin Ltd have asked. Justify your answers, where appropriate, by reference to accounting concepts, SSAPs and or FRSs.

(a)   Why are we carrying forward development costs of £351,572 on the balance sheet? Should these costs be written off in the profit and loss account in the year in which they are incurred? Under what circumstances can these costs be carried forward in the balance sheet and how will they be treated in the future?

(b)   The auditors have asked us to reduce the value of some of our stock – from the cost of £147,213 to £60,648, the amount at which we sold stock after the year end. Why should something that happened after the year end be at all relevant to the balances at the year end?

7.15 You have been assigned to assist in the preparation of the financial statements of Dowango Ltd for the year ended 31 March 20-6. The company is a cash and carry operation that trades from a large warehouse on an industrial estate.

You have recently received a letter from the directors of Dowango Ltd, the contents of which are listed below.

DOWANGO LTD

Dear AAT student,

In preparation for discussions about a possible loan to Dowango Ltd, the bank has asked to see the latest financial statements of Dowango Ltd. We wish to ensure that the financial statements show the company in the best light. In particular, we wish to ensure that the assets of the business are shown at their proper value. We would like to discuss with you the following issues:

1   The fixed assets of our company are undervalued. We have received a professional valuation of the land and buildings which shows that they are worth more than is stated in

our financial statements. The land has a current market value of £641,000 and the buildings are valued at £558,000.

2   The investments are recorded in our trial balance at cost. We realise that the market value of the investment is less than the cost, but since we have not yet sold it, we have not made a loss on it and so we should continue to show it at cost.

3   Stocks are recorded in our balance sheet at cost. Most of our stock is worth more than this as we could sell it for more than we paid for it. Only a few items would sell for less than we paid for them. We have worked out the real value of our stock as follows:

	Cost £000	Sales price £000
Undervalued items	340	460
Overvalued items	25	15
Total	365	475

We have set out a number of questions we would like answered at our meeting in an appendix to this letter. We would also like you to advise us at that meeting on the profitability and return on capital of the two companies targeted for takeover (whose financial statements we have already sent to you) and on the reporting implications if we purchase one of the companies.

Yours sincerely

The Directors

Dowango Limited

Tasks

The questions from the appendix to the directors' letter are shown below. Write a memo to the directors answering these questions, which relate to the financial statements of Dowango Ltd. Explain your answers, where relevant, by reference to company law, accounting concepts and applicable accounting standards.

1   (a)   Can we show the land and buildings at valuation rather than cost?

     (b)   If we did so, how would the valuation of land and buildings be reflected in the financial statements?

     (c)   Would revaluing the land and buildings have any effect upon the gearing ratio of the company and would this assist us in our attempt to get a loan from the bank?

     (d)   What effect would a revaluation have upon the future results of the company?

2   Can we continue to show the investments at cost?

     The investments consist of shares in a retail company that were purchased with a view to resale at a profit. Dowango Ltd owns 2 per cent of the share capital of the company. At the end of the year a valuation of the shares was obtained with a view to selling the shares in the forthcoming year. The shares were valued at £56,000, but originally cost Dowango Ltd £64,000.

3   What is the best value for stock that we can show in our balance sheet in the light of the information we have given you about sales price?

8 ACCOUNTING FOR LIABILITIES AND PROFIT AND LOSS ACCOUNT

this chapter covers . . .

This chapter focuses on the accounting standards (SSAPs and FRSs) that impact mainly on the way in which liabilities are accounted for in both the profit and loss account and balance sheet. We then turn our attention to those standards that affect principally the profit and loss account.

For the liabilities side of the balance sheet we consider standards that cover:

*   taxation, including VAT (FRS 16, FRS 19 and SSAP 5)

*   hire purchase and leasing (SSAP 21)

*   capital instruments (FRS 4)

*   provisions and contingencies (FRS 12)

*   accounting for post balance sheet events (SSAP 17)

Accounting standards which affect mainly the profit and loss account include:

*   tangible fixed assets (FRS 15)

*   reporting financial performance (FRS 3)

*   earnings per share (FRS 14)

*   segmental reporting (SSAP 25)

*   foreign currencies (SSAP 20)

*   retirement benefits (FRS 17)

*   related party disclosures (FRS 8)

NVQ PERFORMANCE CRITERIA COVERED

unit 11: DRAFTING FINANCIAL STATEMENTS

element 2

draft limited company, sole trader and partnership year end financial statements

●   *financial statements are accurately drafted from the appropriate information*

●   *subsequent adjustments are correctly implemented*

●   *draft accounts comply with domestic standards and legislation and, where relevant, partnership agreement*

- *year end financial statements are presented for approval to the appropriate person in clear form*

- *confidentiality procedures are followed at all times*

- *the organisation's policies, regulations, procedures and timescales relating to financial statements are observed at all times*

- *discrepancies, unusual features or queries are identified and either resolved or referred to the appropriate person*

ACCOUNTING STANDARDS COVERING TAXATION

There are three standards which show how aspects of taxation, including VAT, are to be accounted for:

- FRS 16 – Current tax
- FRS 19 – Deferred tax
- SSAP 5 – Accounting for value added tax

FRS 16 – Current tax

The profits of limited companies are subject to corporation tax at various rates set out by the Chancellor of the Exchequer in budget announcements.

The date (or dates) of payment of corporation tax due vary depending on the size of the company. For example, a small company pays all its corporation tax to the Inland Revenue (the tax collector) nine months after the company's year-end; thus a small company with a financial year-end of 31 December 2002 will pay the corporation tax due on its profits for 2002 by the end of September 2003. Larger companies pay part of their tax due every three months, with some amounts due to be paid in the following accounting period.

In the financial statements there will be shown:

- in profit and loss account, an estimate of corporation tax due on the year's profits (there may also be an entry in the statement of total recognised gains and losses – see below)
- in balance sheet, a current liability for the estimated amount of corporation tax to be paid (or remaining to be paid) on the year's profits

FRS 16 requires that current tax (ie the amount of tax estimated to be due on the profits of the accounting period) is to be recognised in profit and loss account. However, where a gain (or loss) has been recognised directly in the statement of total recognised gains and losses, the tax relating to the gain (or loss) is recognised directly in that statement.

The amount of current tax is to be measured in the financial statements using the tax rates applicable at the balance sheet date.

The Case Study on page 215 illustrates how corporation tax is dealt with in the financial statements of a company.

FRS 19 – Deferred tax

The standard defines deferred tax as 'estimated future tax consequences of transactions and events recognised in the financial statements of the current and previous periods'.

Deferred tax comes about because the taxable profit of a business is often different from the net profit shown in profit and loss account. One reason for this is because the Inland Revenue disallows depreciation and amortisation shown in profit and loss account and, instead, allows a capital allowance against tax for the purchase of fixed assets.

An example of a capital allowance is 25 per cent reducing balance, which is allowed on office equipment, machinery and most vehicles. For example, the capital allowances on a machine costing £10,000 will be:

	£
Cost price	10,000
Year 1 capital allowance at 25%	2,500
	7,500
Year 2 capital allowance at 25%	1,875
	5,625
Year 3 capital allowance at 25%	1,406
	4,219

and so on . . .

If the company owning the machine had a net profit of £15,000 in year 1 after allowing for depreciation on the machine of, say, £1,000, the taxable profit would be calculated as follows:

	£
Net profit in year 1	15,000
Add back depreciation charge	1,000
	16,000
Less capital allowance	2,500
Taxable profit	13,500

Thus the company would pay tax on profits of £13,500 rather than £15,000. This is because the capital allowance is higher than the depreciation charge. As the tax benefit of the capital allowance has been received earlier than the depreciation charge, the company will make a transfer from profit and loss account to deferred tax account to record a possible liability to the Inland Revenue. The transfer will be for £2,500 – £1,000 = £1,500 x the company's tax rate. The possible liability to the Inland Revenue is that, if the machine was sold at the end of year 1 for £9,000 (ie cost, less depreciation to date), the Inland Revenue would claim for a balancing charge of £1,500, ie £9,000 – (£10,000 – £2,500 capital allowance) x the company's tax rate.

In the ordinary course of events, amounts transferred to deferred tax account will reverse (ie be transferred back to profit and loss account) over time – see Case Study below.

In the circumstances described above, the balance of deferred tax account is shown as a liability on the balance sheet under the heading of 'provisions for liabilities and charges'.

Deferred tax account can also be an asset – for example, where a company has taxable losses in the past and is carrying them forward to reduce future taxable profits.

CASE STUDY

RAVEN LIMITED
ACCOUNTING FOR DEFERRED TAX

situation

Raven Limited buys a machine for £10,000. The machine is expected to last for ten years and have a nil scrap value. The company uses straight-line depreciation.
The Inland Revenue gives capital allowances of 25 per cent reducing balance on the machine.
Raven Limited pays corporation tax at the rate of 30 per cent.

solution

• Depreciation is at £1,000 per year (ie 10 per cent, using the straight-line method).

• Capital allowances are at 25 per cent reducing balance.

• The amounts are shown in the table below:

YEARS	1	2	3	4	5	6	7	8	9	10
	£	£	£	£	£	£	£	£	£	£
depreciation	1,000	1,000	1,000	1,000	1,000	1,000	1,000	1,000	1,000	1,000
capital allow'nce	2,500	1,875	1,406	1,054	791	593	445	334	250	188
difference	(1,500)	(875)	(406)	(54)	209	407	555	666	750	812

■ The difference multiplied by the tax rate is transferred (to) or from deferred tax account, as follows:

Dr	**Deferred tax account**	Cr
	Year 1 Transfer from profit	
	and loss	450*

* £1,500 difference x 30%

■ The year 1 profit and loss account will show a transfer to deferred tax of £450, as follows:

Profit and loss account – year 1

	£
Net profit for year	x
Less corporation tax	(x)
Transfer to deferred tax account	(450)
Transfer from deferred tax account	x
Profit after tax	x

■ The balance sheet will show a potential liability to the Inland Revenue of £450 under the heading of 'provisions for liabilities and charges', as follows:

Balance sheet – year 1

	£
Fixed Assets	x
Current Assets	x
Current Liabilities	(x)
Long-term Liabilities	(x)
Provisions for Liabilities and Charges	
Provision for deferred tax	(450)
Net assets	x

■ In years 2, 3 and 4, further transfers will be debited to profit and loss account and credited to deferred tax account. From year 5 onwards, the capital allowances will begin to reverse by debiting deferred tax account with the difference multiplied by the tax rate, and crediting profit and loss account with a 'transfer from deferred tax account'.

■ When the machine is finally sold any small discrepancies between capital allowances and the sale proceeds will be resolved by means of a balancing charge or allowance.

SSAP 5 – Accounting for value added tax

This accounting standard applies to organisations which are registered for Value Added Tax (VAT).

VAT is a tax on the supply of goods and services, which is eventually borne by the final consumer but is collected at each stage of the production and distribution chain.

The treatment of VAT in the accounts of a business should reflect the business' role as a tax collector, and VAT should not be included in income and expenditure – whether for capital or revenue items (although there are some exceptions, such as the purchase of cars, where VAT cannot be reclaimed and the tax is therefore included as part of the cost of the items).

SSAP 5 requires that:

- the turnover figure in profit and loss account is to be shown net of VAT
- irrecoverable VAT on fixed assets (eg cars) is to be included in their cost
- the net amount due to, or from, HM Customs and Excise (the VAT authority) is to be included in the figures for creditors and debtors respectively, and need not be disclosed separately

CASE STUDY

SANTA PLC
SHOWING THE TAX LIABILITIES:

situation
The following balances are taken from the accounting system of Santa plc as at 31 December 2002:

	£	£
Value Added Tax payable		20,800
Provision for deferred tax		8,000
Stock	51,200	
Tangible fixed assets at cost or revaluation	250,000	
Bank	24,500	
Issued ordinary shares		100,000
Share premium account		25,000
Creditors		75,400
Debtors	102,800	
Revaluation reserve		50,000
Loan (repayable in 2007)		20,000
Net profit for year before taxation		68,300
Retained profit at start of year		61,000
	428,500	428,500

Notes:

• Corporation tax liability on the profits for the year is estimated to be £25,400

- £4,000 is to be transferred to deferred tax account
- The company proposes to pay a final dividend on its ordinary shares of £30,000

You are helping with the year-end accounts and are asked to prepare:

- profit and loss account, starting with net profit
- balance sheet, using the Companies Act layout or the financial year ended 31 December 2002.

solution

SANTA PLC

Profit and loss account (extract) for the year ended 31 December 2002

	£
Net profit for year before taxation	68,300
Less: corporation tax	25,400
transfer to deferred tax account	4,000
Profit for year after taxation	38,900
Less proposed final ordinary dividend	30,000
Retained profit for year	8,900
Add balance of retained profits at beginning of year	61,000
Balance of retained profits at end of year	69,900

Balance sheet as at 31 December 2002

	£	£
Fixed Assets		
Tangible assets at cost or revaluation		250,000
Current Assets		
Stock	51,200	
Debtors	102,800	
Bank	24,500	
	178,500	
Creditors: amounts falling due within one year		
Creditors	75,400	
VAT payable	20,800	
Corporation tax payable	25,400	
Proposed dividends	30,000	
	151,600	
Net current assets		26,900
Total assets less current liabilities		276,900
Creditors: amounts falling due after one year		20,000
Provisions for liabilities and charges		
Provision for deferred tax		*12,000
NET ASSETS		244,900

* £8,000 + £4,000 transfer = £12,000

Financed by:	£
Issued share capital	100,000
Share premium account	25,000
Revaluation reserve	50,000
Profit and loss account	69,900
	244,900

LIABILITIES SIDE OF BALANCE SHEET

Four further accounting standards impact mainly on the liabilities side of the balance sheet:

SSAP 21 – Leases and hire purchase contracts

FRS 4 – Capital instruments

FRS 12 – Provisions, contingent liabilities and contingent assets

SSAP 17 – Accounting for post balance sheet events

Note that these standards often also have an effect on both profit and loss account and on the assets side of the balance sheet.

SSAP 21 – Leases and hire purchase contracts

This standard has already been looked at in detail in Chapter 7 (pages 187-188).

With finance leases and hire purchase agreements, the liabilities side of the balance sheet shows the amount due to the finance company for the capital amount (ie excluding interest); the amount is split between long-term and current liabilities, as appropriate.

FRS 4 – Capital instruments

Capital instruments is the term used to describe the means of financing a business – shares, debentures, loans and debt instruments.

The objective of FRS 4 is to ensure that financial statements provide a clear, coherent and consistent treatment of capital instruments – in particular the classification into debt, ordinary shares, and other classes of shares.

The standard defines capital instruments as 'all instruments that are issued by reporting entities as a means of raising finance, including shares, debentures, loans and debt instruments, options and warrants that give the holder the right to subscribe for or obtain capital instruments'.

FRS 12 – Provisions, contingent liabilities and contingent assets

These three items – provisions, contingent liabilities, contingent assets – represent uncertainties that may have an effect on future financial statements. They need to be accounted for consistently so that users of accounts can have a fuller understanding of their effect on financial statements.

The objective of FRS 12 is to ensure that appropriate recognition criteria and measurement bases are applied to provisions, contingent liabilities and contingent assets and that sufficient information is disclosed in the notes to the financial statements to enable users to understand their nature, timing and amount.

provisions

A **provision** is a liability that is of uncertain timing or amount, to be settled by the transfer of economic benefits.

A provision should be recognised (ie recorded) as a liability in the financial statements when:

- an entity has a present obligation as a result of a past event
- it is probable that a transfer of economic benefits will be required to settle the obligation
- a reliable estimate can be made of the amount of the obligation

Unless all of these conditions are met, no provision should be recognised.

FRS 12 uses the word 'probable', in connection with the transfer of economic benefits, as being more likely to occur than not, ie a more than 50% likelihood of its occurrence.

The 'reliable estimate' of the amount of the obligation should be the best estimate of the expenditure required to settle the present obligation at the balance sheet date.

FRS 12 identifies and lists a number of specific classes of provision:

- future operating losses: provisions should not be recognised
- onerous contracts, where the unavoidable costs of meeting the obligations of the contract exceed the economic benefits expected to be received under it: provisions should be recognised for the present obligation under the contract
- restructuring, such as the sale or termination of part of the business, and changes in the management structure; restructuring costs can only be recognised as a provision when the business has an obligation to restructure

The amount of a provision is recorded as an overhead in profit and loss account, and a liability is shown on the balance sheet (under the heading 'provisions for liabilities and charges').

Disclosure in the notes to the financial statements requires:

– details of changes in the amount of provisions between the beginning and end of the year

– a description of the provision(s) and expected timings of any resulting transfers

– an indication of the uncertainties regarding the amount or timing of any resulting transfers

contingent liabilities

A **contingent liability** is either

– a possible obligation arising from past events whose existence will be confirmed only by the occurrence of one or more uncertain future events not wholly within the entity's control; or

– a present obligation that arises from past events but is not recognised because:

(a) it is not probable that a transfer of economic benefits will be required to settle the obligation; or

(b) the obligation cannot be measured with sufficient reliability

Note that a contingent liability is a *possible* obligation, ie less than 50% likelihood of its occurrence (contrast this with the *probable* obligation of a provision, ie more than 50% likelihood of its occurrence).

A contingent liability is not recognised (ie recorded) in the financial statements; however, it should be disclosed as a note which includes:

– a brief description of the nature of the contingent liability

– an estimate of its financial effect

– an indication of the uncertainties relating to the amount or timing of any outflow

– the possibility of any re-imbursement

Note that where a contingent liability is considered to be remote (contrast with 'possible') then no disclosure is required.

contingent assets

A **contingent asset** is a possible asset arising from past events whose existence will be confirmed only by the occurrence of one or more uncertain future events not wholly within the entity's control.

A business should not recognise (ie record) a contingent asset in its financial statements (because it could result in the recognition of profit that may never be realised). However, when the realisation of the profit is virtually certain, then the asset is no longer contingent and its recognition is appropriate.

A contingent asset is disclosed where an inflow of economic benefits is probable; disclosure should include:

- – a brief description of the nature of the contingent asset
- – an estimate of its financial effect

summary

The diagram below summarises the ways in which provisions, contingent liabilities and contingent assets are to be handled in the financial statements.

PROVISIONS (more than 50% likelihood of occurrence)	CONTINGENT LIABILITIES (less than 50% likelihood of occurrence)	
Probable • provision recognised in financial statements as a liability • disclosure of provision in notes	**Possible** • no liability recognised in financial statements • disclosure of contingent liability in notes	**Remote** • no liability recognised in financial statements • no disclosure in notes
CONTINGENT ASSETS		
Virtually certain • no longer contingent • accrue asset in financial statements	**Probable** • no asset recognised in financial statements • disclosure of contingent asset in notes	**Not probable** • no asset recognised in financial statements • no disclosure of contingent asset in notes

CASE STUDY

WYVERN WATER – WHAT SHOULD BE SHOWN IN THE FINANCIAL STATEMENTS?

situation

Wyvern Water Limited is a producer of spa water which is bottled at source high in the Wyvern Hills. The company also produces a very successful high energy drink – with a secret mix of Wyvern Water, glucose, and vitamins – marketed under the 'Dr Wyvern' label to sports enthusiasts.

You are helping to prepare the year-end financial statements and have been asked to decide how the following should be reported in the accounts to 31 December 2002.

1   Earlier in the year, a small batch of bottles of spa water was contaminated with oil from the bottling machinery. Although the problem was spotted by quality control checks, and most bottles were withdrawn from sale, some were sold to the public. In a few instances consumers of the water suffered severe stomach upsets and had to spend a night in hospital. These consumers are currently suing Wyvern Water for damages. The company's legal representatives consider that it is probable that the company will lose the case and that damages of £50,000 will be awarded against the company.

2   Wyvern Water holds worldwide patents and trademarks for the 'Dr Wyvern' energy drink. However, it has recently had letters from somebody claiming to be a Dr Wyvern who says that he devised the secret formula for the drink over fifty years ago. The mysterious Dr Wyvern is claiming royalties on sales of the drink for the past fifty years and says he will sue the company for £10m if he is not paid. Wyvern Water has checked carefully and found that the formula for the high energy drink was devised ten years ago by its own development team and that all applicable patents and trademarks are held. The company has sought legal advice and been advised that it is extremely unlikely that the claimant's case, if it gets to court, will be successful.

3   During the year Wyvern Water Limited has formed a separate company, Wyvern Foods Limited, to manufacture 'homestyle' pies and cakes. Wyvern Water has given a guarantee to the Mercia Bank in respect of bank overdraft facilities provided to Wyvern Foods. At 31 December 2002 it is not considered probable that Wyvern Water will have to make payment under the guarantee.

solution

1   Court case for damages

- The present obligation is the potential liability to pay damages from a past event, ie the sale of contaminated bottled water.
- It is probable that the company will lose the case and have to pay damages.
- The amount of damages is reliably estimated at £50,000.
- The company will record a provision as an expense in its profit and loss account and will record a liability in its balance sheet (under the heading 'provisions for liabilities and charges').
- Details of the provision will be given in the notes to the financial statements.

2   Claim for past royalties

- This is a possible obligation arising from past events, ie the sale of 'Dr Wyvern' energy drink.
- However, the possible obligation will be confirmed only by a future event – a court case.
- Legal advice considers the claimant's chances of success in a court case to be remote.
- This is a contingent liability, which will not be recognised in the accounts.
- Because the likelihood of losing the case is remote, there will be no disclosure of the contingent liability in the notes.

3 Bank guarantee

- The guarantee is a present obligation arising from a past event, ie the giving of the bank guarantee.

- However, at 31 December 2002, no transfer of economic benefits is probable to settle the obligation.

- This is a contingent liability, which will not be recognised in the accounts.

- Because the likelihood of having to meet the terms of the guarantee is probable, details of the contingent liability will be given in the notes to the financial statements.

SSAP 17 – Accounting for post balance sheet events

This standard recognises that there may be

- events which occur, or
- information that becomes available

after the end of the financial year that need to be reflected in the financial statements. For example, if a debtor becomes insolvent after the year-end and the amount of the debt is material, it may be necessary to make changes in the financial statements for the year to reflect this.

Any such changes can only be made in the period

- after the end of the financial year, and
- before the financial statements are approved by the board of directors

Once the financial statements have been approved by the board of directors, they cannot be altered.

SSAP 17 distinguishes between

- adjusting events, and
- non-adjusting events

Adjusting events relate directly to something that existed at the balance sheet date. If material, changes should be made to the amounts shown in the financial statements. Examples of adjusting events include:

- fixed assets, the subsequent determination of the purchase price, or sale price, of assets bought or sold before the year-end
- property, where a valuation shows a permanent fall in value
- investments, where there has been a permanent fall in value
- stocks, where net realisable value falls below cost price
- debtors, where a customer has become insolvent

Non-adjusting events arise after the balance sheet date and have no direct link with something that existed at the balance sheet date. No adjustment is made to the financial statements; instead they are disclosed by way of notes in order to ensure that the financial statements are not misleading. Examples of non-adjusting events include:

- mergers and acquisitions
- issue of shares and debentures
- purchases and sales of fixed assets and investments
- losses of fixed assets and stocks caused by events such as fire or flood
- opening new, or extending existing, trading activities
- closing a significant part of the business
- changes in rates of foreign exchange
- strikes and labour disputes

PROFIT AND LOSS ACCOUNT

In this section we look at accounting standards that affect mainly the profit and loss account:

FRS 15	– Tangible fixed assets
FRS 3	– Reporting financial performance
FRS 14	– Earnings per share
SSAP 25	– Segmental reporting
SSAP 20	– Foreign currency translation
FRS 17	– Retirement benefits
FRS 8	– Related party disclosures

Note that these standards often also have an effect on the balance sheet – affecting either assets or liabilities.

FRS 15 – Tangible fixed assets

We have already seen – in Chapter 7 – how this standard sets out the principles of accounting for tangible fixed assets. Thus the standard affects both balance sheet and profit and loss account.

Profit and loss account is mainly affected by the depreciation charge, where the objective of depreciation is to reflect in operating profit the cost of the use of the tangible fixed assets in the period.

All tangible fixed assets having a known useful economic life are to be depreciated (the most common exception is land).

Further details of FRS 15 are given on pages 183-184.

FRS 3 – Reporting financial performance

The accounting requirements of FRS 3 have already been considered in Chapter 6 (pages 136 - 140).

The standard distinguishes between three categories of non-recurring profits and losses:

– exceptional items

– extraordinary items

– prior period adjustments

FRS 3 requires that the profit and loss account must distinguish between:

– results of continuing operations (including acquisitions – shown as a separate figure)

– results of discontinued operations

– exceptional items

– extraordinary items

The standard also requires that a statement of total recognised gains and losses is included in the year-end financial statements.

In addition to the accounting requirements of FRS 3 which we have already seen in Chapter 6, the standard requires two notes to the accounts to be shown:

– the reconciliation of movements in shareholders' funds

– the note of historical cost profit and losses

reconciliation of movements in shareholders' funds

This statement explains how shareholders' funds have changed from the beginning of the financial year to the end. Note that the term 'shareholders' funds' means the issued share capital (including preference shares, if any), plus all the reserves (capital reserves, eg share premium account, revaluation reserve and revenue reserves, eg profit and loss account, general reserve).

At its most simple, the statement will show (using example figures):

	£
Profit for the financial year (after tax)	50,000
Dividends	(30,000)
Addition to shareholders' funds	20,000
Opening shareholders' funds	150,000
Closing shareholders' funds	170,000

The statement, therefore, shows the link between profit and loss account and the shareholders' stake recorded on the balance sheet.

A more complex statement will also include:

- items from the statement of total recognised gains and losses
- other changes to shareholders' funds, such as a new issue of shares, or the repayment of shares

A further statement (using example figures) shows:

	£
Profit for the financial year (after tax)	50,000
Dividends	(30,000)
	20,000
Other recognised gains and losses (from the statement of total recognised gains and losses)	10,000
New share capital	25,000
Net addition to shareholders' funds	55,000
Opening shareholders' funds	150,000
Closing shareholders' funds	205,000

note of historical cost profit and losses

- This note is required only where there is a material difference between:
  - profit or loss figure shown in profit and loss account, and
  - historical cost profit or loss (prepared on the basis that no asset revaluations have taken place)

- Where this note is required, it commences with the reported profit on ordinary activities before tax and, after adjustments, concludes with the historical cost profit on ordinary activities before tax. The two most common adjustments shown in the note are:
  - the difference between depreciation charges based on the historical cost of fixed assets and those based on revalued amounts (note that where fixed assets have been revalued upwards, the depreciation charge will be higher than that based on historical cost)
  - gains which have been recognised in the statement of total recognised gains and losses in previous years, but which have been realised (ie the asset has been sold) in the current year (note that, if the assets had been kept at historical cost, then the full amount of the gain would be shown in the current year's profit and loss account)

- The note will appear as follows (using example figures):

	£
Reported profit on ordinary activities before taxation	90,000
Difference between historical cost depreciation charge and actual depreciation charge of the year calculated on the revalued amount	*10,000
Realisation of property revaluation gains of previous years	*18,000
Historical cost profit on ordinary activities before taxation	118,000
Historical cost profit for the year retained after taxation, minority interests, extraordinary items and dividends	70,000

* Both of these are added because

– historical cost depreciation is lower than that based on revalued (upwards) amounts, ie historical cost will be higher as a result of a lower depreciation figure

– under historical cost accounting the full amount of realised gains is reported through profit and loss account, ie no part of the gain would be recognised in earlier years through the statement of total recognised gains and losses

The note requires the historical cost profit figure to be stated both before tax and after tax, minority interests (see Chapter 11), extraordinary items and dividends.

The main reason why FRS 3 requires this note is to enable comparison of the historical cost profit figures of similar companies. It would be almost impossible to make meaningful comparison if one company had kept fixed assets at historical costs whilst the other was using revaluations.

FRS 14 – Earnings per share

Earnings per share (EPS) is an accounting ratio that is widely used by investors to measure the performance of a company (see Chapter 10, page 276). The figure is given in all published accounts of public limited companies and is widely quoted in the financial press – the *Financial Times*, for example, quotes the EPS figure for those companies listed on its share prices pages.

The main method of calculating earnings per share allowed by FRS 14 is the *basic method* which is calculated as follows:

$$\frac{\text{net profit after tax and preference dividends}}{\text{number of issued ordinary shares}}$$

Note that the profit used in the calculation is the amount that is attributable to ordinary shareholders, ie after deducting:

– taxation

- minority interests (see Chapter 11)
- preference dividends

As well as stating a figure for EPS calculated using the basic method, other methods can be used by companies (eg the exclusion of extraordinary items, if any) but they have to:

- explain the method of calculation
- apply the method on a consistent basis
- provide a reconciliation of their method with the basic method

It is important to note that EPS is affected by the issue of additional ordinary shares during a financial year:

- when the issue has been at full market price, EPS is calculated on the basis of the average number of shares in issue during the period, using the weighted average; for example:

start of year (1 January)	100,000	ordinary shares
new issue (1 July)	50,000	ordinary shares
average number of shares in issue	*125,000	

* 100,000 + (50,000 ÷ 2 [ie half a year])

- when a bonus issue (see page 155) has been made during the year, EPS is calculated on the basis of the number of shares in issue *after* the bonus issue (this is done because, with a bonus issue, there is no inflow of cash to the company – it has the same net assets before and after the bonus issue)

CASE STUDY

MARTLEY SERVICES: CALCULATING EARNINGS PER SHARE

situation

The profit and loss account (extract) of Martley Services Ltd for 2002 is as follows:

Profit and loss account (extract) for the year ended 31 December 2002

	£
Profit before taxation	8,200
Corporation tax	2,300
	5,900
Dividends:	
Ordinary shares	2,000
Preference shares	1,400
Retained profit for year	2,500

The 'financed by' section of the balance sheet at 31 December 2002 was:

Balance sheet (extract) as at 31 December 2002

FINANCED BY	£
Issued Share Capital	
Ordinary shares of £1 each	10,000
7% preference shares of £1 each	20,000
Retained profits	35,100
SHAREHOLDERS' FUNDS	65,100

(a) You are asked to calculate the basic earnings per share figure of Martley Services Ltd for 2002 based on the information given above.

(b) What would the basic EPS figure be if Martley Services had made a new issue of 5,000 ordinary shares of £1 each at full market value on 1 October 2002?

(c) What would the basic EPS figure be if Martley Services had made, on 1 July 2002, a bonus issue of three fully paid ordinary shares for every ordinary share previously held?

Note: the ordinary dividend payable for 2002 will be the same for all three circumstances.

solution

(a) Basic earnings per share

$$\frac{\text{net profit after tax} - \text{preference dividend}}{\text{number of issued ordinary shares}} = \frac{£5,900 - £1,400}{10,000} = 45\text{p per share}$$

(b) New issue at full market value

EPS is calculated on the basis of the weighted average number of shares in issue during the period:

$$\frac{£5,900 - £1,400}{10,000 + (5,000 \div 4)} = \frac{£4,500}{11,250} = 40\text{p per share}$$

(c) Bonus issue

EPS is calculated on the basis of the number of shares in issue *after* the bonus issue:

$$\frac{£5,900 - £1,400}{10,000 + 30,000} = \frac{£4,500}{40,000} = 11.25\text{p per share}$$

SSAP 25 – Segmental reporting

In order to help the user of accounts, SSAP 25 requires businesses to disclose information from their accounts in two principal ways:

- by class of business (eg hotels, pubs, clubs)
- by geographical segment (eg United Kingdom, European Union, North America)

A class of business is a distinguishable part of a business that provides a separate product or service.

A geographical segment is a geographical area comprising an individual country or group of countries.

SSAP 25 requires that, where a business has two or more classes of business, or operates in two or more geographical segments, it should disclose for each class of business and geographical segment:

- turnover
- profit
- net assets

An extract of the disclosure requirements from the accounts of The Body Shop International PLC is shown below:

Turnover and operating profit based on destination of goods and services

	2000 £m	Turnover 1999 £m	2000 £m	Operating profit 1999 £m
UK & Republic of Ireland	137.4	123.9	8.6	5.7
Americas	99.5	97.8	6.5	(3.7)*
Europe & Middle East	57.9	48.0	7.5	6.3
Asia Pacific	35.3	34.0	10.4	11.8
	330.1	303.7	33.0	20.1
Restructuring costs			(2.7)	(16.6)
Net interest			(1.5)	(0.1)
Profit before taxation			28.8	3.4

*After exceptional costs of £4.5 million relating to the USA

Turnover by origin

	Total sales £m	Intra group £m	2000 Third party £m	Total sales £m	Intra group £m	1999 Third party £m
UK & Republic of Ireland	243.9	(28.0)	215.9	221.4	(16.8)	204.6
Americas	88.1	–	88.1	86.6	–	86.6
Europe & Middle East	19.9	–	19.9	6.9	–	6.9
Asia Pacific	6.2	–	6.2	5.6	–	5.6
	358.1	(28.0)	330.1	320.5	(16.8)	303.7

Note that, for calculating segmental profits, common costs (ie those that relate to more than one segment) can be apportioned between segments – for example on the basis of turnover. If, however, such apportionment would be misleading, common costs should be deducted from the total of the segment results.

Segmental reporting enables the user of accounts to assess and compare the performance of the various segments of the business – especially in terms of turnover/assets and profit/assets.

SSAP 20 – Foreign currency translation

This standard applies

- firstly, to companies which carry out business transactions denominated in foreign currencies

- secondly, where business is conducted through a foreign company, such as a subsidiary (see Chapter 11) which trades in its own currency

Currencies fluctuate against other currencies and the problem in accounting is to determine the rate of exchange to be used for transactions in foreign currencies.

The term **translation**, when used in connection with foreign currency transactions, means the process whereby financial data denominated in one currency are expressed in terms of another currency (**conversion** is the process of exchanging ownership of a sum of money in one currency for a sum of money in another currency).

SSAP 20 is concerned with the translation of assets, liabilities, revenues and costs denominated in foreign currencies.

The standard refers to two methods of translation:

- the closing rate method, which is based on the exchange rate at the balance sheet date

- the temporal method, which is based on historical exchange rates ruling at the date on which the amount recorded in the accounts was established

The closing rate method is referred to in the standard as 'closing rate/net investment'; it is the preferred method for translating the value of an investment in an overseas subsidiary company. The term '**net investment**' refers to the fact that such an investment is in the net worth of the foreign enterprise, rather than a direct investment in the separate assets and liabilities of that enterprise.

FRS 17 – Retirement benefits

As more and more companies provide pension schemes as part of the remuneration package of their employees, it is necessary to have a standard accounting practice which deals with the accounting for, and the disclosure of, retirement benefit costs and obligations in the financial statements.

The objectives of FRS 17 are to ensure that:

- financial statements reflect fairly the assets and liabilities of an employer's retirement benefit obligations and any related funding
- the operating costs of providing retirement benefits to employees are recognised in the accounting periods in which the benefits are earned by the employees, and the related finance costs; any changes in value of the assets and liabilities are recognised in the accounting periods in which they arise
- the financial statements contain adequate disclosure of the cost of providing retirement benefits and the related gains, losses, assets and liabilities

There are two main retirement benefits schemes considered by the standard:

- **defined contribution scheme**, into which an employer pays regular contributions fixed as an amount or percentage of the employee's pay; the amount of retirement benefits payable to the employee is not guaranteed and will depend on the return achieved by the investments of the scheme
- **defined benefit scheme**, where the scheme rules define the benefits independently of the contributions payable, and the benefits are not directly related to the investments of the scheme

Profit and loss account is debited with the employer's pension costs for the accounting period.

With defined benefit schemes, because the pension benefits payable are independent of the value of the pension share investments, there has to be a regular valuation of the two, ie the pension scheme liabilities and the value of pension scheme assets. There may be a surplus (assets exceed liabilities) or a deficit (liabilities exceed assets).

For defined benefit schemes any surplus or deficit is shown in the accounts as follows:

- the statement of total recognised gains and losses is credited with the surplus, or debited with the deficit, of the scheme
- balance sheet shows the pension scheme surplus or deficit

An example of how a defined benefit pension scheme surplus will be reported in the balance sheet is shown on the next page.

BALANCE SHEET AS AT 31 DECEMBER 2002

Assets	£000s
Pension asset*	<u>250</u>

Reserves	
Pension reserve**	<u>250</u>

* Pension scheme investments (valued at market values, eg current share price of investment), less pension scheme liabilities (valued by an actuary – at least every three years – to reflect the retirement benefits that the employer will have to provide).

** The amount of the pension scheme surplus at the balance sheet date, any changes having been reported through the statement of total recognised gains and losses.

When a defined benefit scheme has a surplus, the employer will usually reduce contributions in the future. With a deficit, the employer may have a legal obligation (under the terms of the pension scheme trust deed) to make good the shortfall – such a liability must be recognised in the financial statements.

FRS 8 – Related party disclosures

As we saw in Chapter 1, many different parties have an interest in the financial statements of companies and other organisations. Where such an interest extends to the ability to control or influence the financial or operating policies then such a party is known as a **related party**.

The objective of FRS 8 is to ensure that financial statements contain the disclosures necessary to draw attention to the existence of related parties, and material transactions with them. Such transactions may have an effect on the results shown by the financial statements.

Related parties exist under any one of the following circumstances:

– one party has direct or indirect control of another party

– the parties are subject to common control from the same source

– one party has influence over the financial or operating policies of the other party to an extent that the other party might be inhibited from pursuing at all times its own separate interests

- the parties, in entering a transaction, are subject to influence from the same source to such an extent that one of the parties to the transaction has subordinated its own separate interests (ie has put its own interests below that of the other)

Some parties are always related parties of the reporting entity. These include companies within the same group (see Chapter 11), associated companies, the entity's directors (and directors of the entity's parent company), pension funds and those who control 20 per cent or more of the voting rights.

Certain parties are presumed to be related parties of the reporting entity unless it can be demonstrated that neither party has influenced the financial and operating policies of the other in such a way as to inhibit the pursuit of separate interests. Examples include the key management of the reporting entity and the key management of its parent undertaking.

FRS 8 requires disclosure of:

- all material related party transactions
- the name of the party controlling the reporting entity

CONFIDENTIALITY PROCEDURES

The Companies Act requires that all large companies (together with some small and medium-sized companies):

- disclose whether the accounts have been prepared in accordance with applicable accounting standards
- give particulars of any material departure from the standards and the reasons for the departure

Thus, such information is readily available to users of accounts. However, other information (which may be available to those involved in the preparation of accounts) is subject to confidentiality procedures which must be observed at all times; for example:

- details of any discussion about accounting standards with the directors
- the application of standards to a particular set of financial statements
- details of any workings used, but not disclosed in the accounts, such as in the calculation of deferred tax, provisions, depreciation, etc
- discussion of whether to treat an item one way rather than another, such as deciding whether to classify something as a provision to be recognised in the financial statements, or as a contingent liability to be disclosed as a note

CHAPTER SUMMARY

- **FRS 16** 'Current tax' requires that current tax is to be recognised in profit and loss account. However, where a gain (or loss) has been recognised directly in the statement of total recognised gains and losses, the tax relating to the gain (or loss) is recognised directly in that statement.

- **FRS 19** 'Deferred tax' requires deferred tax to be recognised on most types of timing differences.

- **SSAP 5** 'Accounting for value added tax' requires that:

  – the turnover figure in profit and loss account is to be shown net of VAT

  – irrecoverable VAT on fixed assets is to be included in their cost

  – the net amount due to, or from, HM Customs and Excise is to be included in the figures for creditors and debtors respectively, and need not be disclosed separately

- **SSAP 21** 'Leases and hire purchase contracts' requires to be shown, on the liabilities side of the balance sheet, the amount due to the finance company for the capital amount – split between long-term and current liabilities, as appropriate. See also pages 187-188.

- **FRS 4** 'Capital instruments' states how capital instruments – shares, debentures, loans and debt instruments – are to be treated in the financial statements.

- **FRS 12** 'Provisions, contingent liabilities and contingent assets' ensures that appropriate recognition criteria and measurement bases are applied to these three types of uncertainties. It requires that sufficient information is disclosed in the notes to financial statements to enable users to understand their nature, timing and amount.

- **SSAP 17** 'Accounting for post balance sheet events' allows for events which may occur, or information that becomes available, in the period between the end of the financial year and the approval of financial statements by the board of directors to be reflected in the financial statements. The standard distinguishes between adjusting events and non-adjusting events.

- **FRS 15** 'Tangible fixed assets' (see also pages 183-184) requires that all tangible fixed assets having a known useful economic life are to be depreciated.

- **FRS 3** 'Reporting financial performance' (see also pages 136-140)

  – distinguishes between three categories of non-recurring profits and losses: exceptional items, extraordinary items and prior period adjustments

- requires that the profit and loss account distinguishes between: results of continuing operations, results of discontinued operations, exceptional items, extraordinary items

- requires that a statement of total recognised gains and losses is included in the year-end financial statements

- requires two notes to the accounts to be shown: reconciliation of movements in shareholders' funds, and a note of historical cost profit and losses

- **FRS 14** 'Earnings per share' requires the EPS figure to be given in the published accounts of public limited companies. The main method of calculating EPS allowed by the standard is called the basic method.

- **SSAP 25** 'Segmental reporting' requires businesses to disclose information from their accounts in two principal ways:

  - by class of business

  - by geographical segment

- **SSAP 20** 'Foreign currency translation' is concerned with the translation of assets, liabilities, revenues and costs denominated in foreign currencies. The standard refers to two methods of translation:

  - the closing rate method

  - the temporal method

  The 'closing rate/net investment' method is seen as the preferred method for translating the value of an investment in an overseas subsidiary company.

- **FRS 17** 'Retirement benefits' distinguishes between two main retirement benefits schemes:

  - defined contribution scheme

  - defined benefit scheme

  The objectives of the standard are to ensure that the financial statements reflect fairly the assets and liabilities, operating costs, and changes in value of assets and liabilities, of an employer's retirement benefit obligations and any related funding.

- **FRS 8** 'Related party disclosures' ensures that financial statements contain the disclosures necessary to draw attention to the existence of related parties, and material transactions with them.

KEY TERMS

current tax
the amount of tax estimated to be due on the profits of the accounting period

deferred tax
'estimated future tax consequences of transactions and events recognised in the financial statements of the current and previous periods' (FRS 19)

Value Added Tax
a tax on the supply of goods and services, which is eventually borne by the final consumer, but is collected at each stage of the production and distribution chain

capital instruments
'all instruments that are issued by reporting entities as a means of raising finance, including shares, debentures, loans and debt instruments, options and warrants that give the holder the right to subscribe for or obtain capital instruments' (FRS 4)

provision
a liability of uncertain timing or amount, to be settled by the transfer of economic benefits

contingent liability
either a possible obligation arising from past events whose existence will be confirmed only by the occurrence of one or more uncertain future events not wholly within the entity's control;

or a present obligation that arises from past events but is not recognised because

– it is not probable that a transfer of economic benefits will be required to settle the obligation; or

– the obligation cannot be measured with sufficient reliability

contingent asset
a possible asset arising from past events whose existence will be confirmed only by the occurrence of one or more uncertain future events not wholly within the entity's control

adjusting event
a post balance sheet event that relates directly to something that existed at the balance sheet date; if material, changes should be made to the amounts shown in the financial statements

non-adjusting event
an event that arises after the balance sheet date and has no direct link with something that existed at the balance sheet date; no adjustment is made to the financial statements, but it is disclosed by way of a note in order to ensure that the financial statements are not misleading

earnings per share

basic method:

$$\frac{\text{net profit after tax and preference dividends}}{\text{number of issued ordinary shares}}$$

class of business

a distinguishable part of a business that provides a separate product or service

geographical segment

a geographical area comprising an individual country or group of countries

foreign currency translation

the process whereby financial data denominated in one currency are expressed in terms of another currency; there are two main methods of translation:

- the closing rate method (based on the exchange rate at the balance sheet date)

- the temporal method (based on historical exchange rates ruling at the date on which the amount recorded in the accounts was established)

defined contribution scheme

pension scheme into which an employer pays regular contributions fixed as an amount or percentage of the employee's pay; the amount of retirement benefits payable to the employee is not guaranteed and will depend on the return achieved by the investments of the scheme

defined benefit scheme

pension scheme where the scheme rules define the benefits independently of the contributions payable, and the benefits are not directly related to the investments of the scheme

related parties

exist under any one of the following:

- one party has direct or indirect control of another party

- the parties are subject to common control from the same source

- one party has influence over the financial or operating policies of the other party to an extent that the other party might be inhibited from pursuing at all times its own separate interests

- the parties, in entering a transaction, are subject to influence from the same source to such an extent that one of the parties to the transaction has subordinated its own separate interests

STUDENT ACTIVITIES

8.1   Which of the following could be charged to the profit and loss account as an expense?

(a)   A non-adjusting post balance sheet event.

(b)   A possible contingent liability

(c)   Non purchased (inherrant) goodwill

(d)   Research and development expenditure

8.2   FRS 12 Provisions, contingent liabilities and contingent assets, states that a contingent liability at the balance sheet date should be provided for in the accounts for that year, if:

(a)   Its occurrence is probable and the loss can be estimated with reasonable certainty.

(b)   Its occurrence is possible.

(c)   Its occurrence is remote.

(d)   Its occurrence is neither probable, possible or remote.

8.3   According to SSAP 17 *Accounting for post balance sheet events*, which one of the following is an adjusting event?

(a)   A flash flood which occurred after the year end ruining a certain amount of stock.

(b)   The signing of a major export contract with Japan on the last day of the financial year.

(c)   A strike by the workforce after the year end, which threatens the profitability of the company

(d)   A customer who was forced into liquidation, after the year end, but the amount due is recorded in the balance sheet as at the actual year end.

8.4   When dealing with current tax (FRS 16) which of the following best describes the amount due to be paid in the accounts?

(a)   Debit Profit and Loss Account   Credit Cash

(b)   Debit Profit and loss Account   Credit Corporation tax payable

(c)   Debit Cash   Credit Corporation tax payable

(d)   Debit Cash   Credit Profit and Loss Account

8.5   Which one of the following statements is correct when dealing with deferred taxation, according to FRS 19?

(a)   The taxable profit and the business profit are one and the same, allowances being based upon depreciation.

(b)   The taxable profit is the same as the bank account balance, ensuring that there is enough cash to pay the tax payable.

(c)   The taxable profit is the same as the NBV of the tangible fixed assets, after adjusting for depreciation.

(d)   The taxable profit is different to the business profit due to the fact that depreciation is replaced by a system of capital allowances.

8.6   Define adjusting and non-adjusting events, giving an example of each.

8.7   State how a material contingent loss and a material contingent gain should be treated and accounted for in financial statements.

8.8   Explain the main purpose of a statement of recognised gains and losses.

8.9   What is the main purpose for issuing SSAP 25 segmental reporting?

8.10   What are the main differences between a defined contribution pension scheme and a defined benefit pension scheme?

8.11   When a company deals abroad in a foreign currency what are the differences as you understand them, between conversion and translation?

9 CASH FLOW STATEMENTS

this chapter covers . . .

In this chapter we study the cash flow statement, which links profit from the profit and loss account with changes in assets and liabilities in the balance sheet, and the effect on the cash of the business.

We will cover:

- an appreciation of the need for a cash flow statement

- the cash flows for the main sections of the statement

- how the cash flows relate to the main areas of business activity

- the interpretation of cash flow statements

NVQ PERFORMANCE CRITERIA COVERED

unit 11: DRAFTING FINANCIAL STATEMENTS

element 2

draft limited company, sole trader and partnership year end financial statements

- a cash flow statement is correctly prepared and interpreted where required

- year end financial statements are presented for approval to the appropriate person in clear form

- confidentiality procedures are followed at all times

- the organisation's policies, regulations, procedures and timescales relating to financial statements are observed at all times

- discrepancies, unusual features or queries are identified and either resolved or referred to the appropriate person

INTRODUCTION

The profit and loss account shows profitability, and the balance sheet shows asset strength. While these two financial statements give us a great deal of information on the progress of a business during an accounting period, profit does not equal cash, and strength in assets does not necessarily mean a large bank balance.

The **cash flow statement** links profit with changes in assets and liabilities, and the effect on the cash of the business.

A cash flow statement uses information from the accounting records (including profit and loss account and balance sheet) to show an overall view of money flowing in and out of a business during an accounting period.

Such a statement explains to the owner or shareholders why, after a year of good profits for example, there is a reduced balance at the bank or a larger bank overdraft at the year-end than there was at the beginning of the year. The cash flow statement concentrates on the liquidity of the business: it is often a lack of cash (a lack of liquidity) that causes most businesses to fail. The importance of the cash flow statement is such that all but small limited companies must include the statement as a part of their accounts. For sole traders and partnerships, the information that the statement contains is of considerable interest to the owner(s) and to a lender, such as a bank.

The format used in this chapter for the cash flow statement follows the guidelines set out in FRS 1 *Cash Flow Statements*.

FORMAT OF THE CASH FLOW STATEMENT

FRS 1 provides a format for cash flow statements which is divided into eight sections:

1   Operating activities

2   Returns on investments and servicing of finance

3   Taxation

4   Capital expenditure and financial investment

5   Acquisitions and disposals

6   Equity dividends paid

7   Management of liquid resources

8   Financing

The cash flows for the year affecting each of these main areas of business activity are shown in the statement, although not every business will have cash flows under each of the eight sections. The final figure at the bottom of the cash flow statement shows the net cash inflow or outflow for the period.

The diagram on the next page shows the main cash inflows and outflows under each heading, and indicates the content of the cash flow statement. The first section – operating activities – needs a word of further explanation, particularly as it is the main source of cash inflow for most businesses.

operating activities

The net cash inflow from operating activities is calculated by using figures from the profit and loss account and balance sheet as follows:

operating profit (ie net profit, before deduction of interest)

add   depreciation for the year

add   loss on sale of fixed assets (or *deduct* profit on sale of fixed assets) – see page 250

add   decrease in stock (or *deduct* increase in stock)

add   decrease in debtors (or *deduct* increase in debtors)

add   increase in creditors (or *deduct* decrease in creditors)

Note that depreciation is added to profit because depreciation is a non-cash expense, that is, no money is paid out by the business in respect of depreciation charged to profit and loss account.

LAYOUT OF A CASH FLOW STATEMENT

A cash flow statement uses a common layout which can be amended to suit the particular needs of the business for which it is being prepared. The example layout shown on page 244 (with specimen figures included) is commonly used – see also the cash flow statement for The Body Shop International PLC shown on page 143.

CASH FLOW STATEMENT

Operating activities
- Operating profit (ie net profit, before deduction of interest)
- Depreciation charge for the year (see page 250 for treatment of a profit or a loss on sale of fixed assets)
- Changes in stock, debtors and creditors

Returns on investments and servicing of finance
- Inflows: interest received, dividends received
- Outflows: interest paid, dividends paid on preference shares (but not ordinary shares – see below)

Taxation
- Outflow: corporation tax paid by limited companies during the year

Capital expenditure and financial investment
- Inflows: sale proceeds from fixed assets and investments
- Outflows: purchase cost of fixed assets and investments

Acquisitions and disposals
- Inflows: sale proceeds from investments and interests in
  - subsidiary companies (where more than 50 per cent of the shares in another company is owned)
  - associated companies (where between 20 per cent and 50 per cent of the shares in another company is owned)
  - joint ventures (where a project is undertaken jointly with another company)
- Outflows: purchase cost of investments in subsidiary companies, associated companies, and of interests in joint ventures

Equity dividends paid
- Outflow: the amount of dividends paid to equity (ordinary) shareholders during the year (where the cash flow statement is for a sole trader or partnership, the amount of drawings will be shown here)

Management of liquid resources
- Inflows: sale proceeds from short-term investments that are almost as good as cash – such as treasury bills (a form of government debt), and term deposits of up to a year with a bank
- Outflows: purchase of short-term liquid investments

Financing
- Inflows: receipts from increase in capital /share capital, raising/increase of loans (note: no cash inflow from a bonus issue of shares – see page 155)
- Outflows: repayment of capital/share capital/loans

Contents of a cash flow statement

ABC LIMITED
CASH FLOW STATEMENT FOR THE YEAR ENDED 31 DECEMBER 2002

	£	£
Net cash inflow from operating activities		89,000
Returns on investments and servicing of finance:		
Interest received	10,000	
Interest paid	(5,000)	
		5,000
Taxation:		
Corporation tax paid (note: amount paid during year)		(6,000)
Capital expenditure and financial investment:		
Payments to acquire fixed assets	(125,000)	
Receipts from sales of fixed assets	15,000	
		(110,000)
Acquisitions and disposals:		
Purchase of subsidiary undertakings	(–)	
Sale of a business	–	
		–
Equity dividends paid: (note: amount paid during year)		(22,000)
Cash outflow before use of liquid resources and financing		(44,000)
Management of liquid resources:		
Purchase of treasury bills	(250,000)	
Sale of treasury bills	200,000	
		(50,000)
Financing:		
Issue of share capital	275,000	
Repayment of capital/share capital	(–)	
Increase in loans	–	
Repayment of loans	(90,000)	
		185,000
Increase in cash		91,000

Reconciliation of operating profit to net cash inflow from operating activities

Operating profit (note: before tax and interest)	75,000
Depreciation for year	10,000
Decrease in stock	2,000
Increase in debtors	(5,000)
Increase in creditors	7,000
Net cash inflow from operating activities	89,000

notes on the cash flow statement

- The separate amounts shown for each section can, if preferred, be detailed in a note to the cash flow statement. The operating activities section is invariably set out in detail as a note below the cash flow statement (see example opposite), with just the figure for net cash flow from operating activities being shown on the statement (see grey line).

- Money amounts shown in brackets indicate a deduction or, where the figure is a sub-total, a negative figure.

- The changes in the main working capital items of stock, debtors and creditors have an effect on cash balances. For example, a decrease in stock increases cash, while an increase in debtors reduces cash.

- The cash flow statement concludes with a figure for the increase or decrease in cash for the period. This is calculated from the subtotals of each of the eight sections of the statement.

CASE STUDY

SAMANTHA SMITH: A SOLE TRADER CASH FLOW STATEMENT

situation

Samantha Smith runs a children's clothes shop in rented premises in a small market town. Her balance sheets for the last two years are as follows:

BALANCE SHEETS AS AT 31 DECEMBER						
	2001			2002		
	£	£	£	£	£	£
	Cost	Dep'n	Net	Cost	Dep'n	Net
Fixed Assets						
Shop fittings	1,500	500	1,000	2,000	750	1,250
Current Assets						
Stock		3,750			4,850	
Debtors		625			1,040	
Bank		220			–	
		4,595			5,890	
Less Current Liabilities						
Creditors	2,020			4,360		
Bank	–			725		
		2,020			5,085	
Working Capital			2,575			805
			3,575			2,055
Less Long-term Liabilities						
Loan from husband			–			1,000
NET ASSETS			3,575			1,055

continued on next page

FINANCED BY		
Capital	£	£
Opening capital	3,300	3,575
Add net profit for year	5,450	4,080
	8,750	7,655
Less drawings	5,175	6,600
	3,575	1,055

Note: Interest paid on the loan and bank overdraft in 2002 was £450.

Samantha Smith says to you: 'I cannot understand why I am overdrawn at the bank by £725 on 31 December 2002 when I made a profit of £4,080 during the year'. She asks you to help her by explaining why this is.

solution
A cash flow statement will give Samantha Smith the answer:

CASH FLOW STATEMENT FOR THE YEAR ENDED 31 DECEMBER 2002		
	£	£
Net cash inflow from operating activities		5,605
Returns on investments and servicing of finance:		
Interest paid		(450)
Taxation:		
Corporation tax paid		not applicable
Capital expenditure and financial investment:		
Payments to acquire fixed assets		(500)
Equity dividends paid: (drawings)		(6,600)
Cash outflow before use of liquid resources and financing		(1,945)
Financing:		
Loan from husband		1,000
Decrease in cash		(945)

Reconciliation of operating profit to net cash inflow from operating activities	
Operating profit (before interest)	4,530
Depreciation for year	250
Increase in stock	(1,100)
Increase in debtors	(415)
Increase in creditors	2,340
Net cash inflow from operating activities	5,605

Tutorial note
When preparing a cash flow statement from financial statements, take a moment or two to establish which is the earlier year and which is the later year. In this Case Study they are set out from left to right, ie 2001 followed by 2002. In some Assessments and Questions, the later year is shown first, ie 2002 followed by 2001.

points to note from the cash flow statement

- Net profit for the year (before interest) is calculated as:

net profit for 2002	£4,080
interest for 2002	£ 450
	£4,530

- Depreciation for the year of £250 is the amount of the increase in depreciation to date shown on the balance sheets, that is, £750 minus £500.

- An increase in stock and debtors reduces the cash available to the business (because stock is being bought, debtors are being allowed more time to pay). By contrast, an increase in creditors gives an increase in cash (because creditors are allowing Samantha Smith more time to pay).

- In this example there is no tax paid (because Samantha Smith is a sole trader who will be taxed as an individual, unlike a company which pays tax on its profits); however, the place where tax would appear is indicated on the cash flow statement.

- Payments to acquire fixed assets £500 is the amount of the increase in the cost of fixed assets shown on the balance sheets, that is, £2,000 minus £1,500.

- As this is a sole trader business, drawings are shown on the cash flow statement in place of equity dividends.

- The change in the bank balance is summarised as follows: from a balance of £220 in the bank to an overdraft of £725 is a 'swing' in the bank of minus £945, which is the amount of the decrease in cash shown by the cash flow statement.

your explanation to Samantha Smith
In this example, the statement highlights the following points for the owner of the business:

- net cash inflow from operating activities is £5,605, whereas owner's drawings are £6,600; this state of affairs cannot continue for long

- fixed assets costing £500 have been purchased

- a long-term loan of £1,000 has been raised from her husband

- over the year there has been a decrease in cash of £945, this trend cannot be continued for long

- by the end of 2002 the business has an overdraft of £725, caused mainly by the excessive drawings of the owner

- in conclusion, the liquidity position of this business has deteriorated over the two years, and corrective action will be necessary

CASE STUDY

NEWTOWN TRADING COMPANY LIMITED: COMPANY CASH FLOW STATEMENT

situation

The balance sheets of Newtown Trading Company Limited for 2001 and 2002 are as follows:

BALANCE SHEETS AS AT 31 DECEMBER

	2001			2002		
	£	£	£	£	£	£
	Cost	Dep'n	Net	Cost or reval'n	Dep'n	Net
Fixed Assets						
Land	75,000	–	75,000	125,000	–	125,000
Vehicles	22,200	6,200	16,000	39,000	8,900	30,100
	97,200	6,200	91,000	164,000	8,900	155,100
Current Assets						
Stock		7,000			11,000	
Debtors		5,000			3,700	
Bank		1,000			500	
		13,000			15,200	
Less Current Liabilities						
Creditors	3,500			4,800		
Proposed dividends	2,000			2,500		
Corporation tax	1,000			1,500		
		6,500			8,800	
Working Capital			6,500			6,400
			97,500			161,500
Less Long-term Liabilities						
Debentures			5,000			3,000
NET ASSETS			92,500			158,500
FINANCED BY						
Ordinary share capital			80,000			90,000
Share premium account			1,500			2,500
Revaluation reserve			–			50,000
Retained profits			11,000			16,000
SHAREHOLDERS' FUNDS			92,500			158,500

Prepare a cash flow statement for the year ended 31 December 2002 and comment on the main points highlighted by the statement. Note the following points:

- Extract from the profit and loss account for 2002:

	£
Operating profit	9,400
Interest paid	400
Net profit	9,000
Less: Corporation tax	1,500
Proposed ordinary dividend	2,500
Retained profit for year	5,000

- During 2002 the land was revalued at £125,000.

solution

NEWTOWN TRADING COMPANY LIMITED
CASH FLOW STATEMENT FOR THE YEAR ENDED 31 DECEMBER 2002

	£	£
Net cash inflow from operating activities		10,700
Returns on investments and servicing of finance:		
Interest paid		(400)
Taxation:		
Corporation tax paid		(1,000)
Capital expenditure and financial investment:		
Payments to acquire fixed assets (vehicles)		(16,800)
Equity dividends paid:		(2,000)
Cash outflow before use of liquid resources and financing		(9,500)
Financing:		
Issue of ordinary shares at a premium		
ie £10,000 + £1,000 =	11,000	
Repayment of debentures	(2,000)	
		9,000
Decrease in cash**		(500)

Reconciliation of operating profit to net cash inflow from operating activities	
Operating profit (before interest)	9,400
Depreciation for year*	2,700
Increase in stock	(4,000)
Decrease in debtors	1,300
Increase in creditors	1,300
Net cash inflow from operating activities	10,700

notes on the cash flow statement

* Depreciation charged: £8,900 – £6,200 = £2,700

** Decrease in cash: from £1,000 to £500 = £500

Both proposed dividends and corporation tax – which are current liabilities at 31 December 2001 – are paid in 2002. Likewise, the current liabilities for dividends and tax at 31 December 2002 will be paid in 2003 (and will appear on that year's cash flow statement).

The revaluation of the land (increase in the value of the fixed asset, and revaluation reserve recorded in the 'financed by' section) does not feature in the cash flow statement because it is a non-cash transaction.

how useful is the cash flow statement?

The following points are highlighted by the statement on the previous page:

• net cash inflow from operating activities is £10,700

• a purchase of vehicles of £16,800 has been made, financed partly by operating activities, and partly by an issue of shares at a premium

• the bank balance during the year has fallen by £500, ie from £1,000 to £500

In conclusion, the picture shown by the cash flow statement is that of a business which is generating cash from its operating activities and using them to build for the future.

PROFIT OR LOSS ON SALE OF FIXED ASSETS

a difference between book value and sale proceeds

When a business sells fixed assets it is most unlikely that the resultant sale proceeds will equal the net book value (cost price, less depreciation to date).

dealing with a profit or loss on sale

The accounting solution is to transfer any small profit or loss on sale – non-cash items – to profit and loss account. However, such a profit or loss on sale must be handled with care when preparing a cash flow statement because, in such a statement we have to adjust for non-cash items when calculating the net cash inflow from operating activities; at the same time we must separately identify the amount of the sale proceeds of fixed assets in the capital expenditure section.

CASE STUDY

H & J WELLS:
PROFIT OR LOSS ON SALE OF FIXED ASSETS

situation

H & J Wells are electrical contractors. For the year ended 30 June 2002 their profit and loss account is as follows:

		£	£
Gross profit			37,500
Less expenses:			
General expenses		23,000	
Provision for depreciation: machinery		2,000	
vehicles		3,000	
			28,000
Net profit			9,500

profit on sale

During the course of the year they have sold the following fixed asset; the effects of the sale transaction have not yet been recorded in their profit and loss account:

		£
Machine:	cost price	1,000
	depreciation to date	750
	net book value	250
	sale proceeds	350

As the machine has been sold for £100 more than book value, this sum is shown in profit and loss account, as follows:

		£	£
Gross profit			37,500
Profit on sale of fixed assets			100
			37,600
Less expenses:			
General expenses		23,000	
Provision for depreciation: machinery		2,000	
vehicles		3,000	
			28,000
Net profit			9,600

The cash flow statement, based on the amended profit and loss account, will include the following figures:

CASHFLOW STATEMENT (EXTRACT) OF H & J WELLS
FOR THE YEAR ENDED 30 JUNE 2002

	£	£
Operating activities (this will be shown as a note)		
Operating profit (here, the same as net profit)	9,600	
Depreciation	5,000	
Profit on sale of fixed assets	(100)	
(Increase)/decrease in stock	. . .	
(Increase)/decrease in debtors	. . .	
Increase/(decrease) in creditors	. . .	
Net cash inflow from operating activities		14,500
Capital expenditure and financial investment:		
Payments to acquire fixed assets	(. . .)	
Receipts from sales of fixed assets	350	
		350

Note that profit on sale of fixed assets is deducted in the operating activities section because it is non-cash income. (Only the sections of the cash flow statement affected by the sale are shown above.)

loss on sale

If the machine in the Case Study had been sold for £150, this would have given a 'loss on sale' of £100. This amount would be debited to profit and loss account, to give an amended net profit of £9,400. The effect on the cash flow statement would be twofold:

1 In the operating activities section, loss on sale of fixed assets of £100 would be added; the net cash inflow from operating activities remains at £14,500 (which proves that both profit and loss on sale of fixed assets are non-cash items)

2 In the capital expenditure section, receipts from sales of fixed assets would be £150

conclusion: profit or a loss on sale of fixed assets

The rule for dealing with a profit or a loss on sale of fixed assets in cash flow statements is:

• add the amount of the loss on sale, or deduct the amount of the profit on sale, to or from the operating profit when calculating the net cash flow from operating activities

• show the total sale proceeds, ie the amount of the cheque received, as receipts from sales of fixed assets in the capital expenditure section

The Case Study of Retail News Limited (see below) incorporates calculations for both a profit and a loss on sale of fixed assets.

REVALUATION OF FIXED ASSETS

From time-to-time some fixed assets are revalued upwards and the amount of the revaluation is recorded in the balance sheet. The most common assets to be treated in this way are land and buildings. The value of the fixed asset is increased and the amount of the revaluation is placed to a revaluation reserve in the 'financed by' section of the balance sheet where it increases the value of the shareholders' investment in the company. As a revaluation is purely a 'book' adjustment, ie no cash has changed hands, it does not feature in a cash flow statement – see the Case Study of Newtown Trading Company Limited on pages 248 to 250.

CASE STUDY

RETAIL NEWS LIMITED:
PREPARING THE CASH FLOW STATEMENTS

Tutorial note

This is quite a complex example of cash flow statements which incorporates a number of points:

- profit on sale of fixed assets

- loss on sale of fixed assets

- issue of shares at a premium

- calculation of corporation tax paid and ordinary dividends paid

As there are two years' cash flow statements to produce, it is suggested that you work through the Case Study seeing how the figures have been prepared for the first year (year ended 2001); then attempt the second year (year ended 2002) yourself, checking against the Case Study.

situation

Martin Jackson is a shareholder in Retail News Limited, a company that operates newsagent shops in the town of Wyvern. Martin comments that, whilst the company is making reasonable profits, the bank balance has fallen quite considerably. He provides you with the following information for Retail News Limited:

Balance sheet as at 31 December

	2000 £000	2000 £000	2001 £000	2001 £000	2002 £000	2002 £000
Fixed Assets at cost		274		298		324
Less depreciation		74		98		118
		200		200		206
Current Assets						
Stock	50		74		85	
Debtors	80		120		150	
Bank	10		–		–	
	140		194		235	
Less Current Liabilities						
Creditors	62		78		82	
Bank	–		15		46	
Final dividends	10		14		12	
Corporation tax	4		5		8	
	76		112		148	
Working Capital		64		82		87
NET ASSETS		264		282		293
FINANCED BY						
Ordinary share capital		200		210		210
Share premium account		–		5		5
Retained profits		64		67		78
SHAREHOLDERS' FUNDS		264		282		293

Profit and loss account extracts for the three years to 31 December 2002

	2000 £000	2001 £000	2002 £000
Operating profit	25	31	50
Interest paid	–	3	15
Net profit	25	28	35
Corporation tax	5	7	10
Profit after tax	20	21	25
Ordinary dividends paid and proposed	15	18	14
Retained profit for year	5	3	11

Notes

- During the year to 31 December 2001, fixed assets were sold for £30,000, the cost of the fixed assets sold was £40,000 and depreciation was £20,000.
- During the year to 31 December 2002, fixed assets with an original cost of £35,000 were sold at a loss on sale of £5,000 below net book value; the depreciation on these fixed assets sold had amounted to £15,000.

REQUIRED: Prepare a cash flow statement for the years ended 2001 and 2002.

RETAIL NEWS LIMITED
CASH FLOW STATEMENT FOR THE YEAR ENDED 31 DECEMBER

	2001 £000	2001 £000	2002 £000	2002 £000
Net cash inflow from operating activities		17		53
Returns on investments and servicing of finance:				
Interest paid		(3)		(15)
Taxation:				
Corporation tax paid (see below)		(6)		(7)
Capital expenditure and financial investment:				
Payments to acquire fixed assets (see below)	(64)		(61)	
Receipts from sales of fixed assets	30		15	
		(34)		(46)
Equity dividends paid: (see below)		(14)		(16)
Cash outflow before use of liquid resources and financing		(40)		(31)
Financing:				
Issue of ordinary shares at a premium (see below)		15		–
Decrease in cash		(25)		(31)
Bank balance at start of year		10		(15)
Bank balance at end of year		(15)		(46)
Decrease in cash		(25)		(31)

Reconciliation of operating profit to net cash inflow from operating activities

	2001 (£000)	2002 (£000)
Operating profit	31	50
Depreciation for year (see below)	44	35
(Profit)/loss on sale of fixed assets (see below)	(10)	5
Increase in stock	(24)	(11)
Increase in debtors	(40)	(30)
Increase in creditors	16	4
Net cash inflow from operating activities	17	53

Points to note from the cash flow statement:
■ **Depreciation for year**

	2001 £000	2002 £000
Depreciation at start of year*	74	98
Less depreciation on asset sold	20	15
	54	83
Depreciation at end of year*	98	118
Depreciation for year	44	35

* figures taken from balance sheet

■ **Profit/(loss) on sale of fixed assets**

	2001 £000	2002 £000
Cost price of assets sold	40	35
Less depreciation to date	20	15
Net book value	20	20
Receipts from sale	30	*15
Profit/(loss) on sale	10	(5)

* Receipt from sale at £5,000 below net book value

Note that profit on sale is *deducted from*, and loss on sale is *added to*, operating profit because they are non-cash income; the receipts from sale are shown in the capital expenditure section

■ **Corporation tax paid**

From the information available we can calculate the amount of corporation tax in the year as follows:

Liability at start of year*	4	5
Profit and loss account transfer	7	10
	11	15
Less liability at end of year*	5	8
Amount paid in year	6	7

* figures taken from balance sheet

■ **Payments to acquire fixed assets**

Fixed assets at cost at start of year	274	298
Less cost price of asset sold	40	35
	234	263
Fixed assets at cost at end of year	298	324
Payments to acquire fixed assets	64	61

■ **Equity (ordinary) dividends paid**

From the information available we can calculate the amount of ordinary dividends paid in the year as follows:

Liability at start of year*	10	14
Profit and loss account transfer	18	14
	28	28
Less liability at end of year*	14	12
Amount paid in year	14	16

* figures taken from balance sheet

■ **Issue of ordinary shares at a premium**

Ordinary share capital at start of year	200
Share premium account at start of year	–
	200
Ordinary share capital at end of year	210
Share premium account at end of year	5
	215
Issue of ordinary shares at a premium	15

conclusion: how useful is the cash flow statement?

The following points are highlighted by the cash flow statements of Retail News Limited for 2001 and 2002:

- a good cash flow from operating profit in both years – well above the amounts paid for corporation tax and dividends

- stock, debtors and creditors have increased each year – in particular the debtors have increased significantly

- interest paid in 2002 is high because of the increasing bank overdraft (and will, most probably, be even higher in 2002)

- new fixed assets have been bought each year – £64,000 in 2001 and £61,000 in 2002. Apart from a share issue of £15,000 in 2001, these have been financed through the bank account

The business appears to be expanding quite rapidly, with large increases in fixed assets and the working capital items. As most of this expansion has been financed through the bank (apart from the share issue of £15,000 in 2001), there is much pressure on the bank account. It would be better to obtain long-term finance – either a loan or a new issue of shares – rather than using the bank overdraft.

LINKS TO OTHER FINANCIAL STATEMENTS

As the cash flow statement is one of the three financial statements prepared at the end of an accounting period, it needs to be read in conjunction with the profit and loss account and balance sheet. In order to provide links to the other financial statements, the accounting standard on cash flow statements, FRS1, requires that there should be two reconciliations – or formal notes – between:

- operating profit and the net cash flow from operating activities
- the increase or decrease in cash and the movement in net debt

operating profit with net cash flow from operating activities

We have already seen in the Case Studies how this reconciliation is prepared: the 'operating activities' section commences with the operating profit and, after adjustments for depreciation and the change in stocks, debtors and creditors, concludes with the net cash flow from operating activities. The figures making up the reconciliation are invariably shown as a note to the cash flow statement with just the figure for net cash flow from operating activities being shown on the face of the statement.

change in cash with movement in net debt

This reconciliation requires us to take the final figure on the cash flow statement – the increase or decrease in cash – and reconcile it with changes in net debt. (Note that net debt is the borrowing of the business – eg debentures, loans and overdrafts – less cash/bank balances and other liquid resources, such as treasury bills). Thus, for ABC Limited (see page 244) the reconciliation could be shown as follows, with specimen figures used:

Analysis of changes in net debt

	Net debt as at 1 Jan 2002	Cash flows year to 31 Dec 2002	Net debt as at 31 Dec 2002
	£	£	£
Cash at bank	(25,000)	91,000	66,000
Loans	(400,000)	90,000	(310,000)
Treasury bills	125,000	50,000	175,000
	(300,000)	231,000	(69,000)

The above indicates that ABC Limited has used a lot of cash this year both to reduce its loans by £90,000 and to increase its liquid resources (in the form of treasury bills) by £50,000. As a consequence, the bottom line of the analysis shows that its net debt has fallen from £300,000 at the start of the year to £69,000 at the end – a reduction of £231,000. (For businesses where borrowings are less than cash/bank balances and other liquid resources, the words 'net funds' are used in place of 'net debt'.)

USING THE CASH FLOW STATEMENT

The cash flow statement is important because it identifies the sources of cash flowing into the business and shows how they have been used. We need to read the statement in conjunction with the other two financial statements – profit and loss account and balance sheet – and also in the context of the previous year's statements. The following points should also be borne in mind:

- Like the other financial statements, the cash flow statement uses the money measurement concept. This means that only items which can be recorded in money terms can be included; also we must be aware of the effect of inflation when comparing one year with the next.

- We are looking for a reasonable cash flow from operating activities each year – this is the cash from the trading activities of the business.

- Changes in the working items of stock, debtors and creditors need to be put into context. For example, it would be a warning sign if there were large increases in these items in a business with a falling operating profit, and such a trend would put a strain on the liquidity of the business.

- The statement will show the amount of investment made during the year (eg the purchase of fixed assets). In general there should be a link between the cost of the investment and an increase in loans and/or capital – it isn't usual to finance fixed assets from short-term sources, such as a bank overdraft.

- Where there has been an increase in loans and/or capital, look to see how the cash has been used. Was it to buy fixed assets or other investments, or to finance stocks and debtors, or other purposes?

- The statement, as a whole, links profit with changes in cash. Both of these are important: without profits the business cannot generate cash (unless it sells fixed assets), and without cash it cannot pay bills as they fall due.

CONFIDENTIALITY PROCEDURES

The accounting standard FRS 1 requires that all but small companies produce a cash flow statement as a part of their financial statements. This means that cash flow statements are readily available to shareholders and interested parties either from the company itself or from Companies House (www.companieshouse.gov.uk). For sole traders, partnerships and small limited companies, as we have seen in this chapter, a cash flow statement provides useful information to the owner(s) and other interested parties.

For those involved in the preparation of cash flow statements, confidentiality procedures must be observed at all times:

– during the preparation of published accounts

– during the period after the accounts have been prepared but before they are sent to shareholders, filed at Companies House, and disclosed to the public

– for detailed information that is needed in the preparation of cash flow statements (eg the calculation of profit or loss on sale of fixed assets, corporation tax paid, dividends paid) but is not disclosed

– for all information concerned with the cash flow statements of sole traders, partnerships and small companies

CHAPTER SUMMARY

KEY TERMS

- The objective of a cash flow statement is to show an overall view of money flowing in and out of a business during an accounting period

- A cashflow statement is divided into eight sections:

  1 operating activities

  2 returns on investments and servicing of finance

  3 taxation

  4 capital expenditure and financial investment

  5 acquisitions and disposals

  6 equity dividends paid

  7 management of liquid resources

  8 financing

- FRS1 'Cash flow statements' provides a specimen layout.

- Larger limited companies are required to include a cash flow statement as a part of their published accounts. They are also useful statements for sole traders, partnerships and smaller limited companies.

cash flow statement	shows an overall view of money flowing in and out of a business during an accounting period
cash flow from operating activities	operating profit (before interest and tax), plus depreciation for the year, plus loss (or minus profit) on sale of fixed assets, together with changes in the working capital items (stock, debtors and creditors)
returns on investments and servicing of finance	interest received and paid; dividends received; dividends paid on preference shares
capital expenditure and financial investment	purchase and/or sale of fixed assets and investments
liquid resources	short term investments that are almost equal to cash
financing	issue or repayment of loans or share capital or capital
net debt	borrowings (debentures, loans and overdrafts), less cash/bank balances and other liquid resources, such as treasury bills

STUDENT
ACTIVITIES

Osborne Books is grateful to the AAT for their kind permission to use Central Assessment task material for the following activities: 9.9, 9.10, 9.11

9.1 The format, guidelines and layout for cash flow statements is set out in which Financial Reporting Statement?
(a) FRS 21
(b) FRS 11
(c) FRS 1
(d) FRS 10

9.2 Which of the following is **not** a standard heading for cash flow statements?
(a) Taxation
(b) Capital expenditure and financial investments
(c) Equity dividends paid
(d) Net profit for the year before taxation

9.3 In the reconciliation of operating activities, depreciation is added back because:
(a) It is not allowable for taxation purposes
(b) It is a non-cash expense
(c) It appears under the heading of Capital expenditure and financial investment
(d) It is a financing activity

9.4 If a business' operating profit is £50,000 and there were the following movements in the year:

Depreciation charges	£7,500
Increase in Stock	£5,000
Decrease in Debtors	£2,500
Increase in Creditors	£4,000

What is the net cash flow from operating activities for the year?
(a) £59,000 inflow
(b) £69,000 inflow
(c) £36,000 inflow
(d) £31,000 inflow

9.5 If a businesses operating loss is £6,000 and there were the following movements in the year:

Depreciation charges	£10,000
Decrease in Stock	£15,000
Increase in Debtors	£12,500
Decrease in Creditors	£14,000

What is the net cash flow from operating activities for the year?
(a) £7,500 inflow
(b) £1,500 outflow
(c) £1,500 inflow
(d) £7,500 outflow

9.6 What are the advantages to a business in producing a cash flow statement in accordance with FRS 1? Why might the creditors of a business be interested in this statement?

9.7 Radion PLC's profit and loss account for the year ended 31 December 20-3 and balance sheets for 20-2 and 20-3 were as follows:

Radion PLC Profit and Loss Account for the year to 31 December 20-3

	£000	£000
Sales turnover		652
Cost of Sales		349
GROSS PROFIT		303
Wages and salaries	107	
Depreciation Charges	30	
Administrative expenses	62	199
OPERATING PROFIT		104
Interest payable		5
PROFIT BEFORE TAX		99
Taxation		22
PROFIT AFTER TAX		77
Dividends		30
RETAINED PROFIT FOR THE YEAR		47

Radion PLC Balance Sheets as at 31 December

	20-3		20-2	
	£000	£000	£000	£000
FIXED ASSETS				
Tangibles at NBV		570		600
CURRENT ASSETS				
Stock	203		175	
Debtors	141		127	
Cash In Hand/ Bank	6			
	350		302	
CURRENT LIABILITIES				
Creditors	142		118	
Taxation	22		19	
Bank Overdraft			16	
Dividends proposed	30		20	
	194		173	
NET CURRENT ASSETS		156		129
		726		729
LONG TERM LIABILITIES				
Loans and Debentures				50
		726		679
CAPITAL AND RESERVES				
Called up Share Capital		300		300
Share Premium Account		60		60
Profit and Loss Account		366		319
		726		679

Notes to the accounts

During the year there were no purchases or sales of fixed assets made.

REQUIRED

Prepare a reconciliation statement between the cash flows from operating activities and operating profit for the year ended 31 December 20-3

Note: you are not required to prepare an actual cash flow statement.

9.8 Pratt PLC has supplied you with the following abridged profit and loss account for the year to 31 October 20-3.

	£000
Operating profit	2,520
Interest payable	168
Taxation	750
Dividends payable	540
RETAINED PROFIT	1,062

Balance Sheets as at 31 October

	20-3		20-2	
	£000	£000	£000	£000
Fixed Assets				
At cost	9,000		8,400	
Dep'n to date	1,800	7,200	1,500	6,900
Current Assets				
Stock	84		69	
Debtors	255		270	
Bank	48		30	
	387		369	
Creditors				
Trade Creditors	108		81	
Taxation	606		285	
Dividends	225		144	
	939		510	
Net Current Liabilities		552		141
		6,648		6,759
Loans		600		2,400
		6,048		4,359
CAPITAL AND RESERVES				
Called up shares		3,000		2,550
Share Premium		177		
Profit and Loss account		2,871		1,809
		6,048		4,359

Additional Information

During the year the company sold a vehicle for £8,000 cash. The vehicle had originally cost £29,000 and had been depreciated by £18,000 at the time of sale.

REQUIRED

Task 1

Prepare a statement to show the net cash flow derived from trading operations for the year to 31 October 20-3.

Task 2

Prepare a cash flow statement complying with FRS1, to highlight the change in the bank balance during the year.

9.9 Sadler PLC's profit and loss account for the year to 30 June 20-3 and balance sheets for 20-2 and 20-3 were as follows:

Sadler PLC abridged Profit and Loss Account for the year to 30 June 20-3

	£000
OPERATING PROFIT	1,100
Interest payable	(100)
PROFIT BEFORE TAX	1,000
Taxation	(200)
PROFIT AFTER TAX	800
Dividends	(400)
RETAINED PROFIT FOR THE YEAR	400

Sadler PLC Balance Sheets as at 30 June

	20-2		20-3	
FIXED ASSETS	£000	£000	£000	£000
At cost	13,600		16,300	
Depreciation to date	(8,160)	5,440	(9,660)	6,640
CURRENT ASSETS				
Stock	300		340	
Debtors	1,200		1,300	
Prepayments	100		80	
Cash in hand/ Bank	40		20	
	1,640		1,740	
CURRENT LIABILITIES				
Creditors	660		800	
Accruals	60		120	
Taxation	360		260	
Dividends proposed	400		200	
	1,480		1,380	

continued on the next page

NET CURRENT ASSETS	160	360
	5,600	7,000
LONG TERM LIABILITIES		
20% Debentures	-	(1,000)
	5,600	6,000
CAPITAL AND RESERVES		
Called up Share Capital	4,000	4,000
Share Premium Account	600	600
Profit and Loss Account	1,000	1,400
	5,600	7,000

Notes to the accounts

During the year the company sold some machinery costing £1,600,000 on which there was accumulated depreciation totalling £400,000. The net proceeds from the sale amounted to £1,400,000.

REQUIRED

Prepare a cash flow statement for Sadler PLC for the year to 30 June 20-3 together with the relevant formal notes, in accordance with FRS1.

9.10 You have been given the following information about George Ltd for the year ending 31 March 20-5.

George Ltd Profit and loss account for the year ended 31 March 20-5

	20-5		20-4	
	£000s	£000s	£000s	£000s
Turnover		2,500		1,775
Opening stock	200		100	
Purchases	1,500		1,000	
Closing stock	(210)		(200)	
Cost of sales		1,490		900
Gross profit		1,010		875
Depreciation		275		250
Other expenses		500		425
Profit on sales of fixed asset		2		–
Operating profit for the year		237		200
Interest paid		20		35
Profit before tax		217		165
Taxation on profit		25		21
Profit after tax		192		144
Proposed dividends		35		30
Retained profit		157		114

George Ltd Balance sheet as at 31 March 20-5

	20-5			20-4	
	£000s	£000s		£000s	£000s
FIXED ASSETS		330			500
CURRENT ASSETS					
Stocks	210			200	
Debtors	390			250	
Cash	–			10	
	600			460	
CURRENT LIABILITIES					
Trade creditors	150			160	
Dividends payable	35			30	
Taxation	25			21	
Bank overdraft	199			–	
	409			211	
NET CURRENT ASSETS		191			249
		521			749
Debentures					500
Long term loan		200			100
		321			149
CAPITAL AND RESERVES					
Called up share capital		40			25
Profit and loss account		281			124
		321			149

Additional information

- In May 20-4 an asset was sold which originally cost £10,000 and was purchased when the company was started up two years ago. A new asset was bought for £110,000 in June 20-4. Fixed assets are depreciated at 25 per cent of cost. The policy is to charge a full year's depreciation in the year of purchase and none in the year of sale.

- Loan interest is charged at 10% p.a. The long-term loan was increased on 1 April 20-4.

- The 5% debentures were redeemed on 1 April 20-4.

- Sales and purchases were on credit. All other expenses, including interest due, were paid in cash.

- On 1 October 20-4 15,000 new ordinary £1 shares were issued at par.

REQUIRED

Task 1
Prepare a cash flow statement.

Task 2
Prepare a reconciliation between cash flows from operating activities and operating profit.

9.11   The book-keeper of Cashedin Ltd has asked for your assistance in producing a cash flow statement for the company for the year ended 30 September 20-5 in accordance with FRS 1.

He has derived the information which is required to be included in the cash flow statement, but is not sure of the format in which it should be presented. The information is set out below:

	£000s
Operating profit before interest and tax	24
Depreciation charge for the year	318
Proceeds from sale of fixed assets	132
Issue of shares for cash	150
Cash received from new loan	200
Purchase of fixed assets for cash	358
Interest paid	218
Taxation paid	75
Dividends paid	280
Increase in stocks	251
Increase in debtors	152
Increase in creditors	165
Decrease in cash	345

REQUIRED

Using the information provided by the book-keeper, prepare a cash flow statement for Cashedin Ltd for the year ended 30 September 20-5 in accordance with the requirements of FRS 1.

Show clearly your reconciliation between operating profit and net cash inflow from operating activities.

10 INTERPRETATION OF FINANCIAL STATEMENTS

this chapter covers . . .

The profit and loss accounts and balance sheets of businesses are often interpreted by means of accounting ratios in order to assess strengths and weaknesses. Comparisons can be made between:

- consecutive years for the same business

- similar businesses in the same industry

- industry averages and the ratios for a particular business

The accounts of a business can be interpreted in the areas of profitability, liquidity, efficient use of resources and financial position.

In this chapter we examine:

- the importance of interpretation of financial statements

- the main accounting ratios and performance indicators

- a commentary on trends shown by the main accounting ratios

- how to report on the financial situation of a business

- limitations in the interpretation of accounts

NVQ PERFORMANCE CRITERIA COVERED

unit 11: DRAFTING FINANCIAL STATEMENTS

element 1

interpret financial statements

- the relationship of elements within financial statements is identified

- the relationship between elements of limited company financial statements is interpreted

- unusual features or significant issues are identified within financial statements

- valid conclusions are drawn from the information contained within financial statements

- conclusions and interpretations are clearly presented

INTERESTED PARTIES

Interpretation of financial statements is not always made by an accountant; interested parties – as we have seen in Chapter 1 (pages 14-15) – include:

- **managers** of the business, who need to make financial decisions affecting the future development of the business

- **banks**, who are being asked to lend money to finance the business

- **creditors**, who wish to assess the likelihood of receiving payment

- **customers**, who wish to be assured of continuity of supplies in the future

- **shareholders**, who wish to be assured that their investment is sound

- prospective **investors**, who wish to compare relative strengths and weaknesses

- **employees** and **trade unions**, who wish to check on the financial prospects of the business

- **government** and **government agencies**, eg Inland Revenue, HM Customs and Excise, who wish to check they are receiving the amount due to them

We saw in Chapter 1 how *Statement of principles for financial reporting* requires that financial statements provide users with details of:

- financial performance
- financial position

From the financial statements the interested party will be able to calculate the main ratios, percentages and performance indicators. By doing this, the strengths and weaknesses of the entity will be highlighted and appropriate conclusions can be drawn.

TYPES OF ACCOUNTING RATIOS & PERFORMANCE INDICATORS

The general term 'accounting ratios' is usually used to describe the calculations aspect of interpretation of financial statements. The term 'ratio' is, in fact, partly misleading because the performance indicators include percentages, time periods, as well as ratios in the strict sense of the word.

Most ratios are applicable to sole traders, partnerships and limited companies; however, as we will see, there are a number which relate specifically to the share capital and reserves of limited companies.

The main themes covered by the interpretation of accounts are:

*   **profitability** – the relationship between profit and sales turnover, assets and capital employed
*   **liquidity** – the stability of the business on a short-term basis
*   **use of resources** – the effective and efficient use of assets and liabilities
*   **financial position** – the way in which the business has been financed

MAKING USE OF ACCOUNTING RATIOS

It is important when examining a set of financial statements and calculating accounting ratios to relate them to reference points or standards. These points of reference might be to:

*   establish trends from past years, to provide a standard of comparison
*   benchmark against another similar business in the same industry
*   compare against industry averages

Above all, it is important to understand the relationships between ratios: one ratio may give an indication of the state of the business, but this needs to be supported by other ratios. Ratios can indicate symptoms, but the cause will then need to be investigated.

Another use of ratios is to estimate forward the likely profit or balance sheet of a business. For example, it might be assumed that the same gross profit percentage as last year will also apply next year; thus, given an estimated increase in sales, it is a simple matter to estimate gross profit. In a similar way, by making use of ratios, net profit and the balance sheet can be forecast.

Whilst all of the ratios calculated in this chapter use figures from the profit and loss account and balance sheet, the cash flow statement is important too. It assists in confirming the views shown by the accounting ratios and provides further evidence of the position.

ACCOUNTING RATIOS FOR PROFITABILITY

■   Study the table and financial statements on the next two pages. They show the ways in which the profitability of a business is assessed.

■   Then read the section entitled 'Profitability' which follows.

■   Note that the accounting ratios from the financial statements of Wyvern Trading Company Limited are calculated and discussed in the Case Study on pages 284-289.

PROFITABILITY

Gross profit/sales percentage = $\dfrac{\text{Gross profit}}{\text{Sales}} \times \dfrac{100}{1}$

Expense/sales percentage = $\dfrac{\text{Specified expense}}{\text{Sales}} \times \dfrac{100}{1}$

Operating profit/sales percentage = $\dfrac{\text{Operating profit*}}{\text{Sales}} \times \dfrac{100}{1}$

* profit before interest and tax

Net profit/sales percentage = $\dfrac{\text{Net profit}}{\text{Sales}} \times \dfrac{100}{1}$

Return on capital employed = $\dfrac{\text{Operating profit}}{\text{Capital employed*}} \times \dfrac{100}{1}$

* share capital + reserves + long-term liabilities

Return on equity = $\dfrac{\text{Profit after tax} - \text{preference dividend (if any)}}{\text{Equity*}} \times \dfrac{100}{1}$

* ordinary share capital + reserves

Earnings per share = $\dfrac{\text{Profit after tax} - \text{preference dividend (if any)}}{\text{Number of issued ordinary shares}}$

Wyvern Trading Company Limited
TRADING AND PROFIT AND LOSS ACCOUNT
for the year ended 31 December 2002

	£000s	£000s
Sales		1,430
Opening stock	200	
Purchases	1,000	
	1,200	
Less Closing stock	240	
Cost of sales		960
Gross profit		470
Less overheads:		
Selling expenses	150	
Administration expenses	140	
		290
Operating profit		180
Less: Debenture interest		10
Net profit for year before taxation		170
Less: Corporation tax		50
Profit for year after taxation		120
Less:		
preference dividend paid	25	
ordinary dividend proposed	75	
		100
Retained profit for the year		20
Add balance of retained profits at beginning of year		180
Balance of retained profits at end of year		200

BALANCE SHEET (extract)

Capital employed (share capital + reserves + long-term liabilities)	1,550
Equity (ordinary share capital + reserves)	1,200
Number of issued ordinary shares (000s)	1,000

Note: Items used in the ratios on the previous page are shown in bold type on a grey background

PROFITABILITY

One of the main objectives of a business is to make a profit. Profitability ratios examine the relationship between profit and sales turnover, assets and capital employed. Before calculating the profitability ratios, it is important to read the profit and loss account in order to review the figures.

The key profitability ratios are illustrated on page 271. We will be calculating and discussing the accounting ratios from these figures in the Case Study on pages 284-289.

gross profit percentage

$$\frac{Gross\ profit}{Sales} \times \frac{100}{1}$$

This expresses, as a percentage, the gross profit (sales minus cost of sales) in relation to sales. For example, a gross profit percentage of 20 per cent means that for every £100 of sales made, the gross profit is £20.

The gross profit percentage should be similar from year-to-year for the same business. It will vary between organisations in different areas of business, eg the gross profit percentage on jewellery is considerably higher than that on food. A significant change from one year to the next, particularly a fall in the percentage, requires investigation into the buying and selling prices.

Gross profit percentage, and also net profit percentage (see next page), need to be considered in context. For example, a supermarket may well have a lower gross profit percentage than a small corner shop but, because of the supermarket's much higher turnover, the amount of profit will be much higher. Whatever the type of business, gross profit – both as an amount and a percentage – needs to be sufficient to cover the overheads (expenses), and then to give an acceptable return on capital.

expense/sales percentage

$$\frac{Specified\ expense}{Sales} \times \frac{100}{1}$$

A large expense or overhead item can be expressed as a percentage of sales: for example, the relationship between advertising and sales might be found to be 10 per cent in one year, but 20 per cent the next year. This could indicate that an increase in advertising had failed to produce a proportionate increase in sales.

Note that each expense falls into one of three categories of cost:

1   fixed costs, or

2   variable costs, or

3   semi-variable costs

Fixed costs remain constant despite other changes. Variable costs alter with changed circumstances, such as increased output or sales. Semi-variable costs combine both a fixed and a variable element, eg hire of a car at a basic (fixed) cost, with a (variable) cost per mile.

It is important to appreciate the nature of costs when interpreting accounts: for example, if sales this year are twice last year's figure, not all expenses will have doubled.

operating profit percentage

$$\frac{Operating\ profit^*}{Sales} \times \frac{100}{1}$$

* profit before interest and tax

Net profit is calculated after loan and bank interest has been charged to profit and loss account. Thus it may be distorted when comparisons are made between two different businesses where one is heavily financed by means of loans, and the other is financed by owner's capital. The solution is to calculate the operating profit percentage which uses profit before interest and tax.

net profit percentage

$$\frac{Net\ profit}{Sales} \times \frac{100}{1}$$

As with gross profit percentage, the net profit percentage should be similar from year-to-year for the same business, and should also be comparable with other firms in the same line of business. Net profit percentage should, ideally, increase from year-to-year, which indicates that the profit and loss account costs are being kept under control. Any significant fall should be investigated to see if it has been caused by

• a fall in gross profit percentage

• and/or an increase in one particular expense, eg wages and salaries, advertising, etc

return on capital employed (ROCE)

Return on capital employed expresses the profit of a business in relation to the capital employed. The percentage return is best thought of in relation to other investments, eg a bank or building society might offer a return of five per cent. A person running a business is investing a sum of money in that business, and the profit is the return that is achieved on that investment. However, it should be noted that the risks in running a business are considerably greater than depositing the money with a bank or building society, and an additional return to allow for the extra risk is needed.

For limited companies, the calculation of return on capital employed must take note of their different methods of financing. It is necessary to distinguish between the ordinary shareholders' investment (the equity) and the capital employed by the company, which includes preference shares and debentures/long-term loans.

The calculation for capital employed is:

	Ordinary share capital
add	*Reserves (capital and revenue)*
equals	*Equity*
add	*Preference share capital*
add	*Debentures/long-term loans*
equals	*Capital Employed*

The reason for including preference shares and debentures/long-term loans in the capital employed is that the company has the use of the money from these contributors for the foreseeable future, or certainly for a fixed time period.

The calculation of return on capital employed is:

$$\frac{Operating\ profit^*}{Capital\ employed^{**}} \quad \times \quad \frac{100}{1}$$

* *profit before interest and tax*

** *ordinary share capital + reserves + preference share capital + debentures/long-term loans*

return on equity

$$\frac{\text{Profit after tax} - \text{preference dividend (if any)}}{\text{Equity*}} \quad x \quad \frac{100}{1}$$

ordinary share capital + reserves

Whilst return on capital employed looks at the overall return on the long-term sources of finance (the capital employed), return on equity focuses on the return for the ordinary shareholders. Also known as 'return on ordinary shareholders' equity', return on equity indicates the return the company is making on their funds, ie ordinary shares and reserves. The decision as to whether they remain as ordinary shareholders is primarily whether they could get a better return elsewhere.

Note that, when calculating return on equity, use the profit after tax and preference dividends (if any), ie the amount of profit available to the ordinary shareholders after all other parties (corporation tax, preference share dividend) have been deducted.

earnings per share

$$\frac{\text{Profit after tax} - \text{preference dividend (if any)}}{\text{Number of issued ordinary shares}}$$

Earnings per share (or EPS) measures the amount of profit – usually expressed in pence – earned by each ordinary share, after corporation tax and preference dividends. Comparisons can be made with previous years to provide a basis for assessing the company's performance.

See also FRS 14 'Earnings per share' on page 226.

ACCOUNTING RATIOS FOR LIQUIDITY, USE OF RESOURCES AND FINANCIAL POSITION

■ Study the ratios table and financial statements on the next two pages. They show the ways in which the liquidity, use of resources, and financial position of a business are assessed.

■ Then read the sections which follow.

■ Note that the accounting ratios from the financial statements of Wyvern Trading Company Limited are calculated and discussed in the Case Study on pages 284 - 289.

LIQUIDITY

Working capital ratio =
(or current ratio)

$$\frac{\text{Current assets}}{\text{Current liabilities}}$$

Liquid capital ratio =
(or quick ratio/acid test)

$$\frac{\text{Current assets} - \text{stock}}{\text{Current liabilities}}$$

USE OF RESOURCES

Stock turnover (days) =

$$\frac{\text{Stock}}{\text{Cost of sales}} \times 365 \text{ days}$$

Debtors' collection period (days) =

$$\frac{\text{Debtors}}{\text{Sales}} \times 365 \text{ days}$$

Creditors' payment period (days) =

$$\frac{\text{Creditors}}{\text{Purchases}} \times 365 \text{ days}$$

Asset turnover ratio =

$$\frac{\text{Sales}}{\text{Net assets*}}$$

* fixed assets + current assets – current liabilities – long-term liabilities

FINANCIAL POSITION

Interest cover =

$$\frac{\text{Operating profit}}{\text{Interest paid}}$$

Gearing =

$$\frac{\text{Debt (long-term loans, including preference shares)}}{\text{Capital employed*}} \times \frac{100}{1}$$

* ordinary share capital + reserves + preference share capital + long-term loans

alternative calculation:

$$\frac{\text{Debt}}{\text{Equity*}} \times \frac{100}{1}$$

* ordinary share capital + reserves

Wyvern Trading Company Limited
BALANCE SHEET
as at 31 December 2002

Fixed Assets	Cost	Dep'n to date	Net
	£000s	£000s	£000s
Premises	1,100	250	850
Fixtures and fittings	300	120	180
Vehicles	350	100	250
	1,750	470	1,280

Current Assets		
Stock		240
Debtors		150
Bank/cash		135
		525

Less Current Liabilities		
Creditors	130	
Proposed ordinary dividend	75	
Corporation tax	50	
		255

Net Current Assets	270
	1,550

Less Long-term Liabilities	
10% Debentures	100
NET ASSETS	1,450

FINANCED BY
Authorised and Issued Share Capital

1,000,000 ordinary shares of £1 each, fully paid	1,000
250,000 10% preference shares of £1 each, fully paid	250
	1,250

Revenue Reserve

Profit and loss account	200
SHAREHOLDERS' FUNDS	1,450

PROFIT AND LOSS ACCOUNT (extract)

Cost of sales	960
Sales	1,430
Purchases	1,000

Note: Items used in ratios are shown in bold type with a grey background.

LIQUIDITY

Liquidity ratios measure the financial stability of a business, ie the ability of a business to pay its way on a short-term basis. Here we focus our attention on the current assets and current liabilities sections of the balance sheet.

The key liquidity ratios are shown on page 277; these are linked to the balance sheet of Wyvern Trading Company Limited. The ratios are calculated and discussed in the Case Study on pages 284 - 289.

working capital

Working capital = Current assets – Current liabilities

Working capital (often called *net current assets*) is needed by all businesses in order to finance day-to-day trading activities. Sufficient working capital enables a business to hold adequate stocks, allow a measure of credit to its customers (debtors), and to pay its suppliers (creditors) as payments fall due.

working capital ratio (or current ratio)

Working capital ratio = Current assets : Current liabilities

Working capital ratio uses figures from the balance sheet and measures the relationship between current assets and current liabilities. Although there is no ideal working capital ratio, an acceptable ratio is about 2:1, ie £2 of current assets to every £1 of current liabilities. However, a business in the retail trade may be able to work with a lower ratio, eg 1.5:1 or even less, because it deals mainly in sales for cash and so does not have a large figure for debtors. A working capital ratio can be too high: if it is above 3:1 an investigation of the make-up of current assets and current liabilities is needed: eg the business may have too much stock, too many debtors, or too much cash at the bank, or even too few creditors.

Note that the current ratio can also be expressed as a percentage. For example, a current ratio of 2:1 is the same as 200 per cent.

liquid capital ratio (or quick ratio, or acid test)

Liquid capital ratio = $\dfrac{\text{Current assets} - \text{stock}}{\text{Current liabilities}}$

The liquid capital ratio uses the current assets and current liabilities from the balance sheet, but stock is omitted. This is because stock is the least liquid current asset: it has to be sold, turned into debtors, and then the cash has to be collected from the debtors. Also, some of the stock included in the balance sheet figure may be unsaleable or obsolete. Thus the liquid ratio provides a direct comparison between debtors/cash/bank and short-term liabilities. The balance between liquid assets, that is debtors and cash/bank, and current liabilities should, ideally, be about 1:1, ie £1 of liquid assets to each £1 of current liabilities. At this ratio a business is expected to be able to pay its current liabilities from its liquid assets; a figure below 1:1, eg 0.75:1, indicates that the firm would have difficulty in meeting pressing demands from creditors. However, as with the working capital ratio, some businesses are able to operate with a lower liquid ratio than others.

The liquid capital ratio can also be expressed as a percentage, eg 1:1 is the same as 100%.

USE OF RESOURCES

Use of resources measures how efficiently the management controls the current aspects of the business – principally stock, debtors and creditors. Like all accounting ratios, comparison needs to be made either with figures for the previous year, or with a similar firm.

stock turnover

$$\frac{Stock}{Cost\ of\ sales} \quad x \quad 365\ days$$

Stock turnover is the number of days' stock held on average. This figure will depend on the type of goods sold by the business. For example, a market trader selling fresh flowers, who finishes each day when sold out, will have a stock turnover of one day. By contrast, a jewellery shop – because it may hold large stocks of jewellery – will have a much slower stock turnover, perhaps sixty or ninety days, or longer. Nevertheless, it is important for a business to keep its stock days as short as possible, subject to being able to meet the needs of most of its customers. A business which is improving in efficiency will generally have a quicker stock turnover comparing one year with the previous one, or with the stock turnover of similar businesses.

Stock turnover can also be expressed as number of times per year:

$$Stock\ turnover\ (times\ per\ year) \quad = \quad \frac{Cost\ of\ sales}{Stock}$$

A stock turnover of, say, twelve times a year means that about thirty days' stock is held. Note that stock turnover can only be calculated where a business buys and sells goods; it cannot be used for a business that provides a service.

debtors' collection period

$$\frac{Debtors}{Sales} \quad x \quad 365 \; days$$

This calculation shows how many days, on average, debtors take to pay for goods sold to them by the business. The debt collection time can be compared with that for the previous year, or with that of a similar business. In the UK, most debtors should make payment within about 30 days; however, sales made abroad will take longer for the proceeds to be received. A comparison from year-to-year of the collection period is a measure of the firm's efficiency at collecting the money that is due to it and we are looking for some reduction in debtor days over time. Ideally debtor days should be shorter than creditor days (see below): this indicates that money is being received from debtors before it is paid out to creditors.

creditors' payment period

$$\frac{Creditors}{Purchases} \quad x \quad 365 \; days$$

This calculation is the opposite aspect to that of debtors: here we are measuring the speed it takes to pay creditors. While creditors can be a useful temporary source of finance, delaying payment too long may cause problems. This ratio is most appropriate for businesses that buy and sell goods; it cannot be used for a business that provides a service; it is also difficult to interpret when a business buys in some goods and, at the same time, provides a service, eg an hotel. Generally, though, we would expect to see the creditor days period longer than the debtor days, ie money is being received from debtors before it is paid out to creditors. We would also be looking for a similar figure for creditor days from one year to the next: this would indicate a stable business.

Note that there is invariably an inconsistency in calculating both debtors' collection and creditors' payment periods: the figures for debtors and creditors on the balance sheet include VAT, while sales and purchases from the trading account exclude VAT. Strictly, therefore, we are not comparing like with like; however, the comparison should be made with reference to the previous year, or a similar company, calculated on the same basis from year-to-year.

asset turnover ratio

$$\frac{Sales}{Net \; assets^*}$$

* fixed assets + current assets – current liabilities – long-term liabilities

This ratio measures the efficiency of the use of net assets in generating sales. An increasing ratio from one year to the next indicates greater efficiency. A fall in the ratio may be caused either by a decrease in sales, or an increase in net assets – perhaps caused by the purchase or revaluation of fixed assets, or increased stockholding, or increased debtors as a result of poor credit control.

Different types of businesses will have very different asset turnover ratios. For example a supermarket, with high sales and relatively few assets, will have a very high figure; by contrast, an engineering business, with lower sales and a substantial investment in fixed and current assets, will have a much lower figure.

FINANCIAL POSITION

Financial position measures the strength and long-term financing of the business. Two ratios are calculated – interest cover and gearing. Interest cover considers the ability of the business to meet (or cover) its interest payments from its operating profit; gearing focuses on the balance in the long-term funding of the business between monies from loan providers and monies from ordinary shareholders.

Both ratios look at aspects of loan finance and it is important to remember that both interest and loan repayments must be made on time; if they are not the loan provider may well be able to seek payment by forcing the company to sell assets and, in the worst case, may well be able to force the company into liquidation.

interest cover

$$\frac{Operating\ profit}{Interest}$$

The interest cover ratio, linked closely to gearing, considers the safety margin (or cover) of profit over the interest payable by a business. For example, if the operating profit of a business was £10,000, and interest payable was £5,000, this would give interest cover of two times, which is a low figure. If the interest was £1,000, this would give interest cover of ten times which is a higher and much more acceptable figure. Thus, the conclusion to draw is that the higher the interest cover, the better (although there is an argument for having some debt).

gearing

$$\frac{Debt\ (long\text{-}term\ loans\ including\ any\ preference\ shares)}{Capital\ employed^*} \times \frac{100}{1}$$

* ordinary share capital + reserves + preference share capital + long-term loans

Whilst the liquidity ratios seen earlier focus on whether the business can pay its way in the short-term, gearing is concerned with long-term financial stability. Here we measure how much of the business is financed by debt (including any preference shares) against capital employed (debt + equity), defined above. The higher the gearing percentage, the less secure will be the financing of the business and, therefore, the future of the business. This is because debt is costly in terms of interest payments (particularly if interest rates are variable). It is difficult to set a standard for an acceptable gearing ratio: in general terms most investors (or lenders) would not wish to see a gearing percentage of greater than 50%.

Gearing can also be expressed as a ratio, ie debt:equity. Thus a gearing percentage of 50% is a ratio of 0.5:1.

An alternative calculation for gearing is to measure debt in relation to the equity of the business:

$$\frac{Debt}{Equity^*} \times \frac{100}{1}$$

* ordinary share capital + reserves

Usually in assessments and questions, either calculation is acceptable; both methods use similar components:

either $\dfrac{Debt}{Capital\ employed}$ or $\dfrac{Debt}{Equity}$

The first calculation will always give a lower gearing percentage than the second when using the same figures. For example:

$$\frac{£50,000\ (debt)}{£50,000\ (debt) + £100,000\ (equity)} \quad = 33\%$$

$$\frac{£50,000\ (debt)}{£100,000\ (equity)} \quad = 50\%$$

When making comparisons from one year to the next, or between different companies, it is important to be consistent in the way in which gearing is calculated in order for appropriate conclusions to be drawn.

INTERPRETATION OF ACCOUNTS

Interpretation of accounts is much more than a mechanical process of calculating a number of ratios. It involves the analysis of the relationships between the figures in the financial statement and the presentation of the information gathered in a meaningful way to interested parties.

There now follow two Case Studies which put into practice the analytical approach explained earlier in this chapter:

1 **Wyvern Trading Company Limited**

    In the first we look at limited company financial statements from the point of view of a potential investor (for clarity, one year's statements are given although, in practice, more than one year would be used to establish a trend). The comments given indicate what should be looked for when analysing and interpreting a set of financial statements.

2 **Surgdressings Limited**

    In the second we consider financial statements from the point of view of a potential buyer of products from the company. The interpretation seeks to assess the risk of switching to the supplier, and to make comparisons with industry average figures.

CASE STUDY

ACCOUNTING RATIOS: WYVERN TRADING COMPANY LIMITED

situation

The following are the financial statements of Wyvern Trading Company Limited. The business trades in office supplies and sells to the public through its three retail shops in the Wyvern area; it also delivers direct to businesses in the area from its modern warehouse on a local business park.

The financial statements and accounting ratios are to be considered from the viewpoint of a potential investor.

solution

We will now analyse the accounts from the point of view of a potential investor. All figures shown are in £000s. The analysis starts on page 287.

Wyvern Trading Company Limited
TRADING AND PROFIT AND LOSS ACCOUNT
for the year ended 31 December 2002

	£000s	£000s
Sales		1,430
Opening stock	200	
Purchases	1,000	
	1,200	
Less Closing stock	240	
Cost of sales		960
Gross profit		470
Less overheads:		
Selling expenses	150	
Administration expenses	140	
		290
Operating profit		180
Less: Debenture interest		10
Net profit for year before taxation		170
Less: Corporation tax		50
Profit for year after taxation		120
Less:		
preference dividend paid	25	
ordinary dividend proposed	75	
		100
Retained profit for the year		20
Add balance of retained profits at beginning of year		180
Balance of retained profits at end of year		200

Wyvern Trading Company Limited
BALANCE SHEET as at 31 December 2002

Fixed Assets	Cost £000s	Dep'n to date £000s	Net £000s
Premises	1,100	250	850
Fixtures and fittings	300	120	180
Vehicles	350	100	250
	1,750	470	1,280
Current Assets			
Stock		240	
Debtors		150	
Bank/cash		135	
		525	
Less Current Liabilities			
Creditors	130		
Proposed ordinary dividend	75		
Corporation tax	50		
		255	
Net Current Assets			270
			1,550
Less Long-term Liabilities			
10% debentures			100
NET ASSETS			1,450

FINANCED BY	
Authorised and Issued Share Capital	
1,000,000 ordinary shares of £1 each, fully paid	1,000
250,000 10% preference shares of £1 each, fully paid	250
	1,250
Revenue Reserve	
Profit and loss account	200
SHAREHOLDERS' FUNDS	1,450

PROFITABILITY

Gross profit/sales percentage

$$\frac{£470}{£1,430} \quad x \quad \frac{100}{1} \qquad = 32.87\%$$

Selling expenses to sales

$$\frac{£150}{£1,430} \quad x \quad \frac{100}{1} \qquad = 10.49\%$$

Operating profit/sales percentage

$$\frac{£180}{£1,430} \quad x \quad \frac{100}{1} \qquad = 12.59\%$$

Net profit/sales percentage

$$\frac{£170}{£1,430} \quad x \quad \frac{100}{1} \qquad = 11.89\%$$

Return on capital employed

$$\frac{£180}{£1,000 + £250 + £200 + £100} \quad x \quad \frac{100}{1} \qquad = 11.61\%$$

Return on equity

$$\frac{£170 - £25}{£1,000 + £200} \quad x \quad \frac{100}{1} \qquad = 12.08\%$$

Earnings per share

$$\frac{£120 - £25}{1,000} \qquad\qquad = 9.5\text{p per ordinary share}$$

The gross and net profit percentages seem to be acceptable figures for the type of business, although comparisons should be made with those of the previous accounting period. A business should always aim at least to hold its percentages and, ideally, to make a small improvement. A significant fall in the percentages may indicate a poor buying policy, poor pricing (perhaps caused by competition), and the causes should be investigated.

Selling expenses seem to be quite a high percentage of sales. As these are likely to be a relatively fixed cost, it would seem that the business could increase sales turnover without a corresponding increase in sales expenses.

The small difference between net profit percentage and operating profit percentage indicates that finance costs are relatively low.

Return on capital employed is satisfactory, but could be better. At 11.61% it is less than two percentage points above the ten per cent cost of the preference shares and debentures (ignoring the taxation advantages of issuing debentures). Return on equity is better at 12.08%, but a potential shareholder needs to compare this with the returns available elsewhere.

The figure for earnings per share indicates that the company is not highly profitable for its shareholders; potential shareholders will be looking for increases in this figure.

LIQUIDITY
Working capital (or current) ratio

$$\frac{£525}{£255} \qquad = 2.06{:}1$$

Liquid capital ratio (or quick ratio/acid test)

$$\frac{(£525 - £240)}{£255} \qquad = 1.12{:}1$$

The working capital and liquid capital ratios are excellent: they are slightly higher than the expected 'norms' of 2:1 and 1:1 respectively (although many companies operate successfully with lower ratios); however, they are not too high which would be an indication of inefficient use of assets.

These two ratios indicate that the company is very solvent, with no short-term liquidity problems.

ASSET UTILISATION
Stock turnover

$$\frac{£240 \times 365}{£960} \qquad = \text{91 days (or 4 times per year)}$$

Debtors' collection period

$$\frac{£150 \times 365}{£1,430} \qquad = \text{38 days}$$

Creditors' payment period

$$\frac{£130 \times 365}{£1,000} \qquad = \text{47 days}$$

Asset turnover ratio

$$\frac{£1,430}{£1,450^{*}} \qquad = 0.99{:}1$$

* fixed assets + current assets – current liabilities – long-term liabilities

This group of ratios shows the main weakness of the company: not enough business is passing through for the size of the company.

Stock turnover is very low for an office supplies business: the stock is turning over only every 91 days – surely it should be faster than this?

Debtors' collection period is acceptable on the face of it – 30 days would be better – but quite a volume of the sales will be made through the retail outlets in cash. This amount should, if known, be deducted from the sales turnover before calculating the debtors' collection period: thus the collection period is, in reality, longer than that calculated.

Creditors' payment period is quite leisurely for this type of business – long delays could cause problems with suppliers in the future.

The asset turnover ratio says it all: this type of business should be able to obtain a much better figure:

- either, sales need to be increased using the same net assets
- or, sales need to be maintained, but net assets reduced

FINANCIAL POSITION

Interest cover

$$\frac{£180}{£10} = 18 \text{ times}$$

Gearing

$$\frac{£250 + £100}{£1,000 + £200 + £250 + £100} \times \frac{100}{1} = 23\% \text{ or } 0.23{:}1$$

The interest cover figure of 18 is very high and shows that the company has no problems in paying interest.

The gearing percentage is low: anything up to 50% (0.5:1) could be seen. With a low figure of 23% this indicates that the company could borrow more money if it wished to finance, say, expansion plans (there are plenty of fixed assets for a lender – such as a bank – to take as security for a loan). At the present level of gearing there is only a low risk to potential investors.

Note that the alternative calculation for gearing is:

$$\frac{£250 + £100}{£1,000 + £200} \times \frac{100}{1} = 29\% \text{ or } 0.29{:}1$$

CONCLUSION

This appears to be a profitable business, although there may be some scope for cutting down somewhat on the profit and loss account selling expenses (administration expenses could be looked at too). The business offers a reasonable return on capital, although things could be improved.

The company is solvent and has good working capital and liquid capital ratios. Interest cover is high and gearing is low – a good sign during times of variable interest rates.

The main area of weakness is in asset utilisation. It appears that the company could do much to reduce the days for stock turnover and the debtors' collection period; at the same time creditors could be paid faster. Asset turnover is very low for this type of business and it does seem that there is much scope for expansion within the structure of the existing company. As the benefits of expansion flow through to the financial statements, the earnings per share figure should show an improvement from its present modest amount. However, a potential investor will need to consider if the directors have the ability to focus on the weaknesses shown by the ratio analysis and to take steps to improve the business.

ACCOUNTING RATIOS: ASSESSING A SUPPLIER – SURGDRESSINGS LIMITED

situation

You work for the Wyvern Hospital Trust. The Trust has been approached by a supplier of surgical dressings, Surgdressings Limited, which is offering its products at advantageous prices.

The Surgical Director of Wyvern Hospital Trust is satisfied with the quality and suitability of the products offered and the Finance Director, your boss, has obtained the latest financial statements from the company which are set out on the next page.

You have been asked to prepare a report for the Finance Director recommending whether or not to use Surgdressings Limited as a supplier of surgical dressings to the Trust. You are to use the information contained in the financial statements of Surgdressings Limited and the industry averages supplied. Included in your report should be:

- comments on the company's
  - profitability
  - liquidity
  - financial position

- consideration of how the company has changed over the two years

- comparison with the industry as a whole

The report should include calculation of the following ratios for the two years:
- return on capital employed
- net profit percentage
- quick ratio/acid test
- gearing

The relevant industry average ratios are as follows:

	2001	2000
Return on capital employed	11.3%	11.1%
Net profit percentage	16.4%	16.2%
Quick ratio/acid test	1.0:1	0.9:1
Gearing (debt/capital employed)	33%	35%

SURGDRESSINGS LIMITED
Summary profit and loss accounts for the year ended 31 December

	2001	2000
	£000s	£000s
Turnover	4,600	4,300
Cost of sales	2,245	2,135
Gross profit	2,355	2,165
Overheads	1,582	1,491
Net profit before tax	773	674

Summary balance sheets as at 31 December

	2001		2000	
	£000s	£000s	£000s	£000s
Fixed Assets		5,534		6,347
Current Assets				
Stock	566		544	
Debtors	655		597	
Bank	228		104	
	1,449		1,245	
Current Liabilities				
Trade creditors	572		504	
Taxation	242		288	
	814		792	
Net Current Assets		635		453
Long-term loan		(1,824)		(3,210)
NET ASSETS		4,345		3,590
Share capital (ordinary shares)		2,300		2,000
Share premium		670		450
Profit and loss account		1,375		1,140
SHAREHOLDERS' FUNDS		4,345		3,590

solution

REPORT

To: Finance Director, Wyvern Hospital Trust

From: A Student

Date: today's date

Re: Analysis of Surgdressings Limited's financial statements 2000/2001

Introduction

The purpose of this report is to analyse the financial statements of Surgdressings Limited for 2000 and 2001 to determine whether the Trust should use the company as a supplier of surgical dressings.

Calculation of ratios

The following ratios have been calculated:

	2001			2000	
	company	industry average	company		industry average
Return on capital employed	$\frac{773}{6,169}$ =12.5%	11.3%	$\frac{674}{6,800}$ = 9.9%		11.1%
Net profit percentage	$\frac{773}{4,600}$ =16.8%	16.4%	$\frac{674}{4,300}$ = 15.7%		16.2%
Quick ratio/acid test	$\frac{883}{814}$ = 1.1:1	1.0:1	$\frac{701}{792}$ = 0.9:1		0.9:1
Gearing	$\frac{1,824}{6,169}$ = 30%	33%	$\frac{3,210}{6,800}$ = 47%		35%

Comment and analysis

■ In terms of profitability, the company has improved from 2000 to 2001.

■ Return on capital employed has increased from 15.7% to 16.8% – this means that the company is generating more profit in 2001 from the available capital employed than it did in 2000. The company has gone from being below the industry average in 2000 to being better than the average in 2001.

■ Net profit percentage has also improved, increasing from 15.7% in 2000 to 16.8% in 2001. This means that the company is generating more profit from sales in 2001 than it did in the previous year. In 2000 the company was below the industry average but in 2001 it is better than the average. As it is now performing better than the average, this suggests that it may continue to be successful in the future.

- The liquidity of the company has improved during the year.

- The quick ratio (or acid test) has gone up from 0.9:1 to 1.1:1. This indicates that the liquid assets, ie debtors and stock, are greater than current liabilities in 2001. The company has gone from being the same as the industry average in 2000 to better than average in 2001. Thus, in 2001, Surgdressings Limited is more liquid than the average business in the industry.

- The financial position of the company has improved considerably during the year.

- In 2000 the gearing ratio was a high 47%. In 2001 the percentage of debt finance to capital employed declined to 30%. A high gearing ratio is often seen as a risk to a company's long-term survival: in times of economic downturn, when profits fall, a high-geared company will have increasing difficulty in making interest payments on debt – in extreme cases, a company could be forced into liquidation. In 2000, the gearing ratio of Surgdressings Limited was much higher than the industry average, making it relatively more risky than the average of companies in the industry. The much improved ratio in 2001 is now below the industry average, making it less risky than the average of other companies in the industry.

CONCLUSION

- Based solely on the information provided in the financial statements of Surgdressings Limited and the ratios calculated, it is recommended that the company is used by the Trust as a supplier of surgical dressings.

- The company has increasing profitability, liquidity and financial position in 2001 when compared with 2000. It also compares favourably with other companies in the same industry and appears to present a lower risk than the average of the sector.

LIMITATIONS IN THE INTERPRETATION OF ACCOUNTS

Although accounting ratios can usefully highlight strengths and weaknesses, they should always be considered as a part of the overall assessment of a business, rather than as a whole. We have already seen the need to place ratios in context and relate them to a reference point or standard. The limitations of ratio analysis should always be borne in mind.

retrospective nature of accounting ratios

Accounting ratios are usually retrospective, based on previous performance and conditions prevailing in the past. They may not necessarily be valid for making forward projections: for example, a large customer may become insolvent, so threatening the business with a bad debt, and also reducing sales in the future.

differences in accounting policies

When the financial statements of a business are compared, either with previous years' figures, or with figures from a similar business, there is a danger that the comparative statements are not drawn up on the same basis as those currently being worked on. Different accounting policies, in respect of depreciation and stock valuation for instance, may well result in distortion and invalid comparisons.

inflation

Inflation may prove a problem, as most financial statements are prepared on an historic cost basis, that is, assets and liabilities are recorded at their original cost. As a result, comparison of figures from one year to the next may be difficult. In countries where inflation is running at high levels any form of comparison becomes practically meaningless.

reliance on standards

We have already mentioned guideline standards for some accounting ratios, for instance 2:1 for the working capital ratio. There is a danger of relying too heavily on such suggested standards, and ignoring other factors in the balance sheet. An example of this would be to criticise a business for having a low current ratio when the business sells the majority of its goods for cash and consequently has a very low debtors figure: this would in fact be the case with many well-known and successful retail companies.

other considerations

Economic: The general economic climate and the effect this may have on the nature of the business, eg in an economic downturn retailers are usually the first to suffer, whereas manufacturers feel the effects later.

State of the business: The chairman's report for a limited company should be read in conjunction with the financial statements (including the cash flow statement) to ascertain an overall view of the state of the business. Of great importance are the products of the company and their stage in the product life cycle, eg is a car manufacturer relying on old models, or is there an up-to-date product range which appeals to buyers?

Comparing like with like: Before making comparisons between 'similar' businesses, we need to ensure that we are comparing 'like with like'. Differences, such as the acquisition of assets – renting premises compared with ownership, leasing vehicles compared with ownership – will affect the profitability of the business and the structure of the balance sheet; likewise, the long-term financing of a business – the balance between debt finance and equity finance – will also have an effect.

CHAPTER SUMMARY

KEY TERMS

> **Tutorial note**
>
> Accounting ratios are summarised in this chapter on pages 271 and 277.

- Accounting ratios are numerical values – percentages, time periods, ratios – extracted from the financial statements of businesses.

- Accounting ratios can be used to measure:
  - profitability
  - liquidity
  - use of resources
  - financial position

- Comparisons need to be made with previous financial statements, or those of similar companies.

- There are a number of limitations to be borne in mind when drawing conclusions from accounting ratios:
  - retrospective nature, based on past performance
  - differences in accounting policies
  - effects of inflation when comparing year-to-year
  - reliance on standards
  - economic and other factors

profitability

measures the relationship between profit and sales turnover, assets and capital employed; ratios include:
- gross profit percentage
- expenses/sales percentage
- operating profit percentage
- net profit percentage
- return on capital employed
- return on equity
- earnings per share

liquidity

measures the financial stability of a business, ie the ability of a business to pay its way on a short-term basis; ratios include:
- working capital (current) ratio
- liquid capital ratio (or quick ratio/acid test)

use of resources
measures how efficiently the management controls the current aspects of the business – principally stock, debtors and creditors; ratios include:

• stock turnover

• debtors' collection period

• creditors' payment period

• asset turnover ratio

financial position
measures the strength and long-term financing of the business; ratios include:

• gearing

• interest cover

STUDENT ACTIVITIES

Osborne Books is grateful to the AAT for their kind permission to use Central Assessment task material for the following activities: 10.9, 10.10

10.1 The net profit/sales percentage measures which of the following?

(a) Liquidity

(b) Return on investment

(c) Risk

(d) Profitability

10.2 The working capital ratio measures which of the following?

(a) Profitability

(b) Use of assets

(c) Liquidity

(d) Return on investment

10.3 The rate of stock turnover in a trading period, is best described by which of the following definitions?

(a) The value of stock at the start of the year

(b) The value of stock at the end of the year

(c) The number of times that the average level of stock has been sold

(d) The average amount of time that stock has been held throughout the year

10.4 Which of the following headings best describes and measures gearing?

(a) Financial position (risk)

(b) Liquidity

(c) Profitability

(d) Performance / efficiency

10.5 Below is the balance sheet of Matlock PLC for the year ended 30 September 20-3

FIXED ASSETS	£000	£000
At NBV		500
CURRENT ASSETS		
Stock	150	
Debtors	95	
Cash in Hand	5	
	250	
CREDITORS: Amounts falling due within one year		
Creditors	175	
Bank Overdraft	25	
	200	
NET CURRENT ASSETS		50
Total assets less current liabilities		550
CREDITORS: Amounts falling due after more than one year		
Bank Loan		100
		450
CAPITAL AND RESERVES		
Called up Ordinary Share Capital		300
Share Premium Account		50
Profit and Loss Account		100
		450

1 What is the acid test ratio for Matlock PLC

(a) 1.25:1

(b) 0.5:1

(c) 1:1

(d) 5:1

2 The gearing ratio for Matlock should be calculated as follows

(a) 300/450 x 100

(b) 350/450 x 100

(c) 125/550 x 100

(d) 100/550 x 100

3   If Matlock PLC's sales for the year (all on credit) were £405,000 what is the asset turnover ratio?

  (a)   0.9:1
  (b)   0.74:1
  (c)   0.81:1
  (d)   1.11:1

4   What is the debtor collection period in days if the credit sales of the business are £405,000 as in 3 above? (You will need to round up to whole days)

  (a)   86 days
  (b)   68 days
  (c)   158 days
  (d)   61 days

5   Which of the following is the correct calculation for interest cover?

  (a)   Total debt / interest payable
  (b)   Interest payable / total debt
  (c)   Operating profit / interest payable
  (d)   Interest payable / operating profit

10.6   Study the financial statements of the two public limited companies listed below and then calculate the accounting ratios in the questions which follow.

PROFIT & LOSS ACCOUNTS	Hanadi PLC		Abeer PLC	
	£000	£000	£000	£000
Sales		350		300
Less Cost of Sales				
Opening Stock	40		20	
Purchases	170		150	
	210		170	
Closing Stock	(110)	(100)	(70)	(100)
GROSS PROFIT		250		200
Expenses		(100)		(50)
NET PROFIT BEFORE TAXATION		150		150
Taxation		(35)		(30)
NET PROFIT AFTER TAXATION		115		120
Dividends		(60)		(45)
RETAINED PROFIT FOR THE YEAR		55		75

BALANCE SHEETS	*Hanadi PLC*		*Abeer PLC*	
	£000	*£000*	*£000*	*£000*
FIXED ASSETS AT NBV		465		325
CURRENT ASSETS				
Stock	110		70	
Debtors	95		60	
Bank	15		30	
	220		160	
CURRENT LIABILITIES				
Creditors	120		60	
Dividends payable	60		45	
Taxation payable	35		30	
	215		135	
NET CURRENT ASSETS		5		25
		470		350
Represented by				
CAPITAL AND RESERVES				
Ordinary Shares £1 each		300		200
Share Premium Account		50		50
		350		250
Profit and Loss Account		120		100
		470		350

REQUIRED

Task 1
Calculate the following ratios for both businesses:
(a)   Gross Profit as a percentage of Sales
(b)   Net Profit as a percentage of Sales
(c)   Net Profit as a percentage return on Capital Employed (ROCE)
(d)   Current ratio
(e)   Acid Test ratio

Task 2
Comment upon what the ratios reveal, and make recommendations as to which business offers the better return from a profitability, efficiency and investment point of view.

10.7   Ratio analysis is a useful way for a business to compare one year's results with another and to highlight trends. It can also be a useful tool when comparing the results of a business with the results of a competitor. However the limitations of ratio analysis should always be kept in mind, when making any realistic judgement concerning the overall performance of any business.

REQUIRED
Discuss the limitations of ratio analysis when assessing and comparing company performance.

10.8   The following summarised information for the year ended 30 June 20-3 relates to three separate companies operating in the same industrial sector.

Profit and Loss Accounts	*Case PLC*	*Hope PLC*	*Mast PLC*
	£000	*£000*	*£000*
Operating profit	10,000	4,500	1,500
Interest payable	(2,500)	(200)	
PROFIT BEFORE TAXATION	7,500	4,300	1,500
Taxation	(2,800)	(1,200)	(650)
PROFIT AFTER TAXATION	4,700	3,100	850
Dividends			
– Ordinary	(1,600)	(400)	(400)
– Preference	(100)		
Retained Profit for the year	3,000	2,700	450

Balance Sheets			
FIXED ASSETS AT NBV	12,000	4,450	1,800
CURRENT ASSETS	56,000	12,500	1,200
CREDITORS amounts falling due within one year	(50,000)	(5,800)	(700)
CREDITORS amounts falling due after more than one year			
Debentures	(4,000)	(1,650)	
	14,000	9,500	2,300
CAPITAL AND RESERVES			
Ordinary shares of £1 each	3,000	1,500	500
Preference Shares	1,000		
Profit and Loss Account	10,000	8,000	1,800
	14,000	9,500	2,300

Required

Calculate the following ratios for each of the three companies:

(a)   Return on capital employed

(b)   Current ratio

(c)   Interest cover

(d)   Earnings per share

(e)   Gearing

10.9 The directors of Dowango Ltd have asked to have a meeting with you. They are intending to ask the bank for a further long-term loan to enable them to purchase a company which has retail outlets. The directors have identified two possible companies to take over and they intend to purchase the whole of the share capital of one of the two targeted companies.

The directors have obtained the latest financial statements of the two companies, in summary form and these are set out below:

Summary profit and loss accounts

	Company A	Company B
	£000	£000
Turnover	800	2,100
Cost of sales	440	1,050
Gross profit	360	1,050
Expenses	160	630
Net profit before interest and tax	200	420

Summary balance sheets

	Company A	Company B
	£000	£000
Fixed assets	620	1,640
Net current assets	380	1,160
Long-term loan	(400)	(1,100)
	600	1,700
Share capital and reserves	600	1,700

REQUIRED

Advise the directors as to which of the two companies targeted for takeover is the more profitable and which one provides the higher return on capital. Your answer should include calculation of the following ratios:

- return on capital employed
- net profit margin
- asset turnover

You should also calculate and comment on at least *one* further ratio of your choice, for which you have sufficient information, which would be relevant to determining which of the companies is more profitable or provides the greater return on capital.

10.10 Bimbridge Hospitals Trust has just lost its supplier of bandages. The company that has been supplying it for the last five years has gone into liquidation. The Trust is concerned to select a new supplier which it can rely on to supply it with its needs for the foreseeable future. You have been asked by the Trust managers to analyse the financial statements of a potential supplier of bandages. You have obtained the latest financial statements of the company, in summary form, which are set out below.

Patch Ltd
Summary Profit and Loss Accounts
for the year ended 30 September 20-8

	20-8	20-7
	£000	£000
Turnover	2,300	2,100
Cost of sales	1,035	945
Gross profit	1,265	1,155
Expenses	713	693
Net profit before interest and tax	552	462

Patch Ltd
Summary Balance Sheets
as at 30 September 20-8

	20-8		20-7	
	£000	£000	£000	£000
Fixed assets		4,764		5,418
Current assets				
Stocks	522		419	
Debtors	406		356	
Cash	117		62	
	1,045		837	
Current liabilities				
Trade creditors	305		254	
Taxation	170		211	
	475		465	
Net current assets		570		372
Long-term loan		(1,654)		(2,490)
		3,680		3,300
Share capital		1,100		1,000
Share premium		282		227
Profit and loss account		2,298		2,073
		3,680		3,300

You have also obtained the relevant industry average ratios which are as follows:

	20-8	20-7
Return on capital employed	9.6%	9.4%
Net profit percentage	21.4%	21.3%
Quick ratio/acid test	1.0:1	0.9:1
Gearing (Debt/Capital Employed)	36%	37%

REQUIRED

Prepare a report for the managers of Bimbridge Hospitals Trust recommending whether or not to use Patch Ltd as a supplier of bandages. Use the information contained in the financial statements of Patch Ltd and the industry averages supplied.

Your answer should:

• comment on the company's profitability, liquidity and financial position;

• consider how the company has changed over the two years;

• include a comparison with the industry as a whole.

The report should include calculation of the following ratios for the two years:

(a) Return on capital employed

(b) Net profit percentage

(c) Quick ratio/acid test

(d) Gearing

11 CONSOLIDATED ACCOUNTS

this chapter covers . . .

This chapter examines the financial statements of groups of companies. The final accounts for a group comprise consolidated profit and loss account and consolidated balance sheet. Such consolidated accounts show the position of the group as if it was a single entity. The chapter covers:

- definitions of parent and subsidiary companies

- accounting for goodwill, post-acquisition profits, and minority interests when using the acquisition method for preparing consolidated balance sheets

- the use of fair values in acquisition accounting

- inter-company adjustments and profits

- consolidated profit and loss accounts

- merger accounting

Towards the end of the chapter we look at incorporating the results of associated companies – where fewer than half of the shares are owned – into the financial statements of the investor company.

NVQ PERFORMANCE CRITERIA COVERED

unit 11: DRAFTING FINANCIAL STATEMENTS

element 2

draft limited company, sole trader and partnership year end financial statements

- financial statements are accurately drafted from the appropriate information

- subsequent adjustments are correctly implemented

- draft accounts comply with domestic standards and legislation and, where relevant, partnership agreement

- year end financial statements are presented for approval to the appropriate person in clear form

- confidentiality procedures are followed at all times

- the organisation's policies, regulations, procedures and timescales relating to financial statements are observed at all times

- discrepancies, unusual features or queries are identified and either resolved or referred to the appropriate person

INTRODUCTION TO CONSOLIDATED ACCOUNTS

In recent years many companies have been taken over by other companies to form groups. Each company within a group maintains its separate legal entity, and so a group of companies may take the following form:

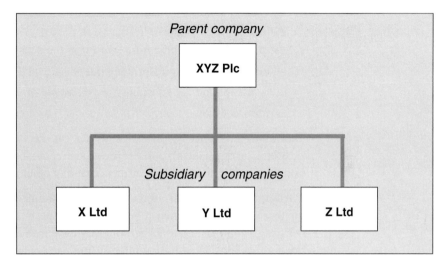

The Companies Act 1985 makes various provisions concerning groups of companies, including:

- A parent company and subsidiary company relationship generally exists where a parent company owns more than 50 per cent of another company's share capital, or controls the composition of its board of directors (see definitions below).

- A parent company is required to produce *group published accounts*.

- Group accounts must include a consolidated profit and loss account and a consolidated balance sheet. Such *consolidated accounts* are designed to show the position of the group as if it was a single entity.

- A parent company, which produces a consolidated profit and loss account, is not legally obliged to produce its own profit and loss account.

PARENT AND SUBSIDIARY COMPANIES DEFINED

FRS 2, *Accounting for subsidiary undertakings*, defines the parent/subsidiary company relationship as a situation where *any* of the following apply:

- the parent holds a majority of the voting rights in the subsidiary

- the parent is a shareholder of the subsidiary and has the right to appoint or remove directors holding a majority of the voting rights at meetings of the board on all, or substantially all, matters

- the parent has the right to exercise a *dominant influence* on the subsidiary either through the memorandum or articles of association, or through a control contract

- the parent is a shareholder of the subsidiary and controls alone, under an agreement with the other shareholders or members, a majority of the voting rights in the subsidiary

- the parent has a *participating interest* in the subsidiary and
  – either actually exercises a *dominant influence* over it
  – or both it and the subsidiary are *managed on a unified basis*
  as explained below . . .

Dominant influence is influence which can be exercised to achieve the operating and financial policies desired by the holder of the influence, notwithstanding the rights or influence of any other party

Participating interest is an interest held by an undertaking in the shares of another undertaking which it holds on a long-term basis for the purpose of securing a contribution to its activities by the exercise of control or influence arising from or related to that interest. In this connection:

– a holding of 20 per cent or more of the shares of an undertaking is presumed to be a participating interest unless the contrary is shown

– an interest in shares includes an interest which is either convertible into shares, or includes an option to convert into shares

Managed on a unified basis occurs when the whole of the operations of two or more undertakings are integrated and they are managed as a single unit.

FRS 2 also covers the situation where a subsidiary is itself the parent of another undertaking, creating a parent, subsidiary and sub-subsidiary relationship:

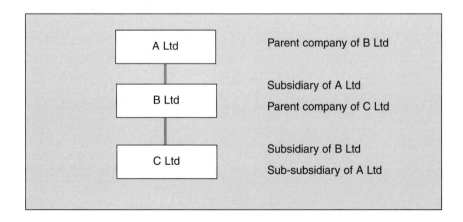

GROUP FINANCIAL STATEMENTS

A group is defined by FRS 2 as 'a parent undertaking and its subsidiary undertakings'. FRS 2 requires a parent undertaking to prepare consolidated financial statements for its group unless it uses one of the exceptions set out in the standard – for example, if the group is defined as being small or medium-sized.

We look firstly at the preparation of consolidated balance sheets, using the **acquisition method** (another method is the **merger method** – see page 330 – which can only be used when certain criteria are complied with).

We then look at the preparation of consolidated profit and loss accounts.

CONSOLIDATED BALANCE SHEETS: ACQUISITION METHOD

The objective of a consolidated balance sheet is to report the affairs of the group of companies as if it was a single entity.

The **acquisition method** regards the business combination as the acquisition of one company by another. Thus the identifiable assets of the company acquired are included in the consolidated balance sheet at the date of acquisition, and its results are included in the profit and loss account (see page 326) from the date of acquisition.

There are three major calculations in the preparation of a consolidated balance sheet under the acquisition method, each with a different relevant date:

1 goodwill – as at the date of acquisition of the subsidiary

2 post-acquisition profits – since the date of acquisition of the shares in the subsidiary

3 minority interests – the stake of the other shareholders in the subsidiary at the date of the consolidated balance sheet

In the Case Studies which follow, we look at the preparation of consolidated balance sheets – starting with simple groups, and then incorporating calculations for goodwill, post-acquisition profits and minority interests. Included in the Case Studies are tutorial notes which explain the calculations.

ACCOUNTING FOR SIMPLE GROUPS OF COMPANIES

situation

The summary balance sheets of Pam Limited, a parent company, and Sam Limited, the subsidiary of Pam, are shown below as at 31 December 2002. Sam Limited was acquired by Pam Limited as a subsidiary company on 31 December 2002.

	Pam Ltd £000	Sam Ltd £000
Investment in Sam:		
20,000 £1 ordinary shares at cost	40	–
Other net assets	40	40
	80	40
Share capital (£1 ordinary shares)	60	20
Reserves: retained profits	20	20
	80	40

solution

The first thing to look at is the percentage of shares owned in the subsidiary by the parent company. Here Pam Limited owns all 20,000 shares of Sam Limited, so the subsidiary is 100 per cent owned. Note that the shares have been bought at the financial year-end, ie the date of the consolidated balance sheet.

The method of preparing the consolidated balance sheet of Pam Limited and its subsidiary Sam Limited is as follows:

1 the £40,000 cost of the investment in Sam (shown on Pam's balance sheet) cancels out directly against the share capital (£20,000) and reserves (£20,000) of Sam and is not shown on the consolidated balance sheet

2 add together the net assets of the two companies

3 show only the share capital and reserves of the parent company

The consolidated balance sheet (CBS) is shown in the far right column:

	Pam Ltd £000	Sam Ltd £000	CBS £000
Investment in Sam:			
20,000 £1 ordinary shares at cost	4̶0̶	–	
Other net assets	40	40	80
	80	40	80
Share capital (£1 ordinary shares)	60	2̶0̶	60
Reserves: retained profits	20	2̶0̶	20
	80	40	80

> **Tutorial Note**
>
> The reason for cancelling out the amount of the investment against the share capital and reserves of the subsidiary is because the amounts record a transaction that has taken place within the group. It does not need reporting because the balance sheet shows the group as if it was a single entity.

CASE STUDY

GOODWILL – POSITIVE AND NEGATIVE

situation

The summary balance sheets of Peeble Limited, a parent company, and Singh Limited and Salvo Limited, its two subsidiaries, as at 31 December 2002 appear below. The investments in Singh Limited and Salvo Limited were bought on 31 December 2002

	Peeble Ltd £000	Singh Ltd £000	Salvo Ltd £000
Fixed assets	30	25	20
Investment in Singh:			
20,000 £1 ordinary shares at cost	50		
Investment in Salvo:			
24,000 £1 ordinary shares at cost	25		
Net current assets	10	15	10
	115	40	30
Share capital (£1 ordinary shares)	70	20	24
Reserves: retained profits	45	20	6
	115	40	30

solution

Peeble Limited owns all the shares of Singh Limited and Salvo Limited – the subsidiaries are 100 per cent owned. The investments have been bought at the financial year-end – the date of the consolidated balance sheet.

As the cost price of the investment in the subsidiaries does not cancel out directly against the share capital and reserves, the difference represents goodwill:

	Singh £000	Salvo £000
cost of investment	50	25
value* of subsidiary at date of acquisition	40	30
goodwill	10	(5)

* share capital + reserves

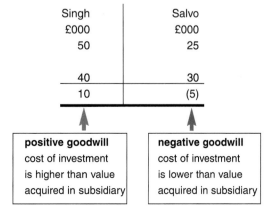

positive goodwill	**negative goodwill**
cost of investment is higher than value acquired in subsidiary	cost of investment is lower than value acquired in subsidiary

The consolidated balance sheet of Peeble Limited and its subsidiaries can now be prepared following the principles outlined in the previous Case Study. Note that positive goodwill is shown on the assets side of the consolidated balance sheet, with negative goodwill also shown on the assets side, but deducted.

PEEBLE LIMITED AND ITS SUBSIDIARIES
Consolidated balance sheet as at 31 December 2002

	£000
Fixed Assets	
Intangible assets:	
Goodwill	10
Negative goodwill	(5)
Tangible assets 30 + 25 + 20	75
Net Current Assets 10 + 15 + 10	35
	115
Share Capital	70
Reserves	
Retained profits	45
	115

Tutorial Note
In future years goodwill – both positive and negative – will most probably be amortised through profit and loss account over its estimated useful economic life, although there are alternative ways of accounting for goodwill (see FRS 10, pages 179-180).

CASE STUDY

PRE-ACQUISITION AND POST-ACQUISITION PROFITS

situation

The summarised balance sheets of Peat Limited, a parent company, and Stone Limited, its subsidiary, as at 31 December 2002 appear as follows:

	Peat Ltd £000	Stone Ltd £000
Fixed assets	80	25
Investment in Stone:		
20,000 £1 ordinary shares at cost	35	
Current assets	25	10
Current liabilities	(10)	(8)
	130	27
Share capital (£1 ordinary shares)	100	20
Reserves: retained profits	30	7
	130	27

Stone Limited was bought by Peat Ltd on 31 December 2001, when Stone's retained profit was £5,000 (note that Stone has earned £2,000 of retained profits since the date of acquisition).

The accounting policy of Peat is to amortise goodwill over an estimated useful economic life of ten years.

Tutorial Note

The reserves held by the subsidiary at the date of acquisition are those that have been earned pre-acquisition: they are included in the goodwill calculation.

The reserves earned by the subsidiary after acquisition – post-acquisition profits – are earned while it is part of the group and are, therefore, part of the consolidated reserves shown on the consolidated balance sheet. Such consolidated reserves are available for distribution as dividends to shareholders – provided that there is sufficient cash in the bank to pay the dividends

---

solution

1   Peat Limited owns all the shares of Stone Limited, ie the subsidiary is 100% owned.

2   The calculation of goodwill in Stone is as follows:

£000

cost of investment	35
value of subsidiary at date of acquisition 20 + 5	*25
positive goodwill	10

* £20,000 of share capital, plus £5,000 of retained profits at date of acquisition (ie pre-acquisition profits)

3   As Peat's accounting policy is to amortise goodwill over an estimated useful economic life of ten years, £1,000 will be written off to profit and loss account in 2002, leaving £9,000 of goodwill to be shown in the balance sheet.

4   The post-acquisition profits of Stone for the consolidated balance sheet are:

£000

reserves at date of consolidated balance sheet	7
reserves at date of acquisition of Stone	5
post-acquisition profits	2

PEAT LIMITED AND ITS SUBSIDIARY
Consolidated balance sheet as at 31 December 2002

£000

Fixed Assets

Intangible asset: goodwill 10 – 1	9
Tangible assets 80 + 25	105
Current Assets 25 + 10	35
Current Liabilities (10) + (8)	(18)
	131
Share Capital	100
Reserves	
Retained profits 30 + 2 – 1*	31
	131

* goodwill amortised

CASE STUDY	MINORITY INTERESTS

The summarised balance sheets of Pine Limited, a parent company, and Spruce Limited, its subsidiary, as at 31 December 2002 are shown below.

The investment in Spruce was bought on 31 December 2001, when Spruce's retained profit was £8,000.

The accounting policy of Pine is to amortise goodwill over an estimated useful economic life of five years.

	Pine Ltd £000	Spruce Ltd £000
Fixed assets	80	25
Investment in Spruce:		
15,000 £1 ordinary shares at cost	26	
Current assets	25	12
Current liabilities	(10)	(5)
	121	32
Share capital (£1 ordinary shares)	100	20
Reserves: retained profits	21	12
	121	32

solution

1 Pine Limited owns 75 per cent of the shares of Spruce Limited, ie 15,000 shares out of 20,000 shares. Thus minority shareholders own 25 per cent of Spruce.

2 The calculation of goodwill in Spruce is as follows:

	£000
cost of investment	26
value of subsidiary at date of acquisition	
20 + 8 = 28 x 75% owned =	21
positive goodwill	5

Note that, for the goodwill calculation, the value of the subsidiary at date of acquisition is reduced to the percentage of shares owned, here 75 per cent.

3   As Pine's accounting policy is to amortise goodwill over an estimated useful economic life of five years, £1,000 will be written off to profit and loss account in 2002, leaving £4,000 of goodwill to be shown in the balance sheet.

4   The post-acquisition profits of Spruce for the consolidated balance sheet are:

	£000
reserves at date of consolidated balance sheet	12
reserves at date of acquisition of Spruce	8
post-acquisition profits	4
75% owned	3

Note that, for the calculation of post-acquisition profits, the amount is reduced to the percentage of shares owned, here 75 per cent.

5   The minority interests of Spruce are:

	£000
value at date of consolidated balance sheet	32
25% minority interests	8

Note that, for the calculation of minority interests, the amount is reduced to the percentage of shares owned by the minority shareholders, here 25 per cent.

PINE LIMITED AND ITS SUBSIDIARY
Consolidated balance sheet as at 31 December 2002

	£000
Fixed Assets	
Intangible asset: goodwill 5 − 1	4
Tangible assets 80 + 25	105
Current Assets 25 + 12	37
Current Liabilities (10) + (5)	(15)
	131
Share Capital	100
Reserves	
Retained profits 21 + 3 − 1*	23
	123
Minority Interests	8
	131

* goodwill amortised

Tutorial Note

When there are minority interests, note that we do not reduce the value of the subsidiary's assets and liabilities in the consolidated balance sheet to allow for minority shareholders – what we are saying is that the parent company has *control* over the subsidiary's assets and liabilities.

The amount shown for minority interests on the consolidated balance sheet is the value of the subsidiary held by them *at the date of the consolidated balance sheet.*

Minority interests are included on the 'financed by' side of the consolidated balance sheet in order to show the overall view of the group.

FAIR VALUES IN ACQUISITION ACCOUNTING

When a parent company acquires a majority holding of shares in a subsidiary company, it acquires both control of the subsidiary and also control of the subsidiary's assets and liabilities. The objective of FRS 7, *Fair values in acquisition accounting*, is to ensure that when a business entity is acquired by another:

- all the assets and liabilities that existed in the acquired entity at the date of acquisition are recorded at fair values reflecting their condition at that date
- all changes to the acquired assets and liabilities, and the resulting gains and losses, that arise after control of the acquired entity has passed to the acquirer are reported as part of the post-acquisition financial performance of the acquiring group

Fair value is defined by the standard as 'the amount at which an asset or liability could be exchanged in an arm's length transaction between informed and willing parties, other than in a forced or liquidation sale'.

FRS 7 gives guidance on valuing individual categories of assets:

- tangible fixed assets – the fair value should be based on either their market value or their depreciated replacement cost
- intangible assets – the fair value should be based on their replacement cost, which is normally their estimated market value
- stocks and work-in-progress – should be valued at the lower of replacement cost and net realisable value
- quoted investments – should be valued at market price
- monetary assets and liabilities (eg debtors and creditors) – should be valued at the amounts expected to be received or paid

Fair value has an effect on the calculations for goodwill, minority interests (where applicable), and sometimes on post-acquisition profits:

- goodwill is the cost of the investment in the subsidiary, less the fair value of the subsidiary's assets and liabilities
- minority interests is the proportion of the subsidiary owned, based on the fair value of the subsidiary's assets and liabilities
- post-acquisition profits will be affected where the use of fair value for fixed assets leads to a different depreciation charge from that based on historic costs

The procedure for dealing with fair values is to restate the subsidiary's balance sheet using fair values. Increases in the valuation of fixed assets and current assets are credited to revaluation reserve; decreases in fixed assets and current assets are debited to revaluation reserve. Any changes to the value of liabilities are also passed through revaluation reserve. The Case Study which follows shows how fair values affect the calculations for the consolidated balance sheet.

One further aspect of FRS 7 to note is that the standard does not allow the liabilities of the acquired company to be increased by the inclusion of provisions for future re-organisation costs and for future operating losses. Such costs are to be dealt with post-acquisition and will be charged to the profit and loss account of the year in which they are incurred. For example, if the acquiring company considers that it will have to spend money on upgrading the computer systems of the subsidiary, it cannot make a provision for this – against which future costs can be charged – at the date of acquisition. Instead, the costs will be charged against post-acquisition profits as they are incurred.

CASE STUDY

FAIR VALUES IN ACQUISITION ACCOUNTING

situation

On 31 December 2002, Pipe Limited bought 75 per cent of the share capital of Soil Limited at a cost of £37,000. At that date the two companies' balance sheets were as follows:

	Pipe Ltd £000	Soil Ltd £000
Fixed assets	60	18
Investment in Soil:		
9,000 £1 ordinary shares at cost	37	
Current assets	20	16
Current liabilities	(13)	(6)
	104	28
Share capital (£1 ordinary shares)	80	12
Reserves: retained profits	24	16
	104	28

At the date of acquisition

– the fair value of Soil's fixed assets was £30,000

– the fair value of Soil's current assets was £12,000

The accounting policy of Pipe is to amortise goodwill over an estimated useful economic life of ten years.

solution

1   We must incorporate the fair values into Soil's balance sheet as follows:

	£000	£000
Fixed assets (increase in value)		
debit fixed assets account	12	
credit revaluation reserve		12
Current assets (reduction in value)		
debit revaluation reserve	4	
credit current assets		4

2   Thus Soil's balance sheet is:

	before	adjustment	after
	£000	£000	£000
Fixed assets	18	+ 12	30
Current assets	16	– 4	12
Current liabilities	(6)	–	(6)
	28	+ 8	36
Share capital	12	–	12
Reserves: revaluation	–	+ 12	
		– 4 ⎬	8
retained profits	16	–	16
	28	+ 8	36

3   Goodwill is:

	£000
cost of investment	37
value of subsidiary at date of acquisition	
fair value of 36 (see above) x 75% owned	27
positive goodwill	10

4   Minority interests are:

	£000
value at date of consolidated balance sheet	36
25% minority interests	9

5   There will be no post-acquisition profits at 31 December 2002, as this is the date at which the investment in the subsidiary is being made.

PIPE LIMITED AND ITS SUBSIDIARY
Consolidated balance sheet as at 31 December 2002

	£000
Fixed Assets	
Intangible asset: goodwill	10
Tangible assets 60 + 30 (at fair value)	90
Current Assets 20 + 12 (at fair value)	32
Current Liabilities (13) + (6)	(19)
	113
Share Capital	80
Reserves	
Retained profits	24
	104
Minority Interests	9
	113

Tutorial Note

Goodwill will be amortised over ten years at £1,000 per year through profit and loss account.

There may be an adjustment each year to post-acquisition profits if the use of fair values leads to an additional depreciation charge.

INTER-COMPANY ADJUSTMENTS

We have already seen the need to cancel out the inter-company balances of investment in the subsidiary company (shown in the parent company's balance sheet) against the share capital and reserves (shown in the subsidiary company's balance sheet). Other inter-company amounts also have to be cancelled out or adjusted against each other when preparing consolidated balance sheets.

debtors, creditors and loans

Where there are debtors, creditors and loans between companies that are part of the same group, they cancel out against each other and do not show on the consolidated balance sheet.

Example 1

Beech Limited has sold goods to Cedar Limited for £5,000. Both Beech and Cedar are subsidiaries of Ash Limited. At the date of the consolidated balance sheet Cedar has not yet paid Beech for the goods, so:

- Beech has an asset of debtors, including the £5,000 due from Cedar
- Cedar has a liability of creditors, including the £5,000 due to Beech

For the consolidated balance sheet of Ash Limited and its subsidiaries, the inter-company balance of debtors and creditors will not be shown because it is between group companies.

Example 2

Ash Limited has made a loan to Beech Limited of £10,000. The loan shows:

- as an asset on Ash's balance sheet
- as a liability on Beech's balance sheet

For the consolidated balance sheet, the loan will not be shown because it is an inter-company balance within the group.

dividends proposed

When a dividend is proposed by a subsidiary company, the amount is shown as a current liability on its balance sheet. In the parent company's balance sheet, the amount of the dividend is shown as a current asset (dividend receivable), having been credited to the parent company's profit and loss account (provided that the dividend represents a distribution of post-acquisition profits). Such inter-company balances will cancel each other out when the consolidated balance sheet is prepared.

Note that, if the subsidiary is partly owned, then the proportion of the proposed dividend that does not belong to the parent company is shown as a current liability due to the minority shareholders.

inter-company profits

Inter-company profits occur when one group company sells goods to another company within the group. If the goods have then been sold to buyers outside the group, then no adjustment to the consolidated balance sheet is necessary as the profit has been realised. However, when some or all of the goods remain in the stock of a group company at the date of the consolidated balance sheet, then an adjustment for unrealised inter-company profits must be made.

For example, Able Limited and Baker Limited are parent company and subsidiary company respectively. Able sells goods which cost it £1,000 to Baker for £1,500. A consolidated balance sheet is prepared before Baker sells any of the stock. The £500 profit made by Able is included in its profit and loss account, whilst the value of the stock held by Baker includes Able's profit. For the consolidated balance sheet:

- the profit and loss account of Able is reduced by £500
- the stock of Baker is reduced by £500

This accounting adjustment ensures that the stocks of the group are stated in the consolidated balance sheet at cost to the group (or net realisable value, if lower) and that no unrealised profit is shown in the group accounts. Note that, if some of the goods had been sold by Baker, then only the profit on the proportion remaining in the group would be adjusted.

When a partly-owned subsidiary has sold goods to another group company and there are unrealised inter-company profits at the date of the consolidated balance sheet, minority interests need to be adjusted for their share of the unrealised profits. This is a requirement of FRS 2, and is illustrated in the Case Study which follows.

CASE STUDY

INTER-COMPANY ADJUSTMENTS

situation

The summary balance sheets of Pearl Limited, a parent company, and Sea Limited, its subsidiary, as at 31 December 2002 are shown below.

The investment in Sea Limited was bought on 31 December 2001, when Sea's retained profit was £10,000. At that date there were no material differences between the book value and fair value of any of the assets of Sea.

The accounting policy of Pearl is to amortise goodwill over an estimated useful economic life of ten years.

In November 2002, Sea sold goods costing £5,000 to Pearl at a price of £7,000. At 31 December 2002 half of those goods were unsold by Pearl.

	Pearl Ltd £000	Sea Ltd £000
Investment in Sea:		
12,000 £1 ordinary shares at cost	28	
Loan to Sea	10	
Net current assets	42	46
Loan from Pearl		(10)
	80	36
Share capital (£1 ordinary shares)	60	20
Reserves: retained profits	20	16
	80	36

solution

1 Pearl Limited owns 60 per cent of the shares in Sea Limited.

2 The calculation of goodwill is as follows:

	£000
cost of investment	28
value of subsidiary at date of acquisition	
20 + 10 = 30 x 60% owned =	18
positive goodwill	10

As Pearl's accounting policy is to amortise goodwill over an estimated useful economic life of ten years, £1,000 will be written off to profit and loss account in 2002, leaving £9,000 of goodwill to be shown in the balance sheet.

3 *Inter-company adjustments:*

Loan

The £10,000 loan from Pearl to Sea cancels out for the consolidated balance sheet, ie the asset on Pearl's balance sheet cancels out against the liability on Sea's balance sheet.

Inter-company profits

Of the £2,000 profit made when Sea sold goods to Pearl at the date of the consolidated balance sheet, £1,000 is unrealised (because the goods remain in Pearl's stock). For the consolidated balance sheet:

– the profit and loss account of Sea is reduced by £1,000

– the stock of Pearl is reduced by £1,000

Tutorial note

It is always advisable to make the inter-company adjustments before calculating post-acquisition profits and minority interests. By doing this, minority shareholders (if any) will be charged or credited with their share of adjustments which affect the subsidiary company, as required by FRS 2.

4 The post-acquisition profits of Sea are:

	£000
reserves at date of consolidated balance sheet:	
16 – 1 unrealised profit	15
reserves at date of acquisition	10
post-acquisition profits	5
60% owned	3

5 The minority interests of Sea are:

	£000
value at date of consolidated balance sheet:	
36 – 1 unrealised profit	35
40% minority interests	14

PEARL LIMITED AND ITS SUBSIDIARY
Consolidated balance sheet as at 31 December 2002

	£000
Fixed Assets	
Intangible asset: goodwill 10 – 1 (amortisation)	9
Net Current Assets 42 – 1 (stock) + 46	87
	96
Share Capital	60
Reserves	
Retained profits 20 – 1 (goodwill amortised) + 3	22
	82
Minority Interests	14
	96

CASE STUDY

PREPARING FOR ASSESSMENT:
THE CONSOLIDATED BALANCE SHEET

Tutorial note

The task which follows is taken from the June 2000 AAT Central Assessment; it is reproduced by kind permission of AAT. We will use it to demonstrate how the calculations for goodwill, post-acquisition profits and minority interests can be presented in a tabular format, which can be used for the calculations..

situation

You have been asked to assist in the preparation of the consolidated accounts of the Norman Group.

Set out on the next page are the balance sheets of Norman Limited and Saxon Limited for the year ended 31 March 2000:

Balance sheets as at 31 March 2000

	Norman Ltd		Saxon Ltd	
Fixed Assets	£000	£000	£000	£000
Tangible assets		12,995		1,755
Investment in Saxon Limited		1,978		–
Current Assets				
Stock	3,586		512	
Debtors	2,193		382	
Cash	84		104	
	5,863		998	
Current Liabilities				
Trade creditors	1,920		273	
Proposed dividend	160		–	
Taxation	667		196	
	2,747		469	
Net Current Assets		3,116		529
Long-term Liabilities				
Loan		–		(400)
		18,089		1,884
Share Capital		2,000		1,000
Reserves				
Share premium		–		200
Profit and loss account		16,089		684
		18,089		1,884

Further information:

- The share capital of both Norman Limited and Saxon Limited consists of ordinary shares of £1 each. There have been no changes to the balances of share capital and share premium during the year. No dividends were paid by Saxon Limited during the year.

- Norman Limited acquired 750,000 shares in Saxon Limited on 31 March 1999.

- At 31 March 1999 the balance on the profit and loss account of Saxon Limited was £424,000.

- The fair value of the fixed assets of Saxon Limited at 31 March 1999 was £2,047,000 as compared with their book value of £1,647,000. The revaluation has not been reflected in the books of Saxon Limited (ignore any depreciation implications).

- Goodwill arising on consolidation is to be amortised using the straight-line method over a period of 10 years.

You are to prepare the consolidated balance sheet of Norman Limited and its subsidiary undertaking as at 31 March 2000.

(Note: an AAT Assessment normally supplies a sample layout for this purpose)..

solution

1 The percentage of shares owned by Norman Limited in Saxon Limited is:

$$\frac{750,000 \text{ shares}}{1,000,000 \text{ shares}} = \underline{75 \text{ per cent}}$$

2 The minority interests in Saxon are, therefore, 100% − 75% = <u>25 per cent.</u>

3 At the date of acquisition (31 March 1999), the fixed assets of Saxon had the following values:

	£000
fair value	2,047
book value	1,647
difference	400

4 As fair value is higher than book value, this increase must be recorded in Saxon's accounts:

	£000	£000
debit fixed assets account	400	
credit revaluation reserve		400

5 Goodwill on consolidation, post-acquisition profits, and minority interests are now calculated using a tabular layout. (Author's note: each of these figures can be calculated separtely as demonstrated on previous pages; the answers will, of course, be the same!)

	total equity	attributable to Norman at acquisition	attributable to Norman after acquisition	minority interests
	100%	75%	75%	25%
	£000	£000	£000	£000
share capital	1,000	750		250
share premium	200	150		50
revaluation reserve (see above)	400	300		100
profit and loss account*				
at acquisition	424	318		106
after acquisition	260		195	65
	†2,284	1,518	195	571
price paid by Norman		1,978		
∴ positive goodwill		460		

• and † – see notes on the next page

Notes on the calculations on the previous page

	£000	
* profit and loss account:	424	at date of acquisition
	260	post-acquisition profits
	684	as shown by Saxon's balance sheet

	£000	
† total equity:	1,884	as shown by Saxon's balance sheet
	400	revaluation reserve (to increase fixed assets to fair value)
	2,284	as shown above

Further calculations

6 The goodwill, an intangible asset, is to be amortised using the straight-line method over ten years:

460	goodwill on consolidation
46	amortisation for year to 31 March 2000 (ie date of consolidated balance sheet)
414	goodwill as at 31 March 2000

7 The amount of goodwill written off is debited to the consolidated profit and loss account as follows:

16,089	Norman's profit and loss account
195	post-acquisition profits of Saxon attributable to Norman (see above)
16,284	
46	less goodwill amortised
16,238	consolidated profit and loss account

8 The consolidated balance sheet can now be prepared as shown on the next page. Note that the workings figures (in £000s) are for guidance only and need not be detailed in the balance sheet.

NORMAN LIMITED AND ITS SUBSIDIARY
Consolidated Balance Sheet as at 31 March 2000

	£000	£000
Fixed Assets		
Intangible assets 460 – 46 goodwill amortised	414	
Tangible assets 12,995 + 1,755 + 400 increase to fair value	15,150	
Investments	–	
		15,564
Current Assets		
Stock 3,586 + 512	4,098	
Debtors 2,193 + 382	2,575	
Investments	–	
Cash at bank and in hand 84 + 104	188	
	6,861	
Creditors: amounts falling due within one year		
Trade creditors 1,920 + 273	2,193	
Proposed dividend	160	
Taxation 667 + 196	863	
	3,216	
Net Current Assets		3,645
Total Assets *less* Current Liabilities		19,209
Creditors: amounts falling due after more than one year		
Loan		400
Provisions for liabilities and charges		–
		18,809
Capital and Reserves		
Share capital		2,000
Profit and loss account (see workings above)		16,238
		18,238
Minority Interests (see tabulation on page 323)		571
		18,809

CONSOLIDATED PROFIT AND LOSS ACCOUNTS

The consolidated profit and loss account, like the consolidated balance sheet, is intended to show the position of the group as if it was a single entity. The consolidated profit and loss account shows the shareholders of the parent company how much profit has been earned by the parent company and the subsidiaries, with a deduction for the proportion of profit due to minority interests. The diagram below shows the format of a consolidated profit and loss account; as the diagram demonstrates, the figures are merged from the profit and loss accounts of the parent company and the subsidiaries.

Format of consolidated profit and loss account

Group turnover	parent + subsidiaries – inter-company sales
Cost of sales*	see below
Gross profit	parent + subsidiaries – inter-company unrealised profit
Distribution costs	parent + subsidiaries
Administrative expenses	parent + subsidiaries
Group operating profit	parent + subsidiaries
Interest receivable/payable	parent + subsidiaries
Profit on ordinary activities before tax	parent + subsidiaries
Tax on profit on ordinary activities	parent + subsidiaries
Profit on ordinary activities after tax	parent + subsidiaries
Minority interests	minority interests' share of subsidiaries' profit
Profit on ordinary activities after tax and minority interests	parent + profit of wholly-owned subsidiaries and/or + parent's share of profit of partly-owned subsidiaries
Dividends	parent
Retained profit/loss for group	to group reserves
* Cost of sales:	
opening stock	parent + subsidiaries
+ purchases	parent + subsidiaries – inter-company purchases
– closing stock	parent + subsidiaries – inter-company unrealised profit

notes on the profit and loss format

- the full profit of subsidiaries is shown, with a separate deduction for the proportion of the profit due to minority interests

- only the dividends paid and proposed of the parent company are shown

- inter-company transactions are deducted for
    - inter-company sales
    - inter-company purchases
    - inter-company unrealised profit

Two Case Studies follow which demonstrate the preparation of consolidated profit and loss accounts – firstly for a simple group, secondly incorporating inter-company transactions. The layout follows that shown in the diagram.

PROFIT AND LOSS FOR SIMPLE GROUPS

situation

The summary profit and loss accounts of Pack Limited, a parent company, and Sack Limited, its subsidiary, for the year-ended 31 December 2002 are shown below.

Pack Limited bought 80 per cent of the ordinary shares of Sack Limited on 1 January 2002.

	Pack Ltd £000	Sack Ltd £000
Turnover (sales)	115	60
Cost of sales	65	28
Gross profit	50	32
Distribution costs	5	8
Administrative expenses	15	12
Profit before tax	30	12
Corporation tax	8	2
Profit after tax	22	10
Dividends	10	–
Retained profits	12	10

solution

1   The figures from the profit and loss accounts are merged.

2   The after-tax profit of Sack is £10,000; of this 20 per cent, ie £2,000 is due to minority interests.

please see next page . . .

PACK LIMITED AND ITS SUBSIDIARY

Consolidated Profit and Loss Account for the year ended 31 December 2002

		£000
Group turnover	115 + 60	175
Cost of sales	65 + 28	93
Gross profit	50 + 32	82
Distribution costs	5 + 8	13
Administrative expenses	15 + 12	27
Group operating profit	30 + 12	42
Interest receivable/payable		–
Profit on ordinary activities before tax		42
Tax on profit on ordinary activities	8 + 2	10
Profit on ordinary activities after tax		32
Minority interests	10 x 20%	2
Profit on ordinary activities after tax and minority interests		30
Dividends		10
Retained profit for group		20

CASE STUDY

GROUP PROFIT AND LOSS WITH ADJUSTMENTS

situation

The summary profit and loss accounts of Perch Limited, a parent company, and Sole Limited and Skate Limited, its subsidiaries for the year-ended 31 December 2002 are shown on the next page.

Perch Limited bought all of the shares of Sole Limited on 1 January 2000, and 75 per cent of the shares of Skate Limited on 1 January 2002.

During the year to 31 December 2002 the following inter-company trading took place:

– Perch sold goods costing £6,000 to Sole at a price of £10,000; all of these goods had been sold by the year-end for £12,000

– Perch sold goods costing £20,000 to Skate at a price of £40,000; at the year-end half of these goods were unsold by Skate

Perch's policy is to take credit for inter-company dividends.

	Perch Ltd £000	Sole Ltd £000	Skate Ltd £000
Turnover (sales)	400	200	150
Opening stock	100	75	50
+ Purchases	300	150	100
− Closing stock	150	100	40
Cost of sales	250	125	110
Gross profit	150	75	40
Distribution costs	40	25	10
Administrative expenses	50	15	10
Dividends from subsidiaries:			
Sole	20		
Skate	9		
Net profit	89	35	20
Corporation tax	20	10	4
Profit after tax	69	25	16
Dividends	50	20	12
Retained profits	19	5	4

solution

> **Tutorial Note**
>
> Inter-company sales, purchases and unrealised profit are deducted from sales, purchases and closing stock respectively before the figures are shown in the consolidated profit and loss account.
>
> Only the dividends of the parent company are shown. The dividends of subsidiary companies have been correctly recorded by Perch to show the proportion due to the parent company – these will not be shown on the consolidated profit and loss account because they are inter-company transactions.
>
> The after-tax profit of Sole is £25,000; as this subsidiary is wholly owned, no deduction is made for minority interests.
>
> The after-tax profit of Skate is £16,000; of this 25 per cent, ie £4,000, is due to minority interests.

please see next page for the consolidated profit and loss account . . .

PERCH LIMITED AND ITS SUBSIDIARIES

Consolidated Profit and Loss Account for the year ended 31 December 2002

		£000
Group turnover	400 + 200 + 150 − 10 − 40	700
Cost of sales*		445
Gross profit		255
Distribution costs	40 + 25 + 10	75
Administrative expenses	50 + 15 + 10	75
Group operating profit		105
Interest receivable/payable		−
Profit on ordinary activities before tax		105
Tax on profit on ordinary activities		34
Profit on ordinary activities after tax		71
Minority interests		4
Profit on ordinary activities after tax and minority interests		67
Dividends		50
Retained profit for group		17
* cost of sales:		
opening stock	100 + 75 + 50	225
+ purchases	300 + 150 + 100 − 10 − 40	500
− closing stock	150 + 100 + 40 − 10 (unrealised profit)	280
		445

CONSOLIDATED BALANCE SHEETS: MERGER METHOD

In the consolidated balance sheets that we have seen earlier in this chapter we have used the **acquisition method** of consolidation. This method is where one company buys a majority of the shares in another, paying for the shares, usually in cash. Another method of consolidation is the **merger method** which can be used, under certain circumstances, when shares in the subsidiary are obtained on a share-for-share exchange basis, with no cash changing hands. For example:

- **acquisition method**

    The parent company buys all the shares in the subsidiary from existing shareholders at a cost of £2.50 per share paid in cash; note that there is a cash outflow.

- **merger method**

  The parent company's offer of one share in the parent for each share in the subsidiary is accepted by most of the subsidiary company's shareholders; note that no cash changes hands, and other criteria apply (see below).

FRS 6, *Acquisitions and mergers*, defines a merger as: 'a business combination that results in the creation of a new reporting entity formed from the combining parties, in which the shareholders of the combining entities come together in a partnership for the mutual sharing of the risks and benefits of the combined entity, and in which no party to the combination in substance obtains control over any other, or is otherwise seen to be dominant, whether by virtue of the proportion of its shareholders' rights in the combined entity, the influence of its directors or otherwise'.

An acquisition is defined by the FRS as 'a business combination that is not a merger.'

The standard states five criteria to determine whether a combination is a merger:

1 no party is portrayed as either acquirer or acquired
2 all parties participate in establishing the management structure for the combined entity
3 the relative sizes of the combining entities are not disparate (ie markedly different)
4 the consideration received by the equity (ordinary) shareholders of each party comprises primarily equity shares in the combined entity
5 no equity shareholders of any of the combined entities retain any material interest in the future performance of only part of the combined entity

Note that the fifth criterion fails if the holders of more than 10 per cent of the equity shares in one of the combining companies do not accept the terms of the merger; ie acceptance by 90 per cent, or more, is required.

All of the above five criteria must be satisfied for merger accounting to be used: if the criteria are met, then merger accounting must be used. If the criteria are not all satisfied, then acquisition accounting must be used.

merger method – accounting treatment

Merger accounting treats the two or more parties as combining on an equal footing, ie no party is seen as the acquirer or the acquired. The parties come together to share in the future risks and benefits of the combined entity. The diagram on the next page shows the main differences between the acquisition method and the merger method. The particular advantage of using the merger method is that all profits of the subsidiary – whenever they were earned – are available for distribution; this contrasts with the acquisition method where pre-acquisition profits are capitalised and go into the goodwill calculation, and only post-acquisition profits are available for distribution.

Acquisition method	Merger method
Parties seen as either the acquirer or the acquired	No party seen as the acquirer or the acquired
Shares in subsidiary bought from existing shareholders and paid for, usually, in cash	Shares in subsidiary obtained on a share-for-share exchange basis
If acquisition is financed by an issue of shares at a premium, a share premium account must be created	No share premium account is used – shares are accounted for at nominal value only
Fair values used to restate assets and liabilities at date of acquisition	Fair values not used – the emphasis is on the continuity of the parties to the combination
Goodwill – positive or negative – must be recognised	Difference on consolidation does not represent goodwill but is deducted from, or added to, reserves through a merger reserve
Pre-acquisition profits of the subsidiary are locked into the group and are no longer available for distribution	All profits of the subsidiary – whenever they were earned – are available for distribution
Minority interests can be a maximum of just under 50 per cent of the equity (ordinary) shares	Minority interests cannot exceed 10 per cent of the equity shares

CASE STUDY

THE MERGER METHOD

Tutorial note

AAT's Guidance Notes for this Unit state that the criteria for treating a business combination as an acquisition or a merger (see above) need to be known; the preparation of merger accounts will not be assessed. Accordingly, this Case Study is provided to give an example – in simple terms – of how the merger method of consolidation is applied; however, you will not be assessed on the preparation of merger method consolidated balance sheets in this way.

situation

The following are the summarised balance sheets of House Limited and Garden Limited before merger:

	House Ltd	Garden Ltd
	£000	£000
Net assets	65	45
Share capital (£1 ordinary shares)	40	30
Reserves: retained profits	25	15
	65	45

House obtains shares in Garden, under the following circumstances, on a share-for-share exchange basis (each circumstance is to be treated separately):

1   House issues 35,000 £1 ordinary shares in exchange for the whole share capital of Garden

2   House issues 25,000 £1 ordinary shares in exchange for the whole share capital of Garden

3   House issues 35,000 £1 ordinary shares in exchange for 27,000 shares in Garden

Assume that the five criteria have been met for merger accounting to be used.

solution
circumstance 1

In merger accounting only the nominal value of shares issued and obtained is considered.

The difference between shares issued and shares obtained is a merger reserve which is
  –   deducted from reserves where shares issued are greater than shares obtained (as here)
  –   added to reserves where shares issued are fewer than shares obtained (see 2, below)

The consolidated balance is as follows:

	£000
Net assets 65 + 45	110
Share capital (£1 ordinary shares) 40 + 35	75
Reserves: retained profits	*35
	110

*	House	25
	Garden	15
		40

continued . . .

Less merger reserve

shares issued	35
shares obtained	30
	5
	35

circumstance 2

In this example, shares issued are fewer than shares obtained:

	£000
shares issued	25
shares obtained	30
merger reserve	5

Here, merger reserve is added to other reserves.

The consolidated balance sheet is as follows:

	£000
Net assets 65 + 45	110
Share capital (£1 ordinary shares) 40 + 25	*65
Reserves: retained profits 25 + 15	40
merger reserve (see above)	5
	110

* Note that all retained profits are available for distribution, this being a key feature of the merger method of consolidation

circumstance 3

In this example, 27,000 out of 30,000 shares in Garden are being obtained, ie 90 per cent. Thus minority interests hold 10 per cent of the shares in Garden – the maximum permitted under the criteria for merger accounting.

Here, £35,000 of shares is being issued in order to obtain £27,000 of shares; this difference of £8,000 is deducted from reserves in the consolidated balance sheet.

The consolidated balance sheet is as follows:

	£000
Net assets 65 + 45	110
Share capital (£1 ordinary shares) 40 + 35	75
Reserves: retained profits	*30
	105
Minority interests 50 x 10%	5
	110
* House	20
Garden 20 x 90%	18
	38
Less merger reserve (see above)	8
	30

ASSOCIATED COMPANIES

participating interest and significant influence

An associated company is defined by FRS 9, *Associates and joint ventures*, as: 'an entity (other than a subsidiary) in which another entity (the investor) has a participating interest and over whose operating and financial policies the investor exercises a significant influence'.

A **participating interest** is a long-term investment held for the purpose of contributing financial benefits to the investor's activities.

The **exercise of significant influence** is where the investor takes part in the process of making policy decisions, such as the expansion or contraction of the business, changes in products, markets, activities, etc.

As a general guideline, an associated company is where an investor owns between 20 per cent and 50 per cent of the ordinary shares of another company. However, ownership of shares by itself is not enough to establish an associated company relationship: ownership must be accompanied by a participating interest and the exercise of significant influence.

As we have seen earlier in this chapter, an ordinary share ownership above 50 per cent usually indicates a subsidiary company relationship; below 20 per cent is classed as a trade investment (see page 339). Thus an investment in an associated company is a substantial investment which is greater than a trade investment, but which is not as significant as a subsidiary company. The relationship is that of investor and investee (the associated company).

Note that FRS 9 also covers joint ventures – AAT's Guidance Notes for this Unit state that accounting for joint ventures is not assessed.

equity method of accounting

The equity method is the usual way of accounting for the results of associated companies. By this method we mean that the investor values its investment so as to reflect its interest in the net assets of the associated company. Initially the associated company is shown on the investor's balance sheet at cost (contrast this with subsidiary companies where assets and liabilities are included with those of the parent); the investor's share of subsequent profits or losses of the associated company are added to, or deducted from, the cost of the investment.

In the investor's financial statements, the key features of the equity method are:

- in the **profit and loss account** (see diagram below) show the investor's share of the associated company's:
  - operating profit (stated separately, immediately after group operating profit)
  - interest receivable/payable (include with amount for group)
  - corporation tax (include with amount for group)
- in the **balance sheet**
  - the investor's share of the net assets of the associated company should be included and separately disclosed
  - goodwill arising on the investor's acquisition of its associate – less any amortisation – should be included in the carrying amount of the associate but should be disclosed separately

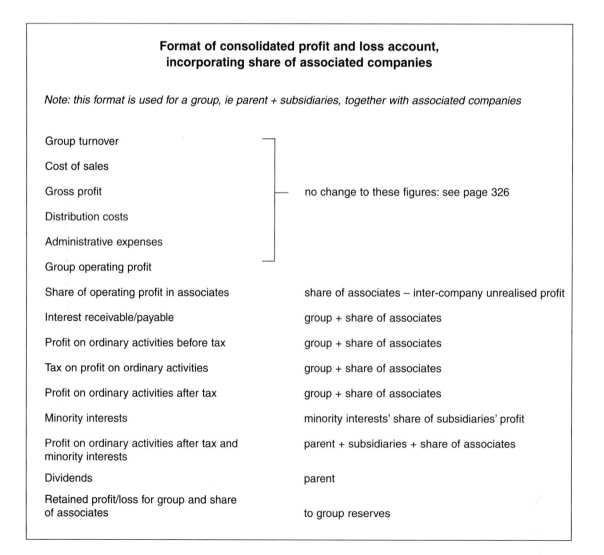

Format of consolidated profit and loss account, incorporating share of associated companies

Note: this format is used for a group, ie parent + subsidiaries, together with associated companies

Group turnover	
Cost of sales	
Gross profit	no change to these figures: see page 326
Distribution costs	
Administrative expenses	
Group operating profit	
Share of operating profit in associates	share of associates – inter-company unrealised profit
Interest receivable/payable	group + share of associates
Profit on ordinary activities before tax	group + share of associates
Tax on profit on ordinary activities	group + share of associates
Profit on ordinary activities after tax	group + share of associates
Minority interests	minority interests' share of subsidiaries' profit
Profit on ordinary activities after tax and minority interests	parent + subsidiaries + share of associates
Dividends	parent
Retained profit/loss for group and share of associates	to group reserves

ASSOCIATED COMPANIES

situation

On 31 December 2001, Icod Limited bought 25 per cent of the share capital of Arona Limited, its associated company, at a cost of £15,000. At that date the balance sheet of Arona was as follows:

	Arona Ltd £000
Fixed assets	28
Current assets	20
Current liabilities	(8)
	40
Share capital (£1 ordinary shares)	30
Reserves: retained profits	10
	40

At 31 December 2002, before including the results of Arona, the balance sheets of Icod and Arona were as follows:

	Icod Ltd £000	Arona Ltd £000
Fixed assets	100	35
Investment in associate at cost	15	–
Current assets	45	45
Current liabilities	(10)	(20)
	150	60
Share capital (£1 ordinary shares)	100	30
Reserves: retained profits at start of year	30	10
retained profits for 2002	20	20
	150	60

An extract from the profit and loss accounts of Icod and Arona for 2002 showed the following:

	Icod Ltd £000	Arona Ltd £000
Operating profit	75	28
Interest payable	5	4
Profit before tax	70	24
Corporation tax	20	4
Profit after tax	50	20
Dividends	30	–
Retained profits	20	20

Notes:

• At the date of acquisition there were no material differences between the book value and fair value of any of the assets of Arona

• The accounting policy of Icod is to amortise goodwill over an estimated useful economic life of five years

solution

Goodwill on acquisition

The calculation of goodwill in Arona is as follows:

	£000
cost of investment	15
value of associate at date of acquisition	
40 (net assets) x 25% owned	10
goodwill	5

Tutorial note

For the goodwill calculation, the value of the associate – using net assets – at the date of acquisition is reduced to the percentage of shares owned, here 25 per cent.

As Icod's accounting policy is to amortise goodwill over an estimated useful economic life of five years, £1,000 will be written off to profit and loss account in 2002, leaving £4,000 of goodwill to be shown in the balance sheet.

Where fair values are different from book values, fair values are used in the calculation of goodwill.

Profit and loss account for 2002

Icod reports its share of the associated company's profits as follows:

	£000	£000	
Operating profit		75	
Share of operating profit in associate	7		28 x 25%
Less amortisation of goodwill on acquisition	1		see goodwill, above
		6	
		81	
Interest payable		6	5 + (4 x 25%)
Profit on ordinary activities before tax		75	
Tax on profit on ordinary activities		21	20 + (4 x 25%)
Profit on ordinary activities after tax		54	
Dividends		30	
Retained profits		24	

Tutorial note

The share of the operating profit of the associate has been shown separately, less the amount for amortisation of goodwill on acquisition

The share of the associate's interest payable, and corporation tax have been included with the amounts of the investing company.

Balance sheet as at 31 December 2002

The value of Arona, the associated company, is calculated as:

				£000
net assets of associated company	x	investor's share		
£60,000	x	25%	=	15
plus goodwill, unamortised, £5,000 – £1,000			=	4
				19

The balance sheet of Icod, incorporating the results of Arona, is as follows (£000):

Fixed assets	100
Investment in associate	19
Current assets	45
Current liabilities	(10)
	154
Share capital (£1 ordinary shares)	100
Reserves: retained profits 30 + 24	54
	154

Tutorial note

An alternative way to calculate the value of Arona is:	£000
cost of investment	15
+ share of retained profits for year 20 x 25%	5
– amortisation of goodwill on acquisition	1
	19
Retained profits for the year are:	
Icod, the investing company	20
+ share of Arona, the associate	5
– amortisation of goodwill on acquisition	1
	24

TRADE INVESTMENTS

A trade investment is where a company holds shares in another company – either for its investment potential, or so as to take an interest in a major supplier or customer. Generally a trade investment is where the investor owns below 20 per cent of the ordinary shares of another company. At this level the percentage owned is not sufficient to make the investee an associated or subsidiary company – either because the investor has limited influence, or the interest is not long-term.

The accounting treatment for trade investments is very simple. The investor records the investment as either a fixed or a current asset – depending on how long the shares are to be held: if more than twelve months from the balance sheet date, the investment is a fixed asset; if less, it is a current asset. Fixed asset trade investments are valued at either cost or valuation; if there is impairment, the fixed asset should be written down to its recoverable amount. Current asset trade investments are valued at the lower of cost and net realisable value.

Income from trade investments – usually in the form of dividends received – is credited in profit and loss account as 'income from investments', while the dividend cheque is debited to bank account.

DISCLOSURE AND CONFIDENTIALITY

the extent of disclosure

The accounting standards FRS 2, *Accounting for subsidiary undertakings*, FRS 6, *Acquisitions and Mergers*, and FRS 7, *Fair values in acquisition accounting*, cover the techniques of consolidated accounting for parent and subsidiary companies and set out the detailed disclosures required in group accounts. FRS 9, *Associates and joint ventures*, deals with accounting for associated companies and joint ventures – note that the latter are not assessed by AAT.

The published accounts of limited companies – which are readily available to shareholders and interested parties – include, where appropriate, group financial statements (profit and loss account, balance sheet and cash flow statement) which disclose the consolidated financial performance and financial position of the parent company and its subsidiary companies; the accounts also incorporate the results of associated companies. Thus the user is assured that the financial statements have been prepared in accordance with the Companies Acts and accounting standards. Nevertheless, only certain information is required to be disclosed in the published accounts; some details do not need to be disclosed.

confidentiality procedures

For those involved in the preparation of the accounts, confidentiality procedures must be observed at all times:

– with the detailed financial statements of subsidiary and associated companies

– with the detailed profit and loss account of the parent company (because, where a consolidated profit and loss account is produced, the parent company is not legally obliged to produce its own profit and loss account)

– during the preparation of published accounts which incorporate the figures from subsidiary and associated companies

– for detailed information that is needed in the preparation of the accounts but is not required to be disclosed under the Companies Acts and accounting standards

CHAPTER SUMMARY

- Consolidated accounts are designed to show the position of a group – parent company and subsidiary companies – as if it was a single entity.

- There are two methods of preparing consolidated balance sheets: the acquisition method and the merger method.

- There are three major calculations in the preparation of a consolidated balance sheet under the acquisition method:
  - goodwill, calculated as at the date of acquisition of the subsidiary
  - post-acquisition profits, calculated since the date of acquisition of the shares in the subsidiary
  - minority interests, calculated at the date of the consolidated balance sheet

- The use of fair values in acquisition accounting affects
  - goodwill, which is calculated as the cost of the investment in the subsidiary, less the fair value of the subsidiary's assets and liabilities
  - minority interests, which is the proportion of the subsidiary, based on the fair value of the subsidiary's assets and liabilities
  - post-acquisition profits, which will be affected where the use of fair value for fixed assets leads to a different depreciation charge from that based on historic costs

- Inter-company adjustments may have to be made when preparing consolidated balance sheets for
  - debtors, creditors and loans, which cancel out between companies within the group
  - dividends proposed, which cancel out between group companies
  - inter-company profits, eg on sale of stock, which are unrealised at the date of the consolidated balance sheet

- When preparing a consolidated profit and loss account
  - the full profit of subsidiaries is shown, with a separate deduction for the proportion of the profit due to minority interests
  - only the dividends paid and proposed of the parent company are shown
  - inter-company transactions are deducted for inter-company sales, inter-company purchases, and inter-company unrealised profit

- The five criteria to determine whether a combination is a merger:
  1. no party is portrayed as either acquirer or acquired
  2. all parties participate in establishing the management structure for the combined entity
  3. the relative sizes of the combining entities are not disparate

4   the consideration received by the equity shareholders of each party comprises primarily equity shares in the combined entity

5   no equity shareholders of any of the combined entities retain any material interest in the future performance of only part of the combined entity

Note: all of the above five criteria must be satisfied for merger accounting to be used.

- An associated company is where an investor owns generally between 20 per cent and 50 per cent of the ordinary shares of another company and has a participating interest and exercises significant influence over its operating and financial policies

- The equity method is the usual way of accounting for the results of associated companies:

  - initially the investment in the associated company is shown at cost on the investor's balance sheet

  - the investor's share of subsequent profits or losses are added to, or deducted from, the cost of the investment

  - the investor's profit and loss account includes the share of the associated companies' operating profit, interest receivable/payable and corporation tax

parent company/ subsidiary company	a parent company has a subsidiary where any of the following apply:
	• holds a majority of voting rights in subsidiary
	• controls composition of board of directors
	• has the right to exercise dominant influence
	• has a participating interest
dominant influence	influence which can be exercised to achieve the operating and financial policies desired by the holder of the influence, notwithstanding the rights or influence of any other party
participating interest	an interest held by an undertaking in the shares of another undertaking which it holds on a long-term basis for the purpose of securing a contribution to its activities by the exercise of control or influence arising from or related to that interest
group	a parent undertaking and its subsidiary undertakings

acquisition method	the business combination is seen as the acquisition of one company by another; defined by FRS 6 as: 'a business combination that is not a merger'
merger method	the two or more parties are treated as combining on an equal footing; defined by FRS 6 as: 'a business combination that results in the creation of a new reporting entity formed from the combining parties, in which the shareholders of the combining entities come together in a partnership for the mutual sharing of the risks and benefits of the combined entity, and in which no party to the combination in substance obtains control over any other, or is otherwise seen to be dominant, whether by virtue of the proportion of its shareholders' rights in the combined entity, the influence of its directors or otherwise'
goodwill	the cost of the investment in the subsidiary, less the fair value of the subsidiary's assets and liabilities
fair value	'the amount at which an asset or liability could be exchanged in an arm's length transaction between informed and willing parties, other than in a forced or liquidation sale' (FRS 7)
post-acquisition profits	profits earned by a subsidiary since the date of acquisition
minority interests	the owners of shares which are not owned by the parent company
associated company	'an entity (other than a subsidiary) in which another entity (the investor) has a participating interest and over whose operating and financial policies the investor exercises a significant influence' (FRS 9)
significant influence	where the investor takes part in the process of making policy decisions, such as the expansion or contraction of the business, changes in products, markets, activities, etc
equity method of accounting	method of accounting for associated companies by which the investing company values its investment so as to reflect its interest in the net assets of the associated company

STUDENT
ACTIVITIES

11.1 Sidney PLC acquires 60% of the ordinary shares in Kidney Ltd on the 1 January 20-3. Kidney Ltd's net profit after tax for the year to 31 December 20-3 is £10,000.

What is the minority interest in the consolidated profit and loss account for the year ended 31 December 20-3?

(a) £6,000
(b) £4,000
(c) £2,000
(d) £10,000

11.2 The Takeover PLC invested £305,000 in 800,000 ordinary shares of 10 pence each in the Subsidiary Co Ltd. The Subsidiary Co Ltd's issued share capital and reserves at the date of acquisition were £100,000 in shares and £200,000 in reserves (£300,000 in total).

What is the value for goodwill arising on the acquisition?

(a) £20,000
(b) £5,000
(c) £65,000
(d) £6,500

11.3 The issued share capital of the Landmark Co Ltd consists of 400,000 ordinary shares of 25 pence each. The reserves of the company currently total £120,000. Seaside PLC currently owns 300,000 ordinary shares in Landmark.

What is the total value for minority interest?

(a) £55,000
(b) £130,000
(c) £165,000
(d) £25,000

11.4 Walkingman Ltd is a subsidiary company which is 80% owned. Its profits for the year after taxation to 31 December 20-3 are £200,000. Out of this profit it has provided its shareholders with a dividend of £60,000 for the year.

What figure will appear in the consolidated profit and loss account for minority interest?

(a) £160,000
(b) £40,000
(c) £28,000
(d) £52,000

11.5 What are group profits commonly referred to as when they are earned and generated whilst under the parent company's control?

(a)   Pre-acquisition profits

(b)   Post-acquisition profits

(c)   Ex-acquisition profits

(d)   Minority interest

11.6 As at 31 December 20-3 the parent company has on its balance sheet trade debtors totaling £85,000. Its subsidiary company on the same day shows trade debtors of £40,000, of which £10,000 is an inter-group debt due from the parent company.

On the consolidated balance sheet for the group what is the correct valuation for trade debtors?

(a)   £125,000

(b)   £45,000

(c)   £135,000

(d)   £115,000

11.7 Which Financial Reporting Statement (FRS) deals with the requirements of Associated Companies?

(a)   FRS 2

(b)   FRS 9

(c)   FRS 10

(d)   FRS 15

11.8 According to FRS 2, Accounting for subsidiary undertakings, what conditions are said to apply if an undertaking is deemed to be a parent undertaking of another undertaking (ie subsidiary undertaking)?

11.9 The directors of Phantom PLC have been in negotiation with the directors/ shareholders of another company, Roover PLC with regard to the purchasing of 80% of the share capital from them. Phantom will pay £2,900,000 for the shares based on the valuation of the company at 30 April 20-3, this being the agreed date for acquisition.

The fair value of the fixed assets in Roover PLC at 30 April 20-3 is £4,200,000. All the other assets and liabilities of the company are stated at fair value (i.e. balance sheet valuation)

Roover PLC Balance sheet as at 30 April 20-3 is as follows:

	£000	£000
FIXED ASSETS AT NBV		3,500
CURRENT ASSETS		
Stocks	450	
Debtors	300	
Cash at bank	100	
	850	

Creditors: amounts falling due within one year

Trade Creditors	250	
Dividends payable	150	
Taxation	200	
	600	
NET CURRENT ASSETS		250
		3,750

Creditors: amounts falling due after more than one year		
10% Debentures		1,000
		2,750

Represented by
CAPITAL AND RESERVES

Called up share capital	800
Share Premium Account	200
Profit and Loss Account	1,750
	2,750

REQUIRED

Calculate the goodwill on consolidation that would arise on acquisition if Phantom PLC purchased an 80% stakeholding in Roover PLC on 30 April 20-3.

What figure for minority interest would appear in the consolidated balance of Phantom PLC as at 30 April 20-3?

11.10 You have been asked to assist in the preparation of the consolidated accounts of the Ringster Group of companies. Set out below are the balance sheets of Ringer PLC and its subsidiary Sterling Ltd, as at 30 April 20-3.

	Ringer PLC		Sterling Ltd	
	£000	£000	£000	£000
Fixed Assets at nbv		6,000		1,600
Investment in Sterling		2,000		
Current Assets				
Stocks	1,900		800	
Debtors	1,500		500	
Cash at Bank	600		100	
	4,000		1,400	
Creditors amounts falling due within one year				
Creditors	1,500		400	
Taxation	400		100	
Dividends	1,000			
Net Current Assets		1,100		900
		9,100		2,500

Creditors: amounts falling due after more than one year		
Long Term Loans	2,000	500
	7,100	2,000
Capital and Reserves		
Called up share Capital	2,000	1,000
Share Premium Account	1,000	500
Profit and Loss Account	4,100	500
	7,100	2,000

Additional information

The share capital of both companies consists of ordinary shares of £1 denomination.

Ringer PLC acquired 600,000 shares in Sterling Ltd on 30 April 20-3.

The fair value of the fixed assets of Sterling Ltd at 30 April 20-3 was £1,900,000.

REQUIRED

Prepare a consolidated Balance Sheet for Ringer PLC as at 30 April 20-3. Any goodwill arising on consolidation should be shown as an intangible asset.

11.11 Crispin PLC purchased 25% of the ordinary share capital in Kingston Ltd for £320,000 on 1 April 20-2. Kingston Ltd is an associate company and the directors would like to know how Kingston Ltd would be included in the results of the Crispin group. Extracts from Kingston Ltd's accounts are listed below:

Profit and loss account for the year to 31 March 20-3

	£000
Net profit before taxation	420
Taxation	120
Net profit after taxation	300

Balance Sheet as at 31 March 20-3	£000
Fixed Assets	900
Net Current Assets	200
	1,100
10% Debentures	100
	1,000
Capital and reserves	
Called up Share Capital	400
Share Premium Account	100
Profit and Loss Account	500
	1,000

Additional Information

Any goodwill is deemed to have an indefinite life and should not be amortised.

REQUIRED

What figures would appear in the consolidated profit and loss account and consolidated balance sheet of the Crispin Group for the year to 31 March 20-3 to account for the results of Kingston Ltd?

11.12 The following summarised balance sheets relate to the Winston group of companies as at 30 November 20-3.

	Winston PLC £000		Churchill Ltd £000	
Fixed Assets at NBV		5,000		600
Investment in Churchill		900		
Current Assets				
Stock	150		30	
Debtors	80		35	
Cash at Bank	10	240	5	70
Current Liabilities				
Creditors		(160)		(120)
		5,980		550
CAPITAL AND RESERVES				
£1 Ordinary Shares		4,000		400
Profit and Loss Account		1,980		150
		5,980		550

Additional Information

Winston PLC purchased a 90% holding in Churchill Ltd on 1 December 20-1 when Churchill's profit and loss account balance was £50,000

During the year to 30 November 20-3 Churchill purchased goods from Winston for £60,000. Winston had invoiced these goods at cost plus 33.3%. A third of these goods were still in stock at the year end.

At 30 November 20-3 the following inter group debt was still outstanding: Churchill owed Winston £10,000.

Any goodwill arising upon consolidation is to be amortised over a 10 year period.

REQUIRED

Prepare the Winston group of companies consolidated balance sheet as at 30 November 20-3.

11.13 The summary profit and loss accounts of Tom Limited, a parent company, and Ben Limited and Sarah Limited, its subsidiaries for the year-ended 31 December 20-2 are as follows:

	Tom Ltd	Ben Ltd	Sarah Ltd
	£000	£000	£000
Turnover (sales)	800	400	300
Opening stock	200	150	100
+ Purchases	600	300	200
– Closing stock	300	200	80
Cost of sales	500	250	220
Gross profit	300	150	80
Distribution costs	80	50	20
Administration expenses	100	30	20
Dividends from subsidiaries:			
Ben	40		
Sarah	18		
Net profit	178	70	40
Corporation tax	40	20	8
Profit after tax	138	50	32
Dividends	100	40	24
Retained profits	38	10	8

Additional information

• Tom Limited bought all of the shares of Ben Limited on 1 January 20-0, and 75 per cent of the shares of Sarah Limited on 1 January 20-2.

• During the year to 31 December 20-2 the following inter-company trading took place:

– Tom sold goods costing £12,000 to Ben at a price of £20,000; Ben had sold all of these goods by the year-end for £24,000.

– Tom sold goods costing £40,000 to Sarah at a price of £80,000; by the year-end half of these goods were unsold by Sarah.

• Tom's policy is to take credit for inter-company dividends.

REQUIRED

Prepare a consolidated profit and loss account of Tom Limited and its subsidiaries for the year ended 31 December 20-2.

CHAPTER 1: PURPOSE OF FINANCIAL STATEMENTS

1.1 (d)

1.2 (a)

1.3 (c)

1.4 Students should list any three of the following:

Existing and potential investors who are interested in:
- Profit
- Liquidity and cash flow
- Annual sales turnover

Lenders who are interested in:
- Profit
- Loan capital and risk
- Asset and balance sheet value
- Liquidity and cash flow

Suppliers and creditors who are interested in
- Cash flow and liquidity
- The value of assets and liabilities

Employees who are interested in
- Profit
- Liquidity and cash flow

Customers who are interested in
- Profit
- The value of assets and liabilities
- Liquidity and cash flow

The government who is interested in
- Profit
- Annual sales turnover

The general public who is interested in:
- Profit
- Liquidity and cash flow

1.5 Stewardship relates to the entity management and the ways in which it is accountable for the safekeeping of the organisation's resources and their proper efficient and profitable use.
Economic decisions are the management's strategy with regard to the business entity covering investment or potential investment decisions on a day-to-day basis..

1.6 (a) Going concern
This assumes that the business will continue to trade for the foreseeable future and there is no intention to downscale or sell off key operations of the business.

(b) Prudence
This concept stipulates that a business should not include in the accounts revenues that have not been realised, and that costs that are likely to be incurred should be included and charged to the profit and loss account.

(c)   Business entity
All financial statements should report and record on its business activities only. Therefore personal transactions are not part of this reporting and recording process and should be kept separate.

(d)   Matching/accruals
This means that revenues and costs are matched to the accounting period to which they relate. Thus revenues and costs incurred are shown in the profit and loss account rather than the amounts received and paid (which is referred to as cash accounting).

1.7   (a)   Business entity concept
Harold's private transactions are his own affairs and nothing to with the business. Therefore the payment of his daughters' school fees should be charged to him as drawings.

(b)   Materiality Concept
A box of pencils in the stationery cupboard is not a material amount and will not have any real significance in the preparation of the annual accounts. Therefore it should not be treated as part of closing stock but written off as an expense to the profit and loss account.

(c)   Going concern concept.
If Harold's business is not likely to continue in the near future then different accounting rules would need to be adopted to reflect this; for example, fixed assets would need to be recorded at their net realisable value rather than a t their net book values. This is often referred to as the going concern principle.

(d)   Matching/Accruals concept
Here expenses and revenues must be matched so that they relate to the same goods and time period. Rent clearly overlaps two accounting periods, the year ending 20-2 and 20-3, part being paid in advance (£1,000) which is carried forward as an asset on the balance sheet.

(e)   Prudence concept.
If the debt is irrecoverable then the £500 should be written off as a bad debt and charged against this year's profit. If there is any doubt to the liquidation question then the £500 should appear as part of the provision for bad and doubtful debts.

(f)   Consistency concept
The stock should continue to be valued on a FIFO basis unless there are any genuine reasons for adopting another method of valuation, which will give a more true and fair view of the businesses accounts. The manipulation of income tax payments does not fall within this category.

1.8   (a)   There is a conflict here between the accruals or matching concept and the prudence concept. The accruals concept states that costs should be matched against revenue which they generate. Thus it might be argued that, since half the revenue expected to result from the advertising campaign will be achieved in 20-6, it might be appropriate to defer half the costs of the advertising campaign until 20-6. However, the concept of prudence states that profits (and revenue) should not be anticipated but that provision should be made for all known losses (and expenses). When prudence and accruals conflict, prudence prevails. Therefore all the cost of the advertising campaign should be written off as an expense in the 20-5 accounts.

(b)   When the proprietor of a business takes stock for his own use, it counts as drawings, which are a deduction from the owner's capital.

(c)   Under the business entity concept the business is a separate entity from Jonathan Brown as a person. This applies for accounting purposes, although not for legal purposes. As the loan was made to the business it should be disclosed in the financial statements.

1.9   Task 1

(a)   The objective of financial statements is to 'provide information about the financial position, performance and financial adaptability of an enterprise that is useful to a wide range of users for assessing the stewardship of management and for making economic decisions'.

(b)   In a profit-making organisation such as a company, financial statements provide information to shareholders to enable them to assess the performance of management, for example in generating profits for the period or in improving the financial position of the company. It may also assist them in deciding whether to continue holding their shares in the business, to acquire more shares or to dispose of all or part of their holding.

In a public sector body like, for example, a local authority, the organisation does not exist to make profits but to provide services to the public. Financial statements may enable payers of Council Tax to assess the level of spending of the authority in relation to the services provided and to determine whether the services have been provided economically, efficiently and effectively.

In not-for-profit organisations like clubs, for example, the aim is not to make a profit but to achieve the objectives of the club. Financial statements can assist the members of the club to assess how the stewards of the club have used the resources entrusted to them to achieve the club's purposes.

Task 2

(a)   The elements of financial statements are:

- assets
- liabilities
- ownership interest
- income
- expenditure
- gains
- losses
- contributions from owners
- distributions to owners

(b)   The accounting equation that underlies the balance sheet of an organisation relates the following elements:

Assets − Liabilities = Ownership interest

In the context of a company, the change in ownership interest in the period is equal to the capital contributed from owners plus gains in the form of revenue and losses in the form of expenses. Revenue less expenses equals profit. Thus the profit and loss account explains how the change in ownership interest arising from sources other than contributions from owners came about (note that some gains or losses are reported only in the statement of total recognised gains and losses and not in the profit and loss account).

(c)   In a profit-making organisation, the ownership interest is referred to as the 'capital' of the business. It is often explained as the amount owing to the owners of the business and includes such things as share capital and undistributed profits earned by the business. In public sector or not-for-profit organisation, the ownership interest is based on the concept of a 'fund'. A fund is established for a particular purpose and the financial statements enable the users to see how the fund has changed in the period and to assist in determining whether the fund has been used for the purposes intended.

1.10   Task 1

(a)   The organisations and their users are as follows:

Profit-making organisations:

Type of organisation	Example of user
Companies	Shareholders
Partnerships	Bank
Sole traders	Creditors

Public sector/not-for-profit organisations

Type of organisation	Example of user
Local authorities	Council taxpayers
National Health Service Trusts	Department of Health
Charities	People making donations
Clubs	Members

(b)   The types of decisions may be as follows:

Profit-making organisations:

User	Example of decisions
Shareholders	To sell or buy more shares
	To assess stewardship of managers
Bank	To decide whether to grant a loan
Creditors	To decide whether to supply goods or services

Public sector/not-for-profit organisations:

User	Example of decisions
Council taxpayers	To decide whether the local authority has given value for money
Department of Health	To decide whether the trust has been efficiently run by the managers
People making donations	To decide whether donations have been effectively used
Members	To decide if the officers have run the club efficiently

Task 2

(a)   "Assets" are rights or other access to future economic benefits controlled by an entity as a result of past transactions or events.

"Liabilities" are obligations of an entity to transfer economic benefits as a result of past transactions or events.

"Ownership interest" is the residual amount found by deducting all of the entity's liabilities from all of the entity's assets.

(b)   In the ownership interest section of the balance sheet of a profit-making organisation capital balances would appear. These can include amounts paid in by owners (such as share capital in the case of companies) plus reserves which are owed to owners (such as the balances in the profit and loss account). In a public sector or not-for-profit organisation fund balances would appear in the ownership interest section of the balance sheet. These are amounts which have been allocated to certain purposes of the organisation.

1.11   NOTES FOR THE DIRECTORS

(a)   The elements in a balance sheet and the balances in Machier Ltd which fall under those elements are as follows:

Elements	Balances
Assets	Fixed assets
	Current assets
Liabilities	Current liabilities
	Long-term liabilities
Ownership interest	Capital and reserves

(b)   The accounting equation is as follows:
(figures in £000)

Assets	−	Liabilities	= Ownership interest
(£4,282 + £975)	−	(£749 + £2,800)	= £1,708
£5,257	−	£3,549	= £1,708

(c)   In not-for-profit organisations the purpose of the organisation is not to make a profit. Hence, a profit and loss account would not be appropriate. Instead an income and expenditure account is used. Expenditure incurred in generating the income is deducted from the income to arrive at a surplus of income over expenditure or an excess of expenditure over income. These figures correspond to the net profit or net loss in a profit and loss account.

(d)   The equivalent of capital balances in a not-for-profit organisation are fund balances. These are amounts which have been allocated to certain purposes of the organisation.

CHAPTER 2: SOLE TRADER FINAL ACCOUNTS

2.1   (b)

2.2   (c)

2.3   (b)

2.4   **Fixed Assets**

These are long-term items which are owned and held by the business for the long term (this is usually perceived to be more than 12 months). Examples include land and buildings, plant and equipment etc.

Current Assets

These are assets with a short life (less than 12 months) . They may change on a day-to–day basis. Such assets tend to represent cash or near cash.

Examples include stock, debtors and cash.

2.5   **Working notes**

	Dr	Cr
	£	£
Stock – Balance Sheet	52,170	
Stock – Trading Account		52,170
Depreciation expense – Premises	1,720	
Accum Dep'n – Premises		1,720
Depreciation expense – Delivery Van	3,072	
Accum Dep'n – Delivery Van		3,072
Depreciation expense – Fixtures & Fittings	2,950	
Accum dep'n – Fixtures & Fittings		2,950
Heat and Light	380	
Accruals		380
Increase in provision for doubtful debts	89	
Provision for doubtful debts		89
Prepayments	560	
Advertising		560
Depreciation Charges		
Premises 2% x £86,000		1,720
Delivery Van 20% x (£24,000 – £8,640)		3,072
Fixtures and Fittings 10% x £29,500		2,950
Increase in provision for doubtful debts		
New provision 4% x £5,350		214
Less already provided		(125)
Net increase in provision		89

Task 1

William Blakeney

Trading, Profit and Loss Account for the year ended 31 July 20-2

	£	£
Sales		198,630
COST OF SALES		
Opening stock	43,750	
Purchases	84,550	
	128,300	
Closing stock	52,170	
		76,130
GROSS PROFIT		122,500
Expenditure:		
Delivery van expenses	6,290	
Shop expenses	3,370	
Heat and Light (2,840 + 380)	3,220	
Postage, Stationery and Telephone	4,910	

Wages and salaries	15,220	
Advertising (2,660 – 560)	2,100	
Bad debts	450	
General expenses	1,080	
Increase in provision for doubtful debts	89	
Depreciation		
– Premises	1,720	
– Delivery van	3,072	
– Fixtures and Fittings	2,950	
		44,471
NET PROFIT FOR THE YEAR		78,029

Task 2

William Blakeney

Balance Sheet as at 31 July 20-2

FIXED ASSETS	COST	DEP'N	NET
	£	£	£
Premises	86,000	10,320	75,680
Delivery Van	24,000	11,712	12,288
Fixtures and Fittings	29,500	17,700	11,800
	139,500	39,732	99,768
CURRENT ASSETS			
Stocks		52,170	
Debtors	5,350		
Less provision for doubtful debts	(214)	5,136	
Prepayments		560	
Cash in Hand		250	
		58,116	
CURRENT LIABILITIES			
Creditors	29,450		
Accruals	380		
Bank overdraft	12,160	(41,990)	
NET CURRENT ASSETS			16,126
Total Assets less current Liabilities			115,894
LONG TERM LIABILITIES			
Bank Loan Account			(35,000)
			80,894
Represented By:			
CAPITAL			
Balance 01.08.01			12,865
Add Net Profit for the Year			78,029
			90,894
Less Drawings			(10,000)
			80,894

2.6   **Working notes**

	Dr	Cr
	£	£
1 Accountancy charges	16,000	
Accruals		16,000
2 Provision for bad and doubtful debts	1,405	
Reduction in provision P/L		1,405
New provision = 3% x £86,500	2,595	
Less already provided	(4,000)	
Reduction in provision adjustment	1,405	

Task 1

Adjusted net profit

Draft net profit for the year	106,250
Less Accountancy charges	16,000
	90,250
Add reduction in provision	1,405
Final net profit for the year	91,655

Task 2

Malcolm Walker Balance Sheet as at 30 September 20-2

FIXED ASSETS	cost	dep'n	net
	£	£	£
Land	133,725		133,725
Premises	300,000	96,000	204,000
Machinery and Equipment	125,800	62,900	62,900
Fixtures and Fittings	55,250	16,575	38,675
Motor vehicles	88,000	53,200	34,800
	702,775	228,675	474,100

CURRENT ASSETS		
Stocks		98,500
Debtors	86,500	
Less provision (4000 – 1405)	2,595	83,905
Prepayments		2,400
		184,805
CURRENT LIABILITIES		
Creditors	72,500	
HMCE – Vat	21,400	
Accruals (3600 + 16000)	19,600	
Bank Overdraft	12,500	126,000
NET CURRENT ASSETS		58,805
Total Assets less current Liabilities		532,905

LONG TERM LIABILITIES

Bank Loan Account	65,000
	467,905
Represented by:	
CAPITAL	
Balance 01.10.01	425,000
Add net profit for the year	91,655
	516,655
Less Drawings	48,750
	467,905

2.7 Working notes

	Dr	Cr
	£	£
Increase in provision for bad debts	520	
Provision for bad debts		520
Depreciation expense – Buildings	5,000	
Accum dep'n – Buildings		5,000
Depreciation expense – Furniture etc	10,000	
Accum dep'n – Furniture		10,000
Depreciation expense – Plant	43,750	
Accum dep'n – Plant		43,750
Depreciation expense – Motors	25,000	
Accum dep'n – Motors		25,000
Provision for bad debts		
New provision (5% x £47,000)		2,350
Less already provided		1,830
Net increase in provision		520
Depreciation:		
Buildings (2% x £250,000)	5,000	
Furniture and Fittings (10% x £100,000)	10,000	
Plant and Equipment (25% x £175,000)	43,750	
Motor vehicles (20% x £125,000)	25,000	

Task 1
Murtagh and Co: Trading, Profit and Loss Account for the year ended 31 August 20-2

	£	£
Sales		480,000
COST OF SALES:		
Opening stock	78,750	
Purchases	260,250	
	339,000	
Closing stock	86,150	
		252,850
GROSS PROFIT		227,150

Interest received	6,720	
Commission received	5,250	11,970
		239,120
EXPENDITURE:		
Wages and NIC	106,190	
Postage and Stationery	5,750	
Rent, Rates and Insurance	35,325	
Telephone	28,920	
Motor Expenses	22,480	
Light and Heat	20,660	
Discounts Allowed	4,800	
Bad debts	7,750	
Increase in provision for bad debts	520	
Repairs to buildings	4,375	
Advertising	22,400	
Depreciation		
– Buildings	5,000	
– Furniture and Fittings	10,000	
– Plant and Equipment	43,750	
– Motor Vehicles	25,000	342,920
NET LOSS FOR THE YEAR		103,800

Task 2
Murtagh and Co: Balance Sheet As At 31 August 20-2

FIXED ASSETS	cost	dep'n	net
	£	£	£
Land	400,000		400,000
Buildings	250,000	35,000	215,000
Furniture and Fittings	100,000	50,000	50,000
Plant and Equipment	175,000	87,500	87,500
Motor Vehicles	125,000	75,000	50,000
	1,050,000	247,500	802,500
CURRENT ASSETS			
Stock		86,150	
Debtors	47,000		
Less Bad debts provision	2,350	44,650	
Prepayments		7,395	
Bank Deposit Account		10,240	
Cash in Hand		500	
		148,935	
CURRENT LIABILITIES			
Creditors	29,150		
HMCE – Vat	8,390		
Inland Revenue	6,250		
Accruals	10,420		
Bank Overdraft	8,350	62,560	

NET CURRENT ASSETS		86,375
		888,875
LONG TERM LIABILITIES		
Loan – Mid West Bank		32,350
		856,525
Represented by:		
CAPITAL		
Balance 01.09.20-1		986,325
Less net loss for the year		103,800
		882,525
Less Drawings		26,000
		856,525

2.8 TAYLORIANA

PROFIT AND LOSS ACCOUNT FOR THE YEAR ENDED 31 MARCH 20-5

	£`000	£`000
Sales	257,350	
Less returns inwards	3,350	
		254,000
Cost of sales		
Opening stock	43,700	
Purchases	162,430	
Carriage inwards	1,320	
Less returns outwards	(7,460)	
	199,990	
Less closing stock	(49,300)	
Cost of Sales		150,690
GROSS PROFIT		103,310
Less expenses		
Wages	39,420	
Depreciation: fixtures and fittings	2,800	
motor vehicles	4,100	
Bad debts (540 + 2,500)	3,040	
Bank charges	320	
Postage, stationery and telephone	2,910	
Carriage outwards	850	
Rent, rates and insurance	8,650	
Discounts allowed	490	
Lighting and heating	1,760	
		64,340
NET PROFIT		38,970

CHAPTER 3: PARTNERSHIP FINAL ACCOUNTS

3.1   (c)

3.2   (c)

3.3   (d)

3.4   (a)

3.5   A partnership is said to exist where there is a relationship subsisting between persons carrying on business in common with a view to a profit.

3.6   If no partnership agreement exists then the following are binding:

(a)   No interest on capital account balances

(b)   Profit and losses are to be shared equally

(c)   No salary is payable to partners

(d)   No interest on drawings is payable

(e)   Interest on Partners loans are at 5% per annum

Nb Any three of the five listed above is permissible.

3.7   **Task 1**

Henry Ian and Simon

Profit and Loss Appropriation Account for the Year ended 30 June 20-2.

	£	£
Net profit for the year		70,000
Interest on Drawings		
Henry	1,200	
Ian	1,000	
Simon	800	3,000
		73,000
Salaries		
Henry	12,000	
Ian	15,000	
Simon	10,000	
	37,000	
Interest on Capital		
Henry	4,800	
Ian	3,200	
Simon	2,000	
		(47,000)
		26,000
Share of Profit		
Henry (4/10)	10,400	
Ian (4/10)	10,400	
Simon (2/10)	5,200	26,000

Task 2: Current Accounts

Note: this layout is for ease of reference – answers should follow the format in the chapter.

Henry	Ian	Simon		Henry	Ian	Simon
£	£	£		£	£	£
		2,000	Balance b/d	6,000	5,000	
26,000	24,000	20,000	Drawings			
1,200	1,000	800	Interest – Drawings			
			Salaries	12,000	15,000	10,000
			Interest – Capital	4,800	3,200	2,000
			Profit Share	10,400	10,400	5,200
6,000	8,600		Balance c/d			5,600
33,200	33,600	22,800		33,200	33,600	22,800
		5,600	Balance b/d	6,000	8,600	

Task 3: disadvantages of a partnership

- Loss of control
- Loss of outright ownership
- Share of profits
- Decisions shared by other partners
- Division of responsibilities and duties

3.8   **Task 1**

Michael Nigel and Elaine

Profit and Loss Appropriation Account for the Year to 30 September 20-2.

	£	£
Net profit for the year		212,240
Salaries		
Michael	36,000	
Nigel	32,000	
Elaine	26,000	
	94,000	
Interest on Capital		
Michael	8,400	
Nigel	6,000	
Elaine	4,800	
		(113,200)
		99,040
Share of Profit		
Michael (4/10)	39,616	
Nigel (3/10)	29,712	
Elaine (3/10)	29,712	99,040

Task 2: Current Accounts

Note: this layout is for ease of reference – answers should follow the format in the chapter.

	Michael	Nigel	Elaine		Michael	Nigel	Elaine
	£	£	£		£	£	£
			2,900	Balance b/d	6,500	1,450	
Drawings	48,000	37,000	58,000	Drawings			
Salaries				Salaries	36,000	32,000	26,000
				Interest – Capital	8,400	6,000	4,800
				Profit Share	39,616	29,712	29,712
Balance c/d	42,516	32,162		Balance c/d			388
	90,516	69,162	60,900		90,516	69,162	60,900
			388	Balance b/d	42,516	32,162	

Task 3: advantages of a partnership
* More expertise
* More capital
* Less risk
* Benefits of small economies of scale
* Benefits from the division of labour
* Potentially more profits
* Better prospects for expansion

3.9   Task 1

Bossman & Stockwell: Trading, Profit and Loss Account for the year to 31 May 20-1

		£	£
Sales		604,400	
Returns Inwards		4,400	600,000
COST OF SALES			
Opening stock		28,690	
Purchases	250,900		
Returns outwards	1,600	249,300	
Carriage inwards		6,780	
		284,770	
Closing stock		32,770	
Cost of sales			252,000
GROSS PROFIT			348,000
Discount received			7,500
			355,500
EXPENDITURE:			
Discount allowed		2,800	
Wages and salaries		164,400	
General expenses		34,000	
Depreciation charges		30,000	231,200
NET PROFIT FOR THE YEAR			124,300

Partners salaries

– Bossman	16,000	
– Stockwell	14,000	
	30,000	

Interest on Capital

– Bossman (£150,000 x 10%)	15,000	
– Stockwell (£70,000 x 10%)	7,000	52,000
		72,300

Share of profit

– Bossman (70%)	50,610	
– Stockwell	21,690	72,300

Task 2
Bossman and Stockwell
Balance sheet as at 31 May 20-1

FIXED ASSETS	cost	dep'n	net
	£	£	£
Premises	200,000	20,000	180,000
Equipment	125,000	79,000	46,000
	325,000	99,000	226,000
CURRENT ASSETS			
Stocks		32,770	
Trade Debtors		64,600	
Cash at Bank and in Hand		6,940	
		104,310	
CURRENT LIABILITIES			
Creditors		40,700	
NET CURRENT ASSETS			63,610
			289,610

Represented by:	Capital account	Current account	
Bossman	150,000	50,630	200,630
Stockwell	70,000	18,980	88,980
			289,610

Working note: Current accounts (summary layout only)

Bossman	Stockwell		Bossman	Stockwell
£	£		£	£
1,080	110	Balance b/d		
29,900	23,600	Drawings		
		Salary	16,000	14,000
		Capital interest	15,000	7,000
		Profit share	50,610	21,690
50,630	18,980	Balance c/d		
81,610	42,690		81,610	42,690
		Balance b/d	50,630	18,980

Task 3

The cost of employing staff and paying wages and salaries is a legitimate business expense which can be deducted against profit. Such expenditure appears in the profit and loss account alongside all the other operating expenses.

By contrast any partner who is a part owner of the business, is assessed on his/her earnings for the year. As such any earnings are deemed to be an appropriation of profit which appears in the partnership appropriation account, after the calculation of the business profits. This profit allocation can be received in a number of ways through salary, commission receivable, interest on capital or via the profit-sharing ratios.

3.10 Task 1

Richmond & Darlington: Trading, Profit and Loss Account for the year ended 31 May 20-1

		£	£
Sales		235,580	
Returns Inwards		4,580	231,000
COST OF SALES			
Opening stock		35,440	
Purchases	140,900		
Returns outwards	2,140	138,760	
Carriage inwards		4,280	
		178,480	
Closing stock		39,240	
Cost of Sales			139,240
GROSS PROFIT			91,760
Discount received			1,960
			93,720
EXPENDITURE:			
Carriage outwards		6,220	
Discount allowed		5,240	
Wages and salaries (47,100 + 2,600)		49,700	
General expenses		8,950	
Insurance (7,230 – 580)		6,650	
Depreciation charges:			
Business premises		1,800	
Motor Vehicles		3,200	
Shop equipment		1,600	83,360
NET PROFIT FOR THE YEAR			10,360
Partners salary and Commission			
– Richmond (10% x £231,000)		23,100	
– Stockwell		28,000	
		51,100	

Interest on Capital
- Richmond (£80K x 12%)   9,600
- Darlington (£60K x 12%)   7,200   67,900
    57,540

Share of losses
- Richmond (50%)   28,770
- Stockwell   28,770   57,540

Task 2

Richmond and Darlington : Balance sheet as at 31 May 20-1

FIXED ASSETS	cost £	dep'n £	net £
Business Premises	90,000	11,800	78,200
Motor Vehicles	20,000	7,200	12,800
Shop Equipment	16,000	5,000	11,000
	126,000	24,000	102,000
CURRENT ASSETS			
Stocks		39,240	
Trade Debtors		14,780	
Prepayments		580	
Cash in Hand		280	
		54,880	
CURRENT LIABILITIES			
Trade Creditors	18,650		
Accruals	2,600		
Bank Overdraft	1,430	22,680	
NET CURRENT ASSETS			32,200
			134,200

Represented by:	Capital Account	Current account	
Richmond	80,000	600	80,600
Darlington	60,000	(6,400)	53,600
			134,200

Working note: Current accounts (summary layout only)

Richmond £	Darlington £		Richmond £	Darlington £
		Balance b/d	18,670	16,770
22,000	29,600	Drawings		
		Salary & Com	23,100	28,000
		Capital int	9,600	7,200
28,770	28,770	Losses share		
600		Balance c/d		6,400
51,370	58,370		51,370	58,370
	6,400	Balance b/d	600	

Task 3

If the commission had been paid to an employee, it would have been treated as revenue expenditure. Therefore in the financial accounts it would have been deducted as a business expense against the annual profit figure in the profit and loss account. However as the commission is attributable to Richmond a partner, this is now recorded as a measure of earnings in the appropriation account, and calculated as part of his overall profit entitlement.

CHAPTER 4: CHANGES IN PARTNERSHIPS

4.1   (b)

4.2   (a)

4.3   (d)

4.4   The rule established in Garner v Murray 1904 states that, when a partner becomes insolvent, then all the other 'bona fide' partners must honour this loss in the ratio of their last agreed capital accounts (for most businesses this relates to the last time a balance sheet was drawn up).

4.5   **Task 1**

Sam, Rick and Cameron: Partners Capital Accounts (summary layout)

	Sam	*Rick*	*Cameron*			*Sam*	*Rick*	*Cameron*
	£	£	£			£	£	£
				Balance b/d		33,000	12,000	30,000
	8,000		8,000	Goodwill		8,000	4,000	4,000
				Revaluation		12,000	6,000	6,000
		22,000		Bank				
Balance c/d	45,000		32,000					
	53,000	22,000	40,000			53,000	22,000	40,000
				Balance b/d		45,000		32,000

Working Notes

Goodwill Account

	£		£
Sam (4/8)	8,000	Sam (2/4)	8,000
Rick (2/8)	4,000	Cameron (2/4)	8,000
Cameron (2/8)	4,000		
	16,000		16,000

Revaluation Account

	£		£
Share of profit		Fixed Assets (£74,000 – £50,000)	24,000
Sam (4/8)	12,000		
Rick (2/8)	6,000		
Cameron (2/8)	6,000		
	24,000		24,000

Task 2

Sam and Cameron: Balance Sheet as at 31 August 20-1

	£
Fixed Assets (£50,000 + £24,000)	74,000
Current Assets	10,000
Cash at Bank (£25,000 – £22,000)	3,000
Creditors	(10,000)
	77,000
Capital Accounts	
Sam	45,000
Cameron	32,000
	77,000

4.6   Task 1

Fame Fortune and Fear: Capital Accounts (summary format)

Fame	Fortune	Fear		Fame	Fortune	Fear
£	£	£		£	£	£
			Balance b/d	110,000	90,000	
			Bank			60,000
30,000	30,000	20,000	Goodwill	40,000	40,000	
120,000	100,000	40,000	Balance c/d			
150,000	130,000	60,000		150,000	130,000	60,000
			Balance b/d	120,000	100,000	40,000

Working note

Goodwill Account

	£		£
Fame (1/2)	40,000	Fame (3/8)	30,000
Fortune (1/2)	40,000	Fortune (3/8)	30,000
		Fear (2/8)	20,000
	80,000		80,000

Task 2

Net Profit adjustment	£
Draft net profit	152,000
Less loan interest	(3,000)
Adjusted net profit	149,000

Task 3
Fame, Fortune and Fear Appropriation Account for the year ended 31 March 20-2

	£	£
Net Profit for the year		149,000
Partners salaries		
Fame	20,000	
Fortune	20,000	
Fear	30,000	
	70,000	
Interest on Capital		
Fame	18,000	
Fortune	15,000	
Fear	6,000	
		109,000
		40,000
Share of profit		
Fame (3/8)	15,000	
Fortune (3/8)	15,000	
Fear (2/8)	10,000	
		40,000

Task 4
Partners current accounts (summary format)

Fame	Fortune	Fear		Fame	Fortune	Fear
£	£	£		£	£	£
			Balance b/d	6,500	7,800	
			Salaries	20,000	20,000	30,000
			Interest on Capital	18,000	15,000	6,000
			Profit share	15,000	15,000	10,000
			Loan Interest		3,000	
28,000	32,000	24,000	Drawings			
31,500	28,800	22,000	Balance c/d			
59,500	60,800	46,000		59,500	60,800	46,000
			Balance b/d	31,500	28,800	22,000

4.7   **Ernest Harvey and Eileen: Realisation Account**

		£		£
Land & Buildings		280,000	Creditors	55,000
Fixtures & Equipment		125,000	Bank – Total proceeds	510,000
Motor Vehicles		40,000		
Stock		35,000		
Debtors		12,000		
Bank – Creditors		50,000		
Profit on realisation				
Ernest (6/10)	13,800			
Harvey (3/10)	6,900			
Eileen (1/10)	2,300	23,000		
		565,000		565,000

Bank Account

	£		£
Balance b/d	23,000	Realisation Account	
Realisation Account		Paid Creditors	50,000
Total receipts	510,000		
		Capital Accounts	
		Ernest	218,800
		Harvey	141,900
		Eileen	122,300
	533,000		533,000

Partners Capital Accounts (summary format)

Ernest	Harvey	Eileen		Ernest	Harvey	Eileen
£	£	£		£	£	£
			Capital b/d	180,000	120,000	100,000
			Current a/c b/d	25,000	15,000	20,000
			Realisation a/c	13,800	6,900	2,300
218,800	141,900	122,300	Bank			
218,800	141,900	122,300		218,800	141,900	122,300

4.8 (a) PROFIT APPROPRIATION ACCOUNT FOR BARROW, MARK, WILLIAMS AND JAMES FOR THE YEAR ENDED 30 JUNE 20-4

	£	£
Profit		40,000
Add back:		
Salaries		13,000
Interest on loan		300
		53,300
Less interest on loan		300
Profit available for appropriation		53,000
Less salaries		
Mark	7,000	
James	6,000	
		13,000
Less interest on capital		
Barrow	1,250	
Mark	750	
Williams	150	
James	500	
		2,650
		37,350
Balance of profit shared in PSR		
Barrow	11,205	
Mark	14,940	
Williams	7,470	
James	3,735	
		37,350

(b)   CAPITAL ACCOUNTS

	Barrow £	Mark £	Williams £	James £		Barrow £	Mark £	Williams £	James £
					Bal b/f	15,000	15,000	3,000	5,000
					Bank	10,000			
Bal c/f	25,000	15,000	3,000	10,000					5,000
	25,000	15,000	3,000	10,000		25,000	15,000	3,000	10,000

CURRENT ACCOUNTS

	Barrow £	Mark £	Williams £	James £		Barrow £	Mark £	Williams £	James £
Bal b/f			1,000		Bal b/f	2,500	1,800		2,000
Drawings	17,000	20,000	5,000	13,000	Loan interest	300			
Bal c/f		4,490	1,620		Salary		7,000		6,000
					Int. on capital	1,250	750	150	500
					Profit	11,205	14,940	7,470	3,735
					Bal c/f	1,745			765
	17,000	24,490	7,620	13,000		17,000	24,490	7,620	13,000

(c)   An appropriation is an allocation of net profit which is credited to the owner of a business. In a partnership appropriations may be in the form of salaries, interest on capital or profit shares.

An expense is business expenditure undertaken by an enterprise, for example loan interest is a tax deductible business expense, and as such is an element in determining the net profit.

4.9   (a)   PARTNERS' CAPITAL ACCOUNTS

	Wordsworth £'000	Quincey £'000	Southey £'000	Taylor £'000		Wordsworth £'000	Quincey £'000	Southey £'000	Taylor £'000
Goodwill (4:3:3)		20	15	15	Balance b/d	138	65	84	
Loan	213				Revaluation (5:3:2)	50	30	20	
Balance c/d		90	99	65	Goodwill (5:3:2)	25	15	10	
					Cash				80
	213	110	114	80		213	110	114	80
					Bal. b/d		90	99	65

(b)   Goodwill, whether originally purchased (being defined as 'the excess of the fair market value of the price paid for a business over the fair market value of the individual assets and liabilities acquired') or whether internally generated, is dependent on a wide variety of factors such as business location, reputation, staff personalities and the ability to earn profits or `super profits'. In the case of Coleridge & Co, goodwill is a genuine asset of the business with a value which could be obtained if the business was sold. In order to give the retiring partner his share of all the net assets of the business he must be given his share of the asset of goodwill. Hence his capital account is credited with the value of this share.

CHAPTER 5: INTRODUCTION TO LIMITED COMPANY ACCOUNTS

5.1   (b)

5.2   (c)

5.3   (a)

5.4   Preference shares have a fixed rate of return and this is the maximum dividend that any such shareholder can receive on their investment.

Preference shares rank above ordinary shares in the case of a winding up or liquidation order. This means that if there are any surplus funds left after paying all the creditors, preference shareholders will receive their money before the ordinary shareholder.

Ordinary shares are often referred to as equity shares as they are the primary risk takers who are rewarded with any surplus (equity) funds. The dividend payable tends to vary from year to year based upon the profits generated, the higher the net profit then the more likelihood of an increased dividend.

Ordinary shareholders are the only type of share normally to receive a vote at an AGM. Therefore as owners they can dictate and vote on company policy and the election of the directors.

5.5   – any four from:

- Directors salaries
- Debenture interest payable
- Corporation tax payable
- Dividends paid and proposed.
- Retained profit for the year

5.6   **Profit and Loss Account for Gretton PLC for the Year to 31 March 20-2**

	£000	£000
Sales Turnover		2,350
COST OF SALES		
Opening stock	140	
Purchases	960	
	1,100	
Closing Stock	180	
Cost of Sales		920
GROSS PROFIT		1,430
Less Expenses:		
Administrative expenses	210	
Distribution costs	420	
Rent Rates and Insurance	487	
Depreciation – plant and Machinery	95	
		1,212
NET PROFIT BEFORE TAXATION		218
Taxation		32
NET PROFIT AFTER TAXATION		186
Dividends – ordinary dividend		60
RETAINED PROFIT FOR THE YEAR		126

Balance Sheet of Gretton PLC as at 31 March 20-2

FIXED ASSETS	Cost	Dep'n	Net
	£000	£000	£000
Plant and Machinery	950	315	635

CURRENT ASSETS			
Stock		180	
Debtors		670	
Cash at Bank		15	
		865	

CURRENT LIABILITIES			
Creditors	260		
Corporation Tax	32		
Dividends Proposed	60		
		(352)	
NET CURRENT ASSETS			513
			1,148

Represented by:

CAPITAL AND RESERVES	
Ordinary Shares	600
Share Premium Account	240
Profit and Loss Account (182 + 126)	308
	1,148

Working notes:

Journal

		Dr	Cr
		£000	£000
1	Stock – Balance Sheet	180	
	Stock – Trading Account		180
2	Taxation – Profit and Loss Account	32	
	Corporation Tax Payable		32
3.	Ordinary dividend Profit and Loss Account	60	
	Dividends proposed		60
4	Depreciation (Plant) – Profit and Loss Account	95	
	Accum Depreciation – Plant		95

5.7   **Profit and Loss Account of Hickson PLC for the Year to 30 September 20-2**

	£	£
Sales Turnover		280,000
COST OF SALES		
Opening stock	25,000	
Purchases	125,000	
	150,000	
Closing Stock	49,000	
Cost of Sales		101,000
GROSS PROFIT		179,000

Less Expenses:

Wages and Salaries	40,000	
Directors fees	29,000	
Printing, Telephone & Stationery	7,000	
General expenses	6,000	
Rent Rates and Insurance	11,000	
Loan Interest payable	4,000	
Depreciation:		
– Equipment	14,000	
– Fixtures and Fittings	6,000	
– Motor Vehicles	12,500	
		129,500
NET PROFIT BEFORE TAXATION		49,500
Taxation		8,000
NET PROFIT AFTER TAXATION		41,500
Dividends		
– Preference Dividend	3,000	
– Ordinary dividend	6,400	
		9,400
RETAINED PROFIT FOR THE YEAR		32,100

Balance Sheet of Hickson PLC as at 30 September 20-2

FIXED ASSETS	Cost	Dep'n	Net
	£	£	£
Equipment	140,000	34,000	106,000
Fixtures and Fittings	40,000	16,000	24,000
Motor Vehicles	80,000	42,500	37,500
	260,000	92,500	167,500

CURRENT ASSETS			
Stock		49,000	
Debtors		26,000	
Cash at Bank		5,000	
Cash In Hand		1,000	
		81,000	
CURRENT LIABILITIES			
Creditors	14,000		
Corporation Tax	8,000		
Dividends Proposed	9,400		
Accruals	4,000		
		35,400	
NET CURRENT ASSETS			45,600
			213,100
LONG TERM LIABILITIES			
8% Debenture Loan			50,000
			163,100

Represented by:
CAPITAL AND RESERVES

Ordinary Shares	80,000
Preference shares	30,000
Share Premium Account	6,000
Profit and Loss Account (15,000 + 32,100)	47,100
	163,100

Working notes
Journal

		Dr £	Cr £
1	Stock – Balance Sheet	49,000	
	Stock – Trading Account		49,000
2.	Interest payable	4,000	
	Accruals		4,000
3	Depreciation – Equipment P/L A/C	14,000	
	Accum Depreciation – Equip		14,000
	Depreciation – Fixtures P/L A/C	6,000	
	Accum Depreciation – Fixtures		6,000
	Depreciation – Motor Vehicles P/L A/C	12,500	
	Accum Depreciation – Vehicles		12,500
4	Preference Dividend –P/L A/C	3,000	
	Ordinary Dividend – P/L A/C	6,400	
	Dividends proposed		9,400
5	Taxation – Profit and Loss Account	8,000	
	Corporation Tax Payable		8,000

5.8 **Profit and loss account of Grayson PLC for the Year to 31 December 20-2**

	£	£
Sales Turnover		2,640,300
COST OF SALES		
Opening stock	318,500	
Purchases	2,089,600	
	2,408,100	
Closing Stock	340,600	
Cost of sales		2,067,500
GROSS PROFIT		572,800
Less Expenses:		
Administration expenses (120,180 – 12,200)	107,980	
Selling & Distribution exp (116, 320 + 21,300)	137,620	
Wages and Salaries	112,800	
Directors Salaries	87,200	
Loan stock Interest payable (10,000 + 10,000)	20,000	
Postage and Telephone	7,900	
Bad debts	8,900	
Motor expenses	12,280	
Bank charges and loan interest	7,720	

Increase in provision for bad debts	2,400	
		504,800
NET PROFIT BEFORE TAXATION		68,000
Taxation		45,000
NET PROFIT AFTER TAXATION		23,000
Dividends		60,000
RETAINED LOSS FOR THE YEAR		(37,000)

Balance Sheet of Grayson PLC as at 31 December 20-2

FIXED ASSETS	Cost	Dep'n	Net
	£	£	£
Office Equipment			110,060
Motor Vehicles			235,000
			345,060
CURRENT ASSETS			
Stock		340,600	
Debtors	415,800		
Less Provision for bad debts	12,474		
		403,326	
Prepayments		12,200	
Cash at Bank		20,640	
		776,766	
CURRENT LIABILITIES			
Creditors	428,250		
Corporation Tax	45,000		
Dividends Proposed	60,000		
Accruals (21,300 + 10,000)	31,300		
		564,550	
NET CURRENT ASSETS			212,216
			557,276
LONG TERM LIABILITIES			
10% Loan Stock		200,000	
Bank Loan Account		50,000	
			250,000
			307,276
Represented by:			
CAPITAL AND RESERVES			
Ordinary Shares			200,000
Reserves			
Profit and Loss Account (144,276 – 37,000)			107,276
			307,276

Working notes
Journal

		Dr £	Cr £
1	Interest payable – Profit & Loss	10,000	
	Accruals – Balance Sheet		10,000
2	Payments in advance – Balance Sheet	12,200	
	Administration expenses – Profit & Loss		12,200
	Selling and Distribution expenses – Profit & Loss	21,300	
	Accruals – Balance Sheet		21,300
3	Increase in provision Bad debts – Profit & Loss	2,400	
	Provision for Bad debts – Balance Sheet		2,400
4	Stock – Balance Sheet	340,600	
	Stock – Profit and Loss Account		340,600
5	Taxation – Profit and Loss Account	45,000	
	Corporation Tax Payable – Balance Sheet		45,000
6	Dividends – Profit and Loss Account	60,000	
	Dividends proposed – Balance Sheet		60,000

Increase in provision for bad debts – working

	£
New Provision (3% x £415,800)	12,474
Less already provided	10,074
Net Increase in provision	2,400

CHAPTER 6: PUBLISHED ACCOUNTS OF LIMITED COMPANIES

6.1 (d)

6.2 (c)

6.3 (b)

6.4 (a)

6.5 A statement of Total Recognised Gains and Losses as prescribed by FRS3 Reporting Financial Performance, acknowledges the fact that not all gains and losses pass through the profit and loss account.

Realised gains and losses are collected in the profit and loss account and these transactions are used to calculate net profit. However, unrealised gains and losses are not accountable here, and these tend to pass exclusively through the balance sheet. Eg the revaluation of tangible fixed assets will be adjusted against the value of tangible fixed assets and a special reserve, that of a revaluation reserve. Any movements in valuation will then be recorded between these two accounts.

6.6 Items that are included in a Directors Report include any four of the following:
- Directors names and their shareholdings
- Dividends proposed
- A review of the previous 12 months activities
- Future developments

- Significant differences between the book value and the market value of Land and Buildings
- Political and Charitable contributions
- Policy on the employment of disabled people
- Health and safety at work of employees
- Action taken on employee involvement and consultation
- Policy on the payment of creditors

6.7   **Task 1**

Journal

	Debit £000	Credit £000
Stock – Balance Sheet	180	
Stock – Trading Account		180
Taxation – Profit & Loss Account	65	
Creditors – CT payable – Balance Sheet		65
Dividends – Profit & Loss Account	280	
Creditors – Dividends payable – Balance Sheet		280

Task 2

Proudlock PLC: Profit and Loss Account for the year ended 31 March 20-2

	£000
Turnover – continuing operations	2,295
Cost of Sales [1]	1,180
GROSS PROFIT	1,115
Distribution costs	500
Administrative expenses	240
OPERATING PROFIT	375
Income from fixed asset investments	75
PROFIT ON ORDINARY ACTIVITIES BEFORE TAXATION	450
Tax on profit on ordinary activities	65
PROFIT ON ORDINARY ACTIVITIES AFTER TAXATION	385
Dividends	280
RETAINED PROFIT FOR THE FINANCIAL YEAR	105

Proudlock PLC

Balance Sheet as at 31 March 20-2

	£000	£000
FIXED ASSETS		
Tangible Assets (1,000–500)		500
Investments		600
		1,100
CURRENT ASSETS		
Stocks	180	
Debtors	600	
Cash at bank and in hand	75	
	855	
CREDITORS:Amounts falling due within one year [2]	740	

NET CURRENT ASSETS   115
                                                                   1,215

CAPITAL AND RESERVES
Called up Share Capital   700
Share Premium Account   200
Profit and Loss Account (210 + 105)   315
                                                                   1,215

Working notes (see profit and loss account and balance sheet)

1	Cost of sales	£
	Opening stock	160
	Purchases	1,200
		1,360
	Closing stock	180
		1,180

2	Creditors: Amounts falling due within one Year	
	Trade Creditors	300
	Accruals	15
	Other Creditors	80
	Corporation Tax payable	65
	Dividends payable	280
		740

6.8   **Task 1**

Journal	*Debit*	*Credit*
	£000	*£000*
Stock – Balance Sheet – Profit and Loss Account	250	
Stock – Trading Account		250
Depreciation – Buildings (210–110 x 5%) – Profit and Loss Account	5	
Accum – Dep'n Buildings – Balance Sheet		5
Depreciation – Plant (125 x 20%)	25	
Accum – Dep'n Plant – Balance Sheet		25
Taxation – Profit & Loss Account	135	
Creditors – Cpn. Tax payable – Balance Sheet		135
Dividends – Profit & Loss Account	300	
Creditors – Dividends payable – Balance Sheet		300

Task 2
Broadfoot PLC: Profit and Loss Account for the year ended 31 March 20-2

	£000
Turnover – continuing operations	1,300
Cost of Sales[1]	388
GROSS PROFIT	912
Distribution costs (240 + 6)	246
Administrative expenses (185 + 6)	191
PROFIT ON ORDINARY ACTIVITIES BEFORE TAXATION	475
Tax on profit on ordinary activities	135
PROFIT ON ORDINARY ACTIVITIES AFTER TAXATION	340
Dividends	300
RETAINED PROFIT FOR THE FINANCIAL YEAR	40

Broadfoot PLC: Balance Sheet as at 31 March 20-2

	£000	£000
FIXED ASSETS		
Tangible Assets[3]		182
CURRENT ASSETS		
Stocks	250	
Debtors	728	
Cash at bank and in hand	15	
	993	
CREDITORS: Amounts falling due within one year[4]	585	
NET CURRENT ASSETS		408
		590
CAPITAL AND RESERVES		
Called up Share Capital		200
Profit and Loss Account (350 + 40)		390
		590

Working notes to the profit and loss account and balance sheet

1	**Cost of sales**	£
	Opening stock	150
	Depreciation[2] (see calculation in note 2 below)	18
	Purchases	470
		638
	Closing stock	250
		388

2   Depreciation

	Total	Cost of sales 60%	Dist'n 20%	Admin 20%
Buildings	5	3	1	1
Plant	25	15	5	5
Total	30	18	6	6

3   Tangible fixed assets

	Land and Buildings £000	Plant and Machinery £000	Total £000
At Cost	210	125	335
Dep'n b/f	48	75	123
Charges	5	25	30
Total	53	100	153
NBV	157	25	182

4   Creditors: amounts falling due within one year

Trade Creditors	60
Accruals	90
Tax payable	135
Dividends payable	300
	585

6.9   Task 1: Journal

	Debit £	Credit £
Interest payable	10,000	
Accruals		10,000
Payments in Advance	12,200	
Administration		12,200
Distribution Costs	21,300	
Accruals		21,300
Increase in provision doubtful debts	2,400	
Provision for Doubtful debts		2,400
Stock – Balance Sheet	340,600	
Stock – Trading Account		340,600
Taxation – Profit & Loss Account	45,000	
Creditors – CT payable		45,000
Dividends – Profit & Loss Account	56,000	
Creditors – Dividends payable		56,000

Task 2: Grandware PLC: Profit and Loss Account for the year ended 31 December 20-2

	£
Turnover – continuing operations	2,640,300
Cost of Sales[1]	2,067,500
GROSS PROFIT	572,800
Distribution costs[2]	237,620
Administrative expenses[2]	219,280

OPERATING PROFIT	115,900
Income from fixed asset investments	2,100
Profit on ordinary activities before interest	118,000
Interest payable and similar charges (10,000 +10,000)	20,000
PROFIT ON ORDINARY ACTIVITIES BEFORE TAXATION	98,000
Tax on profit on ordinary activities	45,000
PROFIT ON ORDINARY ACTIVITIES AFTER TAXATION	53,000
Dividends	56,000
RETAINED (LOSS) FOR THE FINANCIAL YEAR	(3,000)

Grandware PLC: Balance Sheet as at 31 December 2002

	£	£
FIXED ASSETS		
Tangible Assets (110,060 + 235,000)		345,060
Investments		20,000
		365,060
CURRENT ASSETS		
Stocks	340,600	
Debtors[3]	415,526	
Cash at bank and in hand	20,640	
	776,766	
CREDITORS: Amounts falling due within one year[4]	560,550	
NET CURRENT ASSETS		216,216
		581,276
CREDITORS: Amounts falling due after more than one year		200,000
		381,276
CAPITAL AND RESERVES		
Called up Share Capital		200,000
Share Premium Account		40,000
Profit and Loss Account (144,276 − 3,000)		141,276
		381,276

Working notes to the profit and loss account and balance sheet

1	**Cost of sales**	*£000*
	Opening stock	318,500
	Purchases	2,089,600
		2,408,100
	Closing stock	340,600
		2,067,500

2 **Distribution costs**

Distribution	216,320
Accruals	21,300
	237,620

Administration	220,180
Prepaid	(12,200)
Bad debts	8,900
Increase in provision for bad debts	2,400
	219,280

3 **Debtors**

Trade Debtors	415,800
Provision for bad debts	(12,474)
Prepayments	12,200
	415,526

4 **Creditors: amounts falling due within one year**

Trade Creditors	428,250
Accruals (10,000 + 21,300)	31,300
Corporation Tax payable	45,000
Dividends payable	56,000
	560,550

6.10

Task 1

		£	£
1	No adjustment required	-	-
2	DR Land (cost)	200,000	
	CR Revaluation reserve		200,000
	(being revaluation of land)		
3	DR Final dividend (approp. A/C)	39,000	
	DR Preference dividend (approp. A/C)	15,200	
	CR Dividends proposed		54,200
	(being provision of ordinary and preference dividends)		

    [Preference dividend: £200,000 x 7.6 per cent = £15,200

    Ordinary dividend: 600,000 x 6.5p per share = £39,000]

		£	£
4	DR Debenture interest	288,000	
	CR Interest payable		288,000
	(being provision for debenture interest payable)		
	((£2,400,000 x 12 per cent = £288,000)		
5	DR Tax charge (appropriation account)	735,157	
	CR Tax payable		735,157
	(being provision of corporation tax payable)		
6	no adjustment required		
7	DR Audit fees	36,573	
	CR Accruals		36,573
	(being provision of audit fees)		

8	DR Cost of sales (closing stock)	86,265	
	CR Stock		86,265
	(being write down of stock to net realisable value)		
9	no adjustment required	-	-
10	no adjustment required	-	-
11	no adjustment required	-	-
12	no adjustment required	-	-
13	no adjustment required	-	-

Task 2 (a)

Financial statements for publication:

Poussin Ltd
Profit and loss account for the year ended 31 December 20-1

	£
Turnover	
Continuing operations[1]	14,858,934
Cost of sales[2]	7,703,617
Gross profit	7,155,317
Distribution costs[3]	3,491,471
Administrative expenses[3]	1,080,120
Operating profit	
Continuing operations	2,583,726
Interest payable and similar charges	288,000
Profit (or loss) on ordinary activities before taxation	2,295,726
Tax on profit (or loss) on ordinary activities	735,157
Profit (or loss) on ordinary activities after taxation	1,560,569
Dividends[4]	103,400
Retained profit for the financial year	1,457,169

Poussin Ltd
Balance Sheet as at 31 December 20-1

	£	£
FIXED ASSETS		
Intangible assets		351,572
Tangible assets (Note to the accounts 1)		1,961,651
		2,313,223
CURRENT ASSETS		
Stock	1,923,215	
Debtors[5]	3,621,466	

Cash and bank and in hand	2,935	
	5,547,616	
CREDITORS: amounts falling due within one year[6]	2,057,426	
Net current assets		3,490,190
Total assets *less* current liabilities		5,803,413
CREDITORS: amounts falling due after more than one year		2,400,000
		3,403,413
CAPITAL AND RESERVES		
Called up share capital[7] (Note to the accounts 2)		800,000
Share premium		231,563
Revaluation reserve		200,000
Profit and loss account[8]		2,171,850
		3,403,413

Working notes (not to be confused with Notes to the Accounts - see Task 2[b])

1   Calculation of turnover:

	£
Sales	15,184,365
Less: returns inwards	325,431
Turnover	14,858,934

2   Calculation of cost of sales:

	£
Opening stock	1,486,955
Purchases	8,201,311
plus carriage inwards	125,219
Less: returns outwards	186,653
	9,626,832
Less: closing stock	1,923,215
Cost of sales	7,703,617

3   Allocation of expenses:

	Distribution costs	Administrative expenses
	£	£
Advertising	593,215	
Salaries and wages	1,092,135	491,016
Increase in provision for doubtful debts		23,134
Discounts allowed		74,187
Motor expense (80/20)	683,010	170,752
Salesmens' commission	603,681	
Rates (75/25)	63,714	21,238

Light and heat (75/25)	94,771	31,590
Insurance (75/25)	16,453	5,484
Audit		36,573
General expenses (80/20)	69,211	17,303
Directors' remuneration	86,521	165,636
Depreciation: motor vehicles (80/20)	127,732	31,933
fixtures and fittings	38,705	
office equipment (60/40)	11,499	7,666
building	10,824	3,608
	3,491,471	1,080,120

4   Dividends

	£
Preference dividends	15,200
Interim dividend paid	49,200
Final dividend proposed	39,000
	103,400

5   Debtors

Debtors are made up as follows:

	£
Trade debtors	3,583,961
Prepayments	37,505
	3,621,466

6   Creditors: amounts falling due within one year

This is made up of:

	£
Bank overdraft	43,465
Trade creditors	850,753
Corporation tax payable	735,157
Dividends payable	54,200
Accruals	373,851
	2,057,426

7   Called up share capital

Issued, allotted and fully paid:

	£
600,000 ordinary shares of £1	600,000
200,000 7.6 per cent preference shares of £1	200,000
	800,000

8   Profit and Loss account

	£
At 01.01.20-3	714,681
Retained profit for the year	1,457,169
At 31.12.20-3	2,171,850

Task 2(b)
Notes to the Accounts
Note 1: Tangible fixed assets

	Land and Buildings	Fixtures & Fittings	Motor Vehicles	Office Equipment	Total
	£	£	£	£	£
Cost 01.01.20-3	1,321,583	365,152	895,322	135,962	
Additions	–	37,415	209,325	12,465	
Revaluation	200,000	–	–	–	
Disposals	–	15,513	183,921	9,460	
	1,521,583	387,054	920,726	138,967	2,968,330
Accumulated depreciation					
01.01.20-3	157,321	183,563	465,990	41,509	
Charge for the year	14,432	38,705	159,665	19,165	
Disposals	–	10,622	57,462	5,587	
	171,753	211,646	568,193	55,087	1,006,679
Net book value	1,349,830	175,408	352,533	83,880	1,961,651

Note 2: Share Capital

Authorised share capital is:

	£
2,000,000 ordinary shares of £1	2,000,000
500,000 7.6 per cent preference shares of £1	500,000
	2,500,000

Issued, allotted and fully paid:

	£
600,000 ordinary shares of £1	600,000
200,000 7.6 per cent preference shares of £1	200,000
	800,000

6.11

Task 1

		£000	£000
1	DR Final dividend	30	
	CR Dividends payable		30
2	DR Tax charge	211	
	CR Corporation tax payable		211
3	DR Interest charges	15	
	CR Interest payable		15
4	DR Distribution expenses	19	
	CR Accruals		19
5	DR Amounts written off investments	8	
	CR Investments		8

Task 2

Financial statements for publication

Dowango Ltd

Profit and loss account for the year ended 31 March 20-6

	£000
Turnover:	
Continuing operations[1]	5,352
Cost of sales[2]	2,910
Gross profit	2,442
Distribution costs	1,123
Administrative expenses	709
Operating profit:	
Continuing operations	610
Amounts written off investments	8
Interest payable and similar charges	30
Profit (or loss) on ordinary activities before taxation	572
Tax on profit (or loss) on ordinary activities	211
Profit (or loss) on ordinary activities after taxation	361
Dividends[3]	50
Retained profit for the financial year	311

Dowango Ltd
Balance sheet as at 31 March 20-6

	£000	£000
FIXED ASSETS[4]		
Tangible assets		1,153
CURRENT ASSETS		
Investments	56	
Stocks	365	
Debtors[5]	613	
Cash at bank and in hand	3	
	1,037	
CREDITORS: amounts falling due within one year[6]	804	
NET CURRENT ASSETS		233
Total assets less current liabilities		1,386
CREDITORS: amounts falling due after more than one year		300
		1,086
CAPITAL AND RESERVES		
Called up share capital		500
Profit and loss account[7]		586
		1,086

Working notes
(All figures £000's)

1   **Sales** 5,391 – Returns inwards 39 = 5,352

2   **Calculation of cost of sales:**

Opening stock	298
Purchases	2,988
plus Carriage inwards	20
less Returns outwards	31
	3,275
less Closing stock	365
Cost of sales	2,910

3   **Dividends:**

Interim dividend	20
Final dividend proposed	30
	50

4   **Fixed assets**

	Cost	Acc. Depn.	NBV
Land	431	–	431
Buildings	512	184	328

Fixtures & fittings	389	181	208
Motor vehicles	341	204	137
Office equipment	105	56	49
	1,778	625	1,153

5   Debtors

Trade debtors	619	
less provision for doubtful debts	27	
		592
Prepayments		21
		613

6   Creditors: amounts falling due within one year

Bank overdraft	157
Trade creditors	331
Corporation tax payable	211
Dividends payable	30
Accruals (41 + 19 + interest 15)	75
	804

7   Profit and loss account

At 01.04.20-5	275
Retained profit for the year	311
At 31.03.20-6	586

CHAPTER 7: ACCOUNTING FOR ASSETS

7.1   (a)

7.2   (b)

7.3   1   (a)   2   (c)

7.4   (b)

7.5   (c)

7.6   (c)

7.7   SSAP4 – *Accounting for Government Grants.*

Many different types of business grant have been obtainable from government departments. Where these relate to revenue expenditure, eg business rates subsidy, they should be credited to the expenses account in the period when it was incurred.

This is based on the fundamental concept of matching.

Where grants relating to capital expenditure are received, then this matching concept is once again observed by crediting the amount over the expected useful life of the asset. This may be achieved in one of two ways:

1 By treating the grant as a deferred credit, a proportion of which is credited to the profit and loss account each year over its anticipated life (in line with depreciation).

2 By crediting the whole of the grant against the actual purchase cost of the asset and then depreciating the net amount over its anticipated lifetime.

For most businesses either of the methods listed above is acceptable, however for Limited Company accounts it is recommended that the first method be used, in accordance with the concept of historic cost accounting whereby the asset is originally recorded at its full purchase cost.

If a company receives a conditional grant where there may be a liability to repay, if not all of the conditions are met, then a formal note to the accounts is required.

7.8 SSAP 13 – *Accounting for research and development.*

SSAP 13 looks at research and development from three perspectives:

- Pure or basic research is experimental or theoretical work undertaken primarily to acquire new scientific or technical knowledge. However, there is no clear commercial end in view and therefore it has no practical application.

- Applied Research is also experimental or theoretical work undertaken primarily to acquire new scientific or technical knowledge, but this has a specific aim and application (eg the effect of baking soda on toothpaste).

- Development expenditure is the use of existing scientific and technical knowledge to produce new or substantially improved products or systems, prior to the commencement of commercial production.

7.9 SSAP 21 – *Accounting for Leases and Hire Purchase contracts.*

SSAP 21 requires that a finance lease (and hire purchase agreement) should be accounted for by the lessee as if it were the purchaser of the asset outright (substance over form). Thus the asset would be capitalised on the balance sheet and then depreciated over its anticipated economic life. Any amounts outstanding on the agreement would be shown as a finance lease creditor, and any interest payments charged, will be transferred to the profit and loss account.

Under an operating lease only the rental will be taken into account by the lessee and these rental charges will be written off and charged to the profit and loss account only.

7.10 FRS 15 and SSAP 19

FRS 15 – *Tangible fixed assets* states that all assets (with the exception of land) have an economic life and are subject to the rigours of depreciation. FRS 15 requires that all tangibles should initially be recorded at cost and some systematic approach to depreciation applied. However the standard also recognises that alternative accounting rules such as revaluation can apply, and so long as revaluation policy is consistent, ie that one asset is revalued, then all assets within that class/category should also be similarly revalued.

If a property is deemed to be an investment property then it falls under the guidelines laid out in SSAP 19 – *Accounting for investment properties*, whereby the asset would not be depreciated each year. Instead the asset would need to be revalued on an annual basis and therefore included in the balance sheet at its current market valuation. Any changes in valuation would then pass to an investment revaluation reserve (or profit and loss account if losses are incurred).

7.11   Task 1 – losses interpreted to be permanent

Fixed Assets at cost

20-0		£000	20-0		£000
Jan 01	Cost – Castle Hamlets	400	Dec 31	Balance c/d	400
		400			400
20-1			20-1		
Jan 01	Balance b/d	400			
Dec 31	Revaluation	40	Dec 31	Balance c/d	440
		440			440
20-2			20-2		
Jan 01	Balance b/d	440			
Dec 31	Revaluation	20	Dec 31	Balance c/d	460
		460			460
20-3			20-3		
Jan 01	Balance b/d	460	Dec 31	Revaluation (40 + 20)	60
				Profit and loss Account	20
				Balance c/d	380
		460			460
20-4					
Jan 01	Balance b/d	380			

Investment revaluation Reserve

20-1		£000	20-1		£000
Dec 31	Balance c/d	40	Dec 31	Investments	40
20-2			20-2		
			Jan 1	Balance b/d	40
Dec 31	Balance c/d	60	Dec 31	Investments	20
		60			60
			20-3		
Dec 31	Investments	60	Jan 01	balance b/d	60

Makeshift Enterprises PLC

Balance sheet extracts as at 31 December

FIXED ASSETS	20-0	20-1	20-2	20-3
	£000	£000	£000	£000
Investments	400	440	460	380
CAPITAL AND RESERVES				
Investment revaluation				
Reserve		40	60	

Makeshift Enterprises PLC

Profit and loss Account for the year ended 31 December

	20-3
	£000
Loss on fixed asset investments	20

Task 2 – if losses interpreted to be temporary

Fixed Assets at cost

20-3		£000	20-3		£000
Jan 01	Balance b/d	460	Dec 31	Revaluation	80
			Dec 31	Balance c/d	380
		460			460
20-4					
Jan 01	Balance b/d	380			

Investment revaluation Reserve

20-3		£000	20-3		£000
Dec 31	Investments	80	Jan 01	Balance b/d	60
			Dec 31	Balance c/d	20
		80			80
20-4					
Jan 01	Balance b/ d	20			

Makeshift Enterprises PLC

Balance sheet extracts as at 31 December

CAPITAL AND RESERVES	20-1	20-2	20-3
	£000	£000	£000
Investment revaluation			
Reserve	40	60	(20)

7.12 (a) Project Xchem has all the attributes of being research expenditure, as laid down in SSAP 13 accounting for research and development. As a consequence, the costs incurred of £295,000 should be written off and charged to the profit and loss account accordingly.

Chemco Company

Profit and loss account (extract) for the year to 31 December 20-3

Expenses	£000
Research and development costs	295

(b) Project Zchem appears to meet all the deferral requirements of SSAP 13 and therefore should be carried forward on this years balance sheet as an intangible asset.

Chemco Company

Balance Sheet (extracts) as at 30 December 20-3

	£000
Fixed Assets	
Intangibles – development costs	435

According to SSAP 13 any deferred development should be written off over a reasonable period and the years 20-4 to 20-8 (five years) seem most appropriate as no competition can enter the market during that time. This means that with the straight line method of amortisation £87,000 (£435,000÷5) will be transferred to the profit and loss account each year, until it is totally written off the balance sheet altogether by the end of 20-8.

7.13 FRS10 – *Goodwill and intangible assets.*

Task 1

Definition of goodwill: the difference between the value of a business as a whole and the aggregate of the fair values of its separable net assets.

Task 2

There are many factors which make up goodwill. Examples include:

• Skilled management team

• Skilled workforce

• Good employer and employee working relations

• Contacts with customers

• Contacts with suppliers

• Strategic location

• Business reputation

• Technical know-how and experience

• Possession of favourable contracts

• Possession of patents, logo's etc.

Any five of the above (or similar) are acceptable.

Task 3

It is usual for the value of a business as a going concern to differ from the aggregate value of its separable net assets. The difference, which can be positive or negative, is described as goodwill. Therefore goodwill is an asset which cannot be realised separately from the business as a whole.

The factors which lead to goodwill, are said to be intangible and it is difficult to place a monetary value on them. For this reason it is not usual to show goodwill as an asset on the balance sheet, unless one business acquires another as a going concern. In such circumstances this is known as purchased goodwill as it has been evidenced by a purchase transaction. Where goodwill is presumed to exist, but no purchase transaction has been undertaken to effect this, it is called non-purchased or inherent goodwill.

Provisions of FRS10:

• Both positive purchased goodwill and purchased intangible assets should initially be capitalised and classed as an asset at cost.

• Inherent or non-purchased goodwill should not be capitalised.

- When intangible assets are acquired as part of a take-over they should be capitalised separately from goodwill if their fair value can be reliably measured. If this is not possible, then they should be subsumed into goodwill.

- If negative goodwill arises, this should be shown on the balance sheet separately and directly underneath any positive goodwill.

- Goodwill and intangible assets should be amortised on a systematic basis over their useful economic lives. If this is considered to be infinite then no amortisation is required.

- The standard presumes that intangibles and goodwill have a life of less than 20 years but accepts that this could be argued against. It is the responsibility of each reporting entity to review the anticipated economic life annually (annual impairment review).

7.14 (a) Development costs may be deferred to future periods if the following criteria given by SSAP 13 are met:
- there is a clearly defined project
- expenditure can be separately identified
- outcome of the project can be assessed with reasonable certainty
- costs will be more than covered by future revenue
- adequate resources exist to complete project

It appears as though the company has considered these criteria and that a case for deferral can be made. The costs will be carried forward in the balance sheet until the project commences commercial production. The costs will then be amortised over the life of the project.

(b) Although the selling of the stock is an event which happened after the year end, under SSAP 17 this is an example of an adjusting event. Adjusting events are 'post balance sheet events which provide additional evidence of conditions existing at the balance sheet date.' The sale of the stock provides evidence as the net realisable value of the stock reported in the financial statements for the year under review. Under SSAP 9, stock is to be valued at the lower of cost and net realisable value.

7.15 **1** (a) The Companies Act 1985 states that historical cost principles constitute the normal basis for preparing financial statements. However, alternative bases are allowed for revaluation of assets.

(b) If the alternative basis was used the land and buildings would be shown in the balance sheet at their valuation of land £641,000 and buildings £558,000. The difference between NRV and valuation would be credited to a 'revaluation reserve' which would form part of the capital and reserves of the company.

(c) Revaluation would improve gearing. The lower gearing would make the company look less risky from the point of view of the bank and thus they may be more willing to lend the company the money to finance the acquisition. However, the fact that the gearing is already fairly low, it may not make too much difference to the bank's attitude.

(d) Future results would be affected because depreciation on the buildings would be calculated on the revalued amount and not on the basis of the original cost.

2 The investment is a current asset, as it was purchased for resale, and, in accordance with the concept of prudence, should be shown at the lower purchase price and net realisable value. The prudence concept says that profits should not be anticipated but foreseeable losses provided for. As we can foresee a loss on the sale of the investment it should be shown at its realisable value of £56,000.

3   SSAP 9 states that stocks should be shown at the lower of cost and net realisable value (NRV). NRV is the expected selling price less any costs of getting them into a saleable condition and selling costs. If NRV is less than cost then, given the prudence concept that requires losses to be provided for as soon as they become probable, the stock should be reduced to NRV. The comparison of cost and NRV should be done for separate items of stock or groups of similar items and not on the total of all stocks. Applying this policy would lead us to value the undervalued items at cost of £340,000 and the overvalued items at the sales price of £15,000. The effect of this is to reduce the value of stock overall from the £365,000 in the accounts to £355,000.

CHAPTER 8: ACCOUNTING FOR LIABILITIES AND PROFIT AND LOSS ACCOUNT

8.1   (d)

8.2   (a)

8.3   (d)

8.4   (b)

8.5   (d)

8.6   Quite often there will be events occurring after the balance sheet date which will provide new evidence about the value of assets and liabilities at that time. Changes can be made to these valuations up until the time the board of directors formally approve the financial statements. After this time it becomes impossible to alter them.

SSAP17 – *Accounting for post balance sheet events*, identifies adjusting and non-adjusting events.

Adjusting events relate directly to something that existed at the balance sheet date. If material, changes should be made to the amounts shown in the financial statements. Examples of adjusting events include:

–   fixed assets – where the purchase price, or sale price, of assets bought or sold before the year-end is fixed after the year-end

–   property, where a subsequent valuation shows a permanent fall in value

Non-adjusting events arise after the balance sheet date and have no direct link with the conditions that existed at the balance sheet date. No adjustment is made to the financial statements; instead changes are disclosed by way of notes in order to ensure that the financial statements are not misleading. Examples of non-adjusting events include:

–   mergers and acquisitions

–   issue of shares and debentures

8.7   These are uncertainties that must be accounted for consistently in financial statements, if user groups are to achieve a full understanding. FRS 12 – *Provisions, Contingent liabilities and Contingent assets* aims to ensure that appropriate recognition and measurement is applied to provisions, contingent liabilities and contingent assets, and that sufficient information is disclosed in the notes to the accounts, to enable users to understand their nature, timing and amount.

FRS12 states that a **provision** should be recognised as a liability in the accounts when:

- an entity has an obligation as a result of a past event
- it is probable (more then 50% likely) that a transfer of economic benefits will be required to settle the obligation (eg cash)
- a reliable estimate can be made of the obligation

The amount of a provision is recorded as an overhead in profit and loss account, and a liability is shown on the balance sheet (under the heading 'provisions for liabilities and charges').

Disclosure in the notes to the financial statements requires:

- details of changes in the amount of provisions between the beginning and end of the year
- a description of the provision(s) and expected timings of any resulting transfers
- an indication of the uncertainties regarding the amount or timing of any resulting transfers

A **contingent liability** is a possible obligation, ie there less than 50% likelihood of its occurrence.

A contingent liability is not recorded in the financial statements but should be disclosed as a note which includes:

- a brief description of the nature of the contingent liability
- an estimate of its financial effect
- an indication of the uncertainties relating to the amount or timing of any outflow
- the possibility of any re-imbursement

Thus in summary:

Provision = Probable = more than 50% likely.

Contingent liability = Possible = less than 50% likely.

8.8   FRS 3 – *Reporting Financial performance*, introduced a new accounting statement, that of the statement of total recognised gains and losses to expand upon the financial information required in the published accounts.

The statement of recognised gains and losses brings together the realised profits of the business, as shown in the profit and loss account, together with other unrealised gains and losses, which tend to pass exclusively through the balance sheet.

A good example of this is the revaluation of land and property, which may increase the value of the fixed asset in the balance sheet which is recognised by the transfer to a revaluation reserve which appears as part of shareholders funds also in the balance sheet.

8.9   Segmental accounting requires that information relating to the accounts should be broken down (segmented) in two principal ways – by class of business and by geographical location.

SSAP 25 requires that, where a business has two or more classes of business, or operates in two or more geographical segments, it should disclose for each class of business and geographical segment:

- turnover
- profit
- net assets

8.10 FRS 17 – *Retirement benefits* identifies two schemes:

A **defined contribution scheme** – here the amount of pension payable to the employee cannot be guaranteed, as it will depend upon how wisely and effectively the pension fund has been invested.

A **defined benefit scheme** – here the amount of pension payable to the employee is guaranteed and predetermined and is usually based upon the employee's salary immediately prior to retirement and the number of years' service.

8.11 SSAP20 – *Foreign Currency translation* deals with the expression of foreign currency amounts in the accounts. There are two terms relating to the valuing of foreign currency amounts:

- **Conversion**, which is the process of exchanging amounts of one foreign currency for another.
- **Translation**, which is required at the end of an accounting period, when a company still holds assets and liabilities in its balance sheet which were obtained or incurred in a foreign currency.
  Two different methods of 'translation' valuation can be used:
  - a 'temporal' method based on historic cost.
  - a 'closing rate' method based on the exchange rate at the year-end

CHAPTER 9: CASH FLOW STATEMENTS

9.1 (c)

9.2 (d)

9.3 (b)

9.4 (a)

9.5 (d)

9.6 Advantages of producing a cash flow statement:

(a) Cash is said to be the life blood of any business, and the survival of a business will depend on its ability to generate sufficient cash in order to fund its activities and meet its day-to-day obligations.

(b) The level of cash is an important indicator of business performance.

(c) Users of financial statements can easily identify with cash (often more so than profit) and employees may look at the level of cash when negotiating the next pay award.

(d) Cash flow accounting can be used to compare business performance against previous periods or against other businesses. Cash flow forecasting can also assume a role in the budgeting process, by reviewing past performance and as a planning tool for future growth.

9.7 **Radion PLC**

Reconciliation of operating profit to net cash flow from operating activities for the year ended 31 December 20-3

	£000
Operating profit	104
Depreciation	30
Increase in stock (203–175)	(28)
Increase in Debtors (141–127)	(14)
Increase in Creditors (142–118)	24
NET CASH FLOW FROM OPERATING ACTIVITIES	116

9.8 **Pratt PLC**

Task 1: Reconciliation of operating profit to net cash flow from operating activities

	£000
Operating profit	2,520
Depreciation[1]	318
Loss on disposal of tangible fixed assets[2]	3
Increase in stock (84–69)	(15)
Decrease in Debtors (270–255)	15
Increase in Creditors (108–81)	27
Net Cash flow from operating activities	2,868

Task 2: Cash Flow Statement: Pratt PLC

Year ending 31 October 20-3.

		£000
Net Cash flow from operating activities		2,868
Returns on investments and servicing of finance		
Interest paid		(168)
Taxation[3]		(429)
Capital expenditure		
Payments to acquire tangible fixed assets[4]	(629)	
Receipts from the sale of tangible fixed assets	8	(621)
		1,650
Equity dividends paid [5]		(459)
		1,191
Management of liquid resources		
Financing		
Issue of Shares[6]	627	
Repayment of loans	(1,800)	(1,173)
Net increase/(decrease) in cash		18

Working notes

1

Depreciation charges

20-3		£000	20-2		£000
Oct 31	Disposal	18	Nov 01	Balance b/d	1,500
Oct 31	Balance c/d	1,800	20-3		
			Oct 31	P/L Account (Bal fig)	318
		1,818			1,818
			20-3		
			Nov 01	Balance b/d	1,800

2

Vehicle disposals

20-3		£000	20-3		£000
Oct 31	At cost	29	Oct 31	Accum Depreciation	18
			Oct 31	Sale proceeds	8
			Oct 31	P/L Account (bal fig)	3*
		29			29

Denotes a loss on sale

3

Taxation

20-3		£000	20-2		£000
Oct 31 Paid (Bal Fig)		429	Nov 01	Balance b/d	285
Oct 31	Balance c/d	606	Oct 31	P/L Account	750
		1,035			1,035
			20-3		
			Nov 01	Balance b/d	606

4

Tangible Fixed Assets

20-2		£000	20-3		£000
Nov 01	Balance b/d	8,400	Oct 31	Disposals	29
20-3			Oct 31	Balance c/d	9,000
Oct 31	Additions (Bal fig)	629			
		9,029			9,029
20-3					
Nov 01	Balance b/d	9,000			

5

Equity Dividends paid

20-3		£000	20-2		£000
Oct 31	Paid (Bal fig)	459	Nov 01	Balance b/d	144
			20-3		
Oct 31	Balance c/d	225	Oct 31	P/L Account	540
		684			684
			20-3		
			Nov 01	Balance b/d	225

6

Issue of Shares	£000
Issue of called up shares (3,000–2,550)	450
At a premium	177
Total sales proceeds from issue	627

9.9 **Cash Flow Statement**: Sadler PLC
Year ended 30 June 20-3

		£000
Net Cash flow from operating activities		2,880
Returns on investments and servicing of finance		
Interest paid		(100)
Taxation[3]		(300)
Capital expenditure		
Payments to acquire tangible fixed assets[4]	(4,300)	
Receipts from the sale of tangible fixed assets	1,400	(2,900)
		(420)
Equity dividends paid[5]		(600)
		(1,020)
Management of liquid resources		
Financing		
Issue of Debenture stock		1,000
Net increase/(decrease) in cash		(20)

Sadler PLC
Formal notes to cash flow statements
Note: these are not the working notes (which follow on the next page).

Note 1: Reconciliation of operating profit to net cash flow from operating activities

	£000
Operating profit	1,100
Depreciation[1]	1,900
Profit on disposal of tangible fixed assets[2]	(200)
Increase in stock (340–300)	(40)
Increase in Debtors (1,300–1,200)	(100)
Increase in Creditors (800–600)	140
Decrease in Prepayments (100–80)	20
Increase in Accruals (120–60)	60
Net Cash flow from operating activities	2,880

Note 2: Reconciliation of net cash flow to movement in net debt

	£000
Net cash inflow (outflow) for the period	(20)
Cash received / paid from loans	(1,000)
Change in net debt	(1,020)
Net debt at start of year	40
Net debt at the end of the year	(980)

Note 3: Analysis of changes in net debt

	At start Of year £000	Cash Flow £000	At end of year £000
Cash in hand	40	(20)	20
Loans etc		(1,000)	(1,000)
Total	40	(1,020)	(980)

Working notes

1

Depreciation charges

20-3		£000	20-2		£000
Jun 30	Disposal	400	Jul 01	Balance b/d	8,160
Jun 30	Balance c/d	9,660	20-3		
			Jun 30	P/L Account (bal fig)	1,900
		10,060			10,060
			20-3		
			Jul 01	Balance b/d	9,660

2

Machinery Disposals

20-3		£000	20-3		£000
Jun 30	At cost	1,600	Jun 30	Accum Depreciation	400
			Jun 30	Sale proceeds	1,400
Jun 30	P/L Account (bal fig)*	200			
		1,800			1,800

* Denotes a Profit on sale

3

Taxation

20-3		£000	20-2		£000
Jun 30	Paid (Bal fig)	300	Jul 01	Balance b/d	360
			20-3		
Jun 30	Balance c/d	260	Jun 30	P/L Account	200
		560			560
			20-3		
			Jul 01	Balance b/d	260

4

Tangible Fixed Assets

20-2		£000	20-3		£000
Jul 01	Balance b/d	13,600	Jun 30	Disposals	1,600
20-3					
Jun 30	Additions (Bal fig)	4,300	Jun 30	Balance c/d	16,300
		17,900			17,900
20-3					
Jul 01	Balance b/d	16,300			

5

Equity Dividends paid

20-3		£000	20-2		£000
Jun 30	Paid (bal fig)	600	Jul 01	Balance b/d	400
			20-3		
Jun 30	Balance c/d	200	Jun 30	P/L Account	400
		800			800
			20-3		
			Jul 01	balance b/d	200

9.10

GEORGE LIMITED

CASH FLOW STATEMENT FOR THE YEAR ENDED 31 MARCH 20-5

	£'000	£'000
Net cash inflow from operating activities		350
Returns on investment and servicing of finance		
Interest paid		(20)
Taxation		
Corporation tax paid (20-4)		(21)
Capital expenditure		
Purchase of fixed asset	(110)	
Receipts from sale of fixed asset[1]	7	
		(103)
		206
Equity dividends paid		(30)
		176
Financing		
Issue of ordinary share capital (40 – 25)	15	
Long term loan (200 – 100)	100	
Redemption of debentures	(500)	
Net cash outflow from financing		(385)
Decrease in cash		(209)

Reconciliation of operating profit to net cash flow from operating activities

	£'000
Operating profit	237
Depreciation	275
Profit on sales of fixed assets	(2)
Increase in stocks (210 – 200)	(10)
Increase in debtors (390 – 250)	(140)
Decrease in creditors (150 – 160)	(10)
Net cash inflow from operating activities	350

Working note

1 **Receipts from sale of fixed assets**

Disposals of fixed assets

	£		£
Fixed assets (cost)	10,000	Accumulated depreciation	5,000
Profit on sale	2,000	Proceeds (bal fig)	7,000
	12,000		12,000

9.11

CASHEDIN LIMITED

CASH FLOW STATEMENT FOR THE YEAR ENDED 30 SEPTEMBER 20-5

	£'000	£'000
Net cash inflow from operating activities		
Returns on investments and servicing of finance		104
Interest paid		(218)
Taxation		(75)
		(189)
Capital expenditure		
Payments to acquire tangible fixed assets	(358)	
Proceeds from sale of fixed assets	132	
		(226)
		(415)
Equity dividends paid		(280)
		(695)
Financing		
Loans	200	
Issue of ordinary share capital	150	
		350
Decrease in cash		(345)

Reconciliation of operating profit and net cash inflow from operating activities

	£'000
Operating profit	24
Depreciation	318
Increase in stock	(251)
Increase in debtors	(152)
Increase in creditors	165
Net cash inflow from operating activities	104

CHAPTER 10: INTERPRETATION OF FINANCIAL STATEMENTS

10.1 (d)

10.2 (c)

10.3 (d)

10.4 (a)

10.5 1 (b)
    2 (d)
    3 (a)
    4 (a)
    5 (c)

10.6 **Task 1**

		Hanadi PLC	**Abeer PLC**
(a)	Gross Profit %		
	$\dfrac{\text{Gross Profit} \times 100}{\text{Sales}}$	$\dfrac{250}{350} \times 100 = 71\%$	$\dfrac{200}{300} \times 100 = 67\%$
(b)	Net Profit %		
	$\dfrac{\text{Net Profit before tax} \times 100}{\text{Sales}}$	$\dfrac{150}{350} \times 100 = 43\%$	$\dfrac{150}{300} \times 100 = 50\%$
(c)	ROCE		
	$\dfrac{\text{Net Profit before tax} \times 100}{\text{Capital Employed}}$	$\dfrac{150}{470} \times 100 = 32\%$	$\dfrac{150}{350} \times 100 = 43\%$
(d)	Current Ratio		
	$\dfrac{\text{Current Assets}}{\text{Current Liabilities}}$	$\dfrac{220}{215} = 1{:}1$	$\dfrac{160}{135} = 1.2{:}1$
(e)	Acid Test Ratio		
	$\dfrac{\text{Current Assets} - \text{Stock}}{\text{Current Liabilities}}$	$\dfrac{220 - 110}{215} = 0.5{:}1$	$\dfrac{160 - 70}{135} = 0.7{:}1$

Task 2

	Hanadi PLC	**Abeer PLC**
Gross Profit	Better performance More sales at a higher margin	
Net Profit		Better performance More control over costs and expenses

406 financial statements tutorial

ROCE

Both results are good but Abeer has a higher return; it is utilising its capital far more effectively than Hanadi.

Current Ratio

Both are on the low side but Abeer has a better margin from which to pay off debt.

Acid Test Ratio

Again both are on the low side but Abeer has more cash in the business to pay off short-term debt whereas Hanadi appears to have too much cash tied up in stock.

Conclusion: Abeer PLC is more attractive than Hanadi PLC from an investment point of view.

10.7 Accounting ratios need to be analysed and interpreted and not just listed as sets of numbers. Ideally they need to be compared with the previous year's figures and wherever possible, with similar organisations to evaluate and highlight trends.

But there are dangers in relying on the numbers without first looking behind the figures:

1   Financial statements present only an overall picture of the business, and the balance sheet is only a snapshot of the business at a particular moment in time. The balance sheet may not actually be representative of the business as a whole, eg the accounting year-end of a business with seasonal trade is typically timed for when the business is least busy.

2   The problem with accounting policy is no more evident than with ratio analysis. Depreciation and stock valuation, for example, involve different methods of valuation and the choice of method can lead to distortion in comparative figures.

3   Larger organisations frequently aggregate operations and this can make comparison of individual areas of activity difficult.

4   Comparisons can be difficult between a business which finances fixed assets by renting them (thus showing the rental as an expense with no asset on the balance sheet) and a business which purchases its assets outright and then depreciates them over the anticipated working life.

5   Ratios should be open to interpretation, as what is good for one company may not be suitable for another. For example it is generally accepted than the ideal current ratio is 2:1. However retailers such as supermarkets can in fact work on a much lower margin because of rapid stock turnover and their predominantly cash sale base (ie few debtors).

6   Whilst in principle inter-firm comparisons are very worthwhile, there may be considerable differences between firms in the same industry. They may, for example, vary in size and in application of accounting policies.

In conclusion, ratios are a very useful way of investigating the performance of a business over a number of years or comparing one business with a similar one. However ratios cannot be relied upon as the absolute answer and should not be used as absolute standards of performance. Care and consideration needs to be given to points 1-6 above.

10.8

		Case PLC	Hope PLC	Mast PLC

(a) ROCE

$$\frac{\text{Operating Profit}}{\text{Capital employed}} \times 100 \qquad \frac{£10,000}{£18,000} \times 100 = 55.6\% \qquad \frac{£4,500}{£11,150} \times 100 = 40.4\% \qquad \frac{£1,500}{£2,300} \times 100 = 65.2\%$$

(b) Current Ratio

$$\frac{\text{Current Assets}}{\text{Current Liabilities}} \qquad \frac{£56,000}{£50,000} = 1.1{:}1 \qquad \frac{£12,500}{£5,800} = 2.2{:}1 \qquad \frac{£1,200}{£700} = 1.7{:}1$$

(c) Interest Cover

$$\frac{\text{Operating Profit}}{\text{Interest Payable}} \qquad \frac{£10,000}{£2,500} = 4 \text{ times} \qquad \frac{£4,500}{£200} = 22.5 \text{ times} \qquad \text{Nil}$$

(d) Earnings per share

$$\frac{\text{Profit after tax} - \text{Preference dividend}}{\text{Number of issued Ordinary shares}}$$

$$\frac{£4,700 - 100}{£3,000} = 153\text{p per share} \qquad \frac{£3,100}{£1,500} = 207\text{p per share} \qquad \frac{£850}{£500} = 170\text{p per share}$$

(e) Gearing

$$\frac{\text{Fixed return capital}}{\text{Total capital employed}} \qquad \frac{£4,000+£1,000}{£14,000+£4,000} \times 100 = 27.8\% \qquad \frac{£1,650}{£9,500+£1,650} \times 100 = 14.8\% \qquad \text{Nil}$$

10.9

	Company A	Company B
Return on capital employed	$\frac{200}{1000} = 20\%$	$\frac{420}{2800} = 15\%$
Net profit margin	$\frac{200}{800} = 25\%$	$\frac{420}{2100} = 20\%$
Asset turnover	$\frac{800}{1000} = 0.8$	$\frac{2100}{2800} = 0.75$

Other possible ratios:

	Company A	Company B
Gross profit margin	$\frac{360}{800} = 45\%$	$\frac{1050}{2100} = 50\%$
Expenses: Sales	$\frac{160}{800} = 20\%$	$\frac{630}{2100} = 30\%$

From the calculations we can see that Company A has both the highest return on capital employed and also the highest profit margin and asset turnover. It would, therefore, be the better company to target for takeover. However, the gross profit margin for Company B is, in fact, higher suggesting that the underlying business is more profitable. It is only because of the expenses of Company B in relation to sales that it has a lower net profit margin. If Company B could be made more efficient in terms of expenses and utilisation of assets by the introduction of a new management team on takeover, then, given the more profitably underlying business, it might be worth considering as a target for takeover.

10.10

REPORT

To:	**Managers of Bimbridge Hospitals Trust**
From:	**AAT Student**
Date:	**3 December 20-8**
Re:	**Analysis of Patch Ltd's financial statements**

Introduction

The purpose of the report is to analyse the financial statements of Patch Ltd for 20-8 and 20-7 to determine whether to use the company as a supplier.

Calculation of Ratios

The following ratios for the company have been computed:

	20-8	Industry Average 20-8	20-7	Industry Average 20-7
Return on capital employed	$\frac{552}{5,334}$ = 10.3%	9.6%	$\frac{462}{5,790}$ = 8.0%	9.4%
Net profit percentage	$\frac{552}{2,300}$ = 24%	21.4%	$\frac{462}{2,100}$ = 22%	21.3%
Quick ratio/acid test	$\frac{523}{475}$ = 1.1:1	1.0:1	$\frac{418}{465}$ = 0.9:1	0.9:1
Gearing: Debt/Capital employed	$\frac{1,654}{5,334}$ = 31%	36%	$\frac{2,490}{5,790}$ = 43%	37%
or				
Debt/Equity	$\frac{1,654}{3,680}$ = 45%		$\frac{2,490}{3,300}$ = 75%	

Comment and Analysis

The overall profitability of the company has improved from 20-7 to 20-8. The return on capital employed has increased from 8% in 20-7 to 10.3% in 20-8. This means that the company is generating more profit from the available capital employed in 20-8 as compared with 20-7. The company was below average for the industry in 20-7, but has performed better than the average in 20-8. The net profit percentage has also improved. It increased from 22% in 20-7 to 24% in 20-8. This means that the company is generating more profit from sales in 20-8 than in the previous year. In both years the company had a higher than average net profit percentage when compared against the industry average. From these ratios it would seem that the company is relatively more profitable in 20-8 as compared with 20-7 and that it now performs better than the average of the industry. This suggests that its long-term prospects for success are higher than the average of the industry.

The liquidity of the company has also improved in the year. The quick ratio shows how many current assets, excluding stock, there are to meet the current liabilities and is often thought of as a better indicator of liquidity than the current ratio. The quick ratio in Patch Ltd has improved from 20-7 to 20-8. It has gone up from 0.9:1 to 1.1:1. This means that in 20-8 there were more than enough quick assets to meet current liabilities. Again, the quick ratio of Patch Ltd is better than the industry average in 20-8, and matched it in 20-7. We can conclude that Patch Ltd is more liquid than the average of the industry in 20-8.

There has been a considerable decline in the gearing of the company in 20-8 as compared with 20-7. In 20-7 the gearing ratio was 43% and this has fallen to 31% in 20-8. This means that the percentage of debt funding to equity funding has declined between the two years. High gearing ratios are often thought of as increasing the risk of the company in that, in times of profit decline, it becomes increasingly difficult for highly geared companies to meet interest payments on debt, and in extreme cases the company could be forced into liquidation. The gearing ratio of Patch Ltd was above the industry average in 20-7, making it relatively more risky, in this respect, than the average of companies in the industry. However, the ratio in 20-8 is considerably less than the industry average and hence may now be considered less risky than the average. There is thus less of a risk from gearing in doing business with the company than the average of companies in the sector.

Conclusions

Overall, based solely on the information provided in the financial statements of the company, it is recommended that you use Patch Ltd as a supplier. The company has increasing profitability and liquidity and a lower level of gearing in 20-8 than in 20-7. It also compares favourably with other companies in the same industry and seems to present a lower risk than the average of the sector.

CHAPTER 11:CONSOLIDATED ACCOUNTS

11.1 (b)

11.2 (c)

11.3 (a)

11.4 (b)

11.5 (b)

11.6 (d)

11.7 (b)

11.8 According to FRS 2 the following conditions are required for a parent/subsidiary relationship:

- The parent undertaking holds a majority of the voting rights in the subsidiary company.

- The parent company is a member of the subsidiary and therefore has the right to have a vote to remove or appoint its directors.

- The parent company can exercise a dominant influence over the subsidiary company:
  - through the contents and provisions of the subsidiary company's memorandum and articles of association, *or*
  - by virtue of a control contract

- The parent undertaking is a member (shareholder) of the subsidiary undertaking and it is the sole controller of that company due to an agreement with all the other members, which constitutes it a majority holder of the voting rights in that company.

- The parent company has a participating interest in the subsidiary and therefore can:
  - exert a dominant influence *or*
  - the parent and subsidiary are managed on a unified basis

- A parent undertaking can be treated as a parent company if its subsidiary also has a subsidiary. By definition the third company (sub-subsidiary) is also a subsidiary of the original parent company.

11.9 Phantom PLC

Calculation for Goodwill	Total Equity
	£000
Shares	800
Share Premium account	200
Revaluation reserve	700
Profit and Loss Account	1,750
	3,450
Group share 80% x £3,450	2,760
Total purchase consideration	2,900
Goodwill on acquisition	140
Minority interest 20% x £3,450	690

11.10 Ringer PLC
Consolidated Balance Sheet as at 30 April 20-3.

	£000	£000
Fixed Assets		
Intangibles	620	
Tangibles (6,000 + 1,900)	7,900	
		8,520
Current Assets		
Stocks (1,900 + 800)	2,700	
Debtors (1,500 + 500)	2,000	
Cash at Bank (600 + 100)	700	
	5,400	

Creditors: Amounts falling due within one Year.

Creditors (1,500 + 400)	1,900	
Taxation (400 + 100)	500	
Dividends	1,000	
	3,400	
Net Current Assets		2,000
		10,520

Creditors: Amounts falling due within one Year

Long Term Loans	2,500
	8,020

Capital and Reserves	
Called up Share Capital	2,000
Share Premium Account	1,000
Profit and Loss Account	4,100
Shareholders funds	7,100
Minority Interest (40% x 2,300)	920
	8,020

Working notes

Ringer holding in Sterling	=	600,000 / 1,000,000	x 100	=	60%

Minority interest	=	400,000 / 1,000,000	x 100	=	40%

Revaluation	Debit Fixed Assets	£300,000
	Credit Revaluation reserve	£300,000

Goodwill

	Total 100% £000	Group 60% £000	Minority 40% £000
Shares	1,000	600	400
Share Prem	500	300	200
Revaluation	300	180	120
P/L A/C	500	300	200
Total	2,300	1,380	920
Cost of investment		2,000	
Goodwill		620	

11.11 Consolidated profit and Loss Account

	£000
Profit before taxation (25% x £420K)	105
Taxation (25% x £120K)	30

Consolidated Balance Sheet

	£000
Share of Net Assets (25% x 1,000K)	250
Purchased Goodwill	145
	395
Share of post acquisition profits (25% x 300)	75

Working Note: Purchased Goodwill

	£000
Share of net assets at acquisition (1,000K − 300K = 700K x 25%)	175
Cost of Investment	320
Purchased Goodwill	145

11.12 Winston PLC

Consolidated Balance Sheet as at 30 November 20-3

	£000	£000
Fixed Assets		
Intangibles – Goodwill (495 – 99)	396	
Tangibles (5,000 + 600)	5,600	
		5,996
Current Assets		
Stocks (150 + 30 – 5)	175	
Debtors (80 + 35 – 10)	105	
Cash at Bank (10 + 5)	15	
	295	
Creditors: Amounts falling due within one Year.		
Creditors (160 + 120 – 10)	270	
Net Current Assets		25
		6,021
Capital and Reserves		
Called up Share Capital		4,000
Profit and Loss Account (1,980 + 90 – 5 – 396)		1,966
Shareholders funds		5,966
Minority Interest (10% x 550)		55
		6,021

Working notes:

▪ Winston **holding** in Churchill = $\dfrac{360,000 \times 100}{400,000}$ = 90%

▪ **Minority interest** = $\dfrac{40,000 \times 100}{400,000}$ = 10%

▪ **Goodwill**

	Total 100% £000	Group 90% £000	Minority 10% £000
Shares	400	360	40
Profit and Loss Account	50	45	5
Total	450	405	45

Cost of investment	900
Goodwill	495

Amortised 20-2 and 20-3, ie 2 years

    £495,000÷10 years = £49,500 per annum

    2 years x £49,500 = £99,000 written off

▪ **Consolidated reserves**

Holding Co P/L Account	1,980	
Post acquisition profit	90	(£150,000 – £50,000 x 90%)
Unrealised stock	(5)	
Goodwill Amortised	(99)	
	1,966	

▪ **Minority Interest**

Shares	40	(£400,000 x 10%)
Profit and Loss Account	15	(£150,000 x 10%)
	55	

11.13   **TOM LIMITED AND SUBSIDIARIES**

Consolidated Profit and Loss Account for the year ended 31 December 20-2

		£000
Group turnover	800 + 400 + 300 – 20 – 80	1,400
Cost of sales*		890
Gross profit		510
Distribution costs	80 + 50 + 20	150
Administrative expenses	100 + 30 + 20	150
Group operating profit		210
Interest receivable/payable		–
Profit on ordinary activities before tax		210
Tax on profit on ordinary activities		68
Profit on ordinary activities after tax		142
Minority interests	32 x 25%	8
Profit on ordinary activities after tax and minority interests		134
Dividends		100
Retained profit for group		34

*	cost of sales:		
	opening stock	200 + 150 + 100	450
	+ purchases	600 + 300 + 200 – 20 – 80	1,000
	– closing stock	300 + 200 + 80 – 20 (unrealised profit)	560
			890

INDEX OF ACCOUNTING STANDARDS

* note that, for *Drafting Financial Statements*, FRS 13 is not assessed

INDEX